16

PREFACE.

THE Talmud has very often been spoken of, but is little known. The very great linguistic difficulties, and the vast size of the work, have up to the present time prevented the effecting of more than the translation of the Mishna only into Latin and, later, in German. At the instance of some friends, we have decided upon publishing a complete textual and generally literal version of the Talmud, that historical and religious work which forms a continuation of the Old and even of the New Testament.[1] We are far from laying claim to a perfect translation of all the delicate shades of expression belonging to an idiom so strange and variable, which is a mixture of neo-Hebrew and Chaldean, and concise almost to obscurity. We wish to take every opportunity of improving this work.

A general introduction will be annexed, treating of the origin, composition, spirit, and history of the Talmud. This introduction will be accompanied by: 1st. An Alphabetical Index of all the incongruous subjects treated of in this vast and unwieldy Encyclopædia; 2nd. An Index of the proper and geographical names; 3rd. Concordantial Notes of the various Bible texts employed, permitting a reference to the commentaries made on them (which will sometimes serve as *Errata*). This general introduction can, for obvious reasons, only appear on the completion of the present version. The commencement, however, gives an idea of the contents. The "Version of the *Berakhoth*" (or Blessing), as Mr. Ad. Franck[2] says, carries us into the bosom of a society and a creed in which everything is a subject of blessing and prayer. God is blessed for the bread and the wine,[3] for the fruit plucked from the trees, and the produce of the

[1] See the works of Messrs. J. Barclay, H. Polano, Js. Hershon (with Preface by Rev. F. Farrar), and Dr. H. Oort.

[2] *Journal des Savants*, September, 1872, pp. 553, 554.

[3] See the Jewish Prayer-book.

earth. Light and fire, the rainbow, the storm, the lightning, the new moon, were so many reasons for blessing God. Every action and event in life was the occasion of blessing and prayer to God; on rising in the morning, on retiring at night, in repose or in labour, at a birth, marriage, or death, in passing a cemetery, on seeing a prince or a king. Once the principle admitted, all possible inferences must be drawn from it. The formulæ of blessing and of prayer, once hallowed and sanctioned by tradition or faith, we shall see under what circumstances and at what hours they are to be recited. Equal care will be taken in defining the various conditions which permit or forbid the blessing or invocation of the Almighty, when man, by reason of his purity, is worthy, or by reason of his legitimate impurity, unworthy to bless or invoke God. This it is that necessitates a Treatise, or what may be called the Science of Blessings (*Berakhoth*).

For general philology, the following is a list of the Greek and Latin terms used in this first volume:—

ἀβάσκαντα, 156.
ἄλιμος, 118.
ἀνάκλιτα, 56.
ἀνθύπατος, 99.
ἀπειδῶν, 158.
ἄριστον, 76.
ἀρχιτέκτων, 151.
ἄρχων, 53, 99.
ἀσθενής, 48, 140.
βαλανείον, 121.
βασιλεύς, 151.
γαρίσματα, 120.
δημοσία, 53, 66.
δισάκκιον, 70.
εἰκόνιον, 57.
ἐπαρχία, 154.
ἐπενδύτης, 170.
εὔθικος, 16.
ἔχιδνα, 144.
ἴησις, 123.
κινάρα, 118.
κλιντήριον, 56.
κόρος, 7.
κοσμικόν 160.
κοσμοκράτωρ, 154.
λευκός, 156.
λῃστής, 18.
λιμὴν, 68.
νοτάριος, 19.
ξενία, 15, 90.
ὄχλος, 153, 157.
πόλεμος, 19.
σπεῖρα, 157.
συγκλητικός, 161.
σχεδία, 93.
τιμή, 150.
capitatus, 119.
cathedra, 122.
circenses, 83, 158
comes, 161.
compendiaria (via), 170.
conditum, 33, 121.
demissus, 168.
domus, 46.
funda, 170.
linteum, 124.
muscus, 124.
nanus, 156.
narthecium, 101.
nicolai, 121.
palatia, 59, 100.
patronus, 152.
quæstionarius, 153.
semita, 68.
speculare, 145.
speculator, 159.
spicula, 168.
stola, 71.
strata, 4, 100.
strategus, 146.
theatrum, 158.
triclinium, 70, 147.
typus, 25.

THE TREATISE OF THE BERAKHOTH.

CHAPTER I.

MISHNÁ.

1. What is the proper moment for reciting the *Shema'*[1] in the evening? From the hour the priests enter (the Temple) to eat their *Troomâ* (heave offerings, or oblations[2]) until the end of the first watch[3]. This is the opinion of R. Eleazar; the (others) sages (wise men[4]) say: until midnight, and Rabban Gamaliel says: until the pillar of the morn ascend (daybreak[5]).

GEMARA.

"What is the proper moment for reading the evening *Shema'*, &c.?"

We have seen (by the Mishná) that it commences from the moment at which

[1] This is the principal formula of the Jewish liturgy, and is so called from the word *Shema'*, "Hear, O Israel," with which it commences. The formula is composed of three sections: 1st, Deut. vi. 4-9; 2nd, Deut. xi. 13-21; 3rd, Num. xv. 37-41; and is recited evening and morning. Evening prayer might be said after 12.30 p.m. (See Acts x. 9.)

[2] In the event of a priest of the Temple (cohen) who was legally unclean (Lev. xxii. 7), he could not eat holy things for a whole day; at sunset he took a bath of purification, he could then eat of the oblations which depended upon his office.

[3] The night was divided, according to the Rabbis, into three or four watches of three or four hours each; this division of the night is retained by the Church under the denomination of Vigils (for its offices). The night, whatever its length, is divided into twelve hours which vary according to the season, for they are not so much hours as fractions of the night of more or less duration; the first hour was from six to seven o'clock, and so on.

[4] Or greater part of the Rabbis, that is to say, the majority of the Assembly.

[5] According to Maimonide's Commentaries, the daybreak precedes sunrise by 1⅕ hours. He attributes the optical phenomenon to vapours which, rising ceaselessly from the earth, bring the solar light, by refraction, nearer to us. He fixes the height of the atmospheric clouds at 51 Talmudick miles, which are, according to some, of 18 minutes, and according to others, of 24 minutes.

the priests enter in order to eat *Troomâ*. R. Ḥiya taught that it is at the hour at which the people usually return home on Friday evening to take their meal. It is added that these two opinions are almost identical. But wait! (we have an objection to offer): When the priests enter to eat *Troomâ*, it is still day, and the stars are not yet out, whilst on the other hand, when the people sit down to the Friday evening's meal, it is generally an hour or two after nightfall. How, then, can we admit that the two opinions coincide? R. Yosse answers that it relates to the small villages, the inhabitants of which leave the fields before nightfall, in order to avoid the wild beasts. It has been taught that "He who recites the evening prayer before that hour has not fulfilled his obligation." If this is so, why is it done at the Synagogue? R. Yosse replies: It is not recited in the Synagogue as a matter of duty, but in order to remain in prayer after the study of the Law.

R. Zeira, speaking in the name of R. Jeremie, says: If one is uncertain of having said *grace* before meals, it must be re-said, for it is a law written in the *Tôrâ*, דאוריתא: "*When thou hast eaten and art full, then thou shalt bless the Lord*" (Deut. viii. 10). If there is a doubt of having said the *prayer*[6], it is not to be said again, for it is only prescribed by the Rabbis. This is contrary to the opinion of R. Yoḥanan, who says: Would to God that man would pray all the day, for prayer (even repeated) is never lost[7]. As regards the question relative to the recital of the Shema', this is a question to be resolved by the following rule: It has been taught that if the Shema' is recited before the appointed time, the duty has not been accomplished. Now, is there not, at the moment preceding the time appointed, a doubt whether it is day or night? Therefore, in case of doubt, the Shema' must certainly be said.

What is the material indication of the hour at which the priests eat *Troomâ*? The appearance of the stars. Nothing proves this in an irrefutable manner, but there is, on this subject, an allusion in the Bible (Neh. iv. 21): "So we laboured in the work; and half of them held the spears from the rising of the morning till the stars appeared;" and further, "That in the night they may be a guard to us, and labour in the day" (Neh. iv. 22). Thus the duration of the day and the night are determined. How many stars should be visible to make it night? R. Pinchas, in the name of R. Abba bar-Papa, says: When only one star is to be seen, it is still day; when two are to be seen, it is doubtful; but when three are to be seen, night has certainly fallen[8]. How can it be maintained, that when two stars are out it is doubtful? Is it not said: "When

[6] By the word *prayer* must be understood the eighteen benedictions called *Shemone-esré* or *'Amida*, which is not prescribed by the *Tôrâ*, but by the Rabbis. Hereafter, we will use the word *'Amida*, which is the shortest.

[7] See hereafter, i. 2, iv. 4; tr. *Sabbat*, i. 2 (5); *Mekhiltin*, chap. xxi.

[8] Cf. B., tr. *Shabbath*, fol. 35 *b*.

the star-s appear," which means at least two stars? Yes, but the first one does not count. If on Friday evening, one star being visible, work is still going on, there is no transgression of the Sabbath; if two stars are out there is a doubt, and the "trespass offering" must be made (Lev. v. 16). If three stars are out, the sin offering must be made (in case of transgression). And therefore, if on Saturday evening work is done while one star is visible, the sin offering is necessary; if two stars are out, the doubt must be atoned for; if there are three stars out, there has been no transgression. R. Yosse bar-Aboon mentions, in support of this (doubtful case): If we admit that there is a doubt when two stars are out, it follows that if a man work on Friday evening after two stars are out, and continues work after having been warned, and if he do the same on Saturday evening, an inevitable dilemma will arise; for, if in the first case it is still day, it must also be admitted to be day in the second case, and therefore there would be transgression of the Sabbath; and if in the second case, night has already set in, the same must be admitted for the previous day, and therefore there would be transgression. And again: If a man cuts half a fig[*] on Friday evening after two stars are visible, and in the morning he cuts the other half, and he again cuts another half on Saturday evening after two stars are out, then we must reason that, if in the first case it is still day, it is also day in the last case; add the half done in the morning to the half done on Saturday evening, the result is a transgression then accomplished; if in the second case it is night, it would be the same in the first case, and by adding the morning's work to that of Friday evening, there would be a transgression in the first case.

What has been said about the stars, applies to those which are not generally seen until nightfall; for, no note is taken of those which appear before the day is terminated. Therefore, R. Yosse bar R. Aboon says: It means three stars not counting, כוכבתא[1]. R. Jacob from Darom[2] (south) says: One star

[*] A transgression of the Sabbath consists in having accomplished an entire task, or two halves of a task in the same day.

[1] These stars must be disposed thus: ∴. According to Z. Fränkel's Commentary, they are three stars similar to one. This expression (כוכבתא) had remained incomprehensible in spite of the Commentaries; but, thanks to Mr. Goldberg's interpretation given in the *Maggid* (25 May, 1870, No. 21, p. 157), it is now clear. He says that in Syriac this expression applies to Venus, called the Queen of the Heavens (Jer. vii. 18, Chaldean version). Now, as she is visible very early by reason of her brightness (from which is derived her Hebrew name נוגה), she cannot be taken as a guide to fix the limits of day and night. Therefore, R. Yosse says that to fix the commencement of the night, three stars must be visible; but Venus does not count, she is often seen before nightfall and also after daybreak.

[2] See Jos. Derenbourg, *Revue Critique*, 24 Feb., 1872, p. 114, n. 3; Neubauer, *Géographie du Talmud*, pp. 46 and 64.

indicates that it is still day; but two stars certainly show that it is night. Is there any doubt of this? No; the doubt can only exist between the stars visible by day, and the other stars.

With regard to this, we are taught[3] that it is still day as long as the sky is red towards the east; if it becomes shadowy, the intermediate period[4] (twilight) has arrived. If darkness has set in, so that the upper atmosphere has become indistinguishable from the lower, night has arrived. Rabbi says: When, at the period of the new moon, the sun commences to go down and the moon to appear, it is twilight. R. Ḥanina says: The sun must have gone down and the moon have commenced to rise. In effect R. Samuel says: The moon cannot shine as long as the sun still lightens, neither can the moon shine after the sun has darted his (morning) beams. R. Samuel bar-Ḥiya, in the name of R. Ḥanina, says: If a man, when the sun has begun to set, descends from the summit of Mount Carmel to bathe in the sea, and re-ascends to partake of the oblations, he has certainly bathed during the daytime[5]. It is, however, only a certainty in the case of one taking cross-roads to shorten the route; but not in the case of one who follows the high road (Strata). What is meant by "the intermediate period"? R. Tanḥooma says: It resembles the delay of a drop of blood placed on the edge of a sword, i.e. the time required for the drop of blood to divide and run down on either side of the blade, is equivalent to the period of transition. According to R. Neḥemias, it means the time it would require for a man to run half a mile, after sunset. R. Yosse says: This twilight lasts no longer than the twinkling of an eye, and not even the men of science could measure it.

Whilst the R. Yossé and R. Aḥa were together, the former said to the latter: Does it not seem to you that the passage of this half a mile (twilight) lasts but a second[6]? It is certainly my opinion, said R. Aḥa. However, R. Ḥiya does not say so, but each twinkling of an eye, measured by the duration of the passage of half a mile (as R. Neḥemias), is doubtful. R. Mena says: I have made an objection in the presence of R. Aḥa: Have we not learnt elsewhere[7], that if an impurity is seen, once during the day and again during the intermediate period, or once in the twilight and again on the morrow[8], when the certainty exists that the impurity dates partly from this day and partly from the next day,

[3] Cf. B., tr. *Shabbath*, fol. 34 *b*; tr. *Abôda Zara*, fol. 41 *b*; J., ibid., chap. iii. § 1.

[4] The spirit of minutiæ is carried to such an extent in these discussions, that it even makes reference to the passage of day to night, which is called "between the two suns," בי' השמשות.

[5] As prescribed in Lev. xxii. 6.

[6] The moment of doubt would therefore be equal to that given by R. Yosse.

[7] Mishnâ, vi., tr. *Zabin*, i. 6.

[8] See hereafter, chap. iii. § 6, and notes.

there is a certainty as to the circumstances of the impurity, and the sacrifice is obligatory. But if the doubt exists, that the sight of the impurity dates partly from to-day and partly from the morrow, the impurity is certain, but the sacrifice uncertain. On account of this, R. Ḥiya bar-Joseph answered in the presence of R. Yoḥanan: Who is it who taught that one of these occasions of impurity can be divided into two? It was R. Yosse. He answered: Thou refutest thus thy own opinion; for thou sayest that each twinkling of an eye of the time accomplished in a half-mile, according to R. Neḥemiah, is doubtful, and not only the end of it. No contradiction can be offered to this; when the Prophet Elias shall return to this world, and will explain to us what this twilight means, no one will contest him. R. Ḥanina argued against the condisciples of the Rabbis: Since, said he, it is night as soon as three stars are visible, be the sun still high in the heavens, the same must apply (before the day) in the morning. R. Abba said: It is written (in Gen. xix. 23): "The sun was risen upon the earth when Lot entered into Zoar;" and is written (in Lev. xxii. 7): "And when the sun is down he shall be clean." The sunrise is compared with the sunset: As sunset corresponds to the disappearance of the sun from the sight of man, so also sunrise is manifested by the appearance of the sun to the eye of man. R. Aḥa said: It is written (in Gen. xliv. 3): "As soon as the morning was light." The *Tórá* calls the light "morning." R. Ismael taught: It is written "every morning[9]," so as to give a limit for him who desires to know when the morning commences. R. Yosse bar R. Aboon said: If you think to call night, the time that the sun takes to traverse the heavens (from dawn to radiancy), it would be equivalent to saying that the day and the night do not resemble each other (the night would lengthen out to the morning by this addition; but we are taught that on the first day of the Equinox of Nissan[1], and on the first day of the Equinox of Tissri, the day and the night are equal). R. Hoona says: One can accept the usual custom as a term of comparison. Thus, when the king starts to go out, he is said to be out; but when he commences to return, he is not said to be returned, until it is an accomplished fact (it is the same with the sun).

In standing up to recite the Prayer ('Amida), the feet must be met. There are two opinions on this subject, viz. that of R. Levi, and that of R. Shimon. The one says: it is to imitate the angels; the other says: it is to imitate the priests. The latter opinion is founded on the verse, "Neither shalt thou go up by steps to mine altar" (Exod. xx. 26); for the priests had to go to the altar[2] by placing the toe beside the heel, and the heel beside the toe (i.e. by taking very little steps).

[9] See *Mekhilta*, sect. *Bô*, chap. vi.; sect. *Beshalaḥ*, chap. iv.

[1] See *Medrash Rabba* on Leviticus, and the *Minḥath cohen*, at the paragraph relating to the sun.

[2] See *Medrash Rabba* on Exod. xxx.; *Mekhilta*, sect. *Yithrô*, chap. xi.

The former opinion is based on the verse, "And their feet were straight feet" (Ezek. i. 7). Now, R. Ḥanina bar-Andira, in the name of R. Samuel bar-Zootai, says: The angels have no knee-joint, according to (Dan. vii. 16), "I came near unto one of them, that stood (always) by." R. Hoona says: If one sees the priests in the Synagogue at the time of their first blessing of the people, one must say: "Bless the Lord, ye his angels" (Ps. ciii. 20); if at the second benediction: "Bless ye the Lord, all ye his hosts" (Ps. ciii. 21); if at the third benediction: "Bless the Lord, all his works" (Ps. ciii. 22). For the Prayer of Mousaph (additional) at the first blessing is said: "Behold, bless ye the Lord, all ye servants of the Lord, which by night stand in the house of the Lord" (Ps. cxxxiv. 1)[3]; at the second blessing: "Lift up your hands in the sanctuary" (Ps. cxxxiv. 2); and at the third blessing: "The Lord that made heaven and earth, bless thee out of Sion" (Ps. cxxxiv. 3). If there are four blessings of the people (as on the day of *Kippur*), the verse used at the first blessing is repeated at the third, and at the fourth blessing the verse used at the second is repeated.

R. Ḥatzna says: From dawn to daylight, a man can accomplish a journey of four miles[4]; and again from then until the sun darts its rays a like distance. How do we know that the last calculation is correct? Because it is written: "And when the morning arose," &c. (Gen. xix. 15); and: "The sun was risen upon the earth when Lot entered into Zoar[5]" (Gen. xiv. 23). But, was it not more than four miles from Sodom to Zoar[6]? R. Zeira answered: The angel accompanying Lot shortened the road (by levelling it). How do we know that from dawn to sunrise there is an interval of four miles? The repetition of the words "and when (as)" shows this, by correlation, to be the case[7]. R. Yosse bar-Aboon said: He who likens the light of dawn with the presence of a star[8], may deceive himself: sometimes it is a little before, sometimes a little after. How is the opening of the dawn to be recognized? It has the appearance of two

[3] There the verses 1 to 3 are considered as gradations.

[4] Jer., tr. *Yôma*, chap. iii. § 2; B., tr. *Pesahim*, fol. 94.

[5] It results, according to this verse, that the sun had risen when Lot had accomplished four miles to Zoar: the time is thus measured.

[6] For according to a passage of the Midrash Rabba, it was five miles (see Bereshith Rabba on this passage).

[7] See last note but one.

[8] Mr. Goldberg's interpretation, as mentioned above (p. 3), serves also to explain this passage: "The presence, at dawn, of the planet Venus may cause an error; sometimes she appears, and may be seen early before the close of the day, and sometimes she is seen late in the morning, after the day has already broken." What then is meant by the term אילת השחר (found in Ps. xxi. 1)? "It resembles two rays starting from the East, &c." There is indeed a musical instrument or lyre, the summit of which is provided with two horns or rays, so to say. See the Jewish Journal *Maggid*, *l.c.*

spots of light starting from the east to diffuse the light. R. Ḥiya Rabba (the great) and R. Simon ben Ḥalaphtâ were one morning walking in the valley of Arbel, and they noticed the dawn darting its rays of light; R. Ḥiya said to his companion: Master, this represents to me the salvation of Israel; at first it is slightly perceptible, but it increases as it advances. Many examples of this are to be seen in the Bible: "When I sit in darkness, the Lord shall be a light unto me" (Micah vii. 8); and again in the history of Esther: Mordecai was at first only seated in the king's gate; then Haman took the king's robe and the horse, &c.; then Mordecai returned to the gate of the king, and again came out from the presence of the king in royal apparel, and the Jews had light and gladness.

The opinion (aforesaid) of R. Ḥiya is conformable with that of R. Juda: for it has been taught, in the name of the latter, that to traverse the firmament it would take fifty years[a]. Now, a man of ordinary speed can traverse forty miles a day; therefore during the time that the sun takes to arrive at the middle of the firmament, that is, a journey of fifty years, a man would have accomplished four miles. This is equivalent to saying that the breadth of the firmament to be traversed (with reference to the sun's progress) represents a tenth part of the day. As the breadth of the firmament is a journey of fifty years, so also the breadth of the earth, including the depths thereof, is a fifty years' journey. Why? The following verses seem to prove it: "It is he that sitteth upon the circle of the earth," &c. (Isa. xl. 22); and: "he walketh in the circuit of heaven" (Job xxii. 14); and again: "when he set a compass upon the face of the depth" (Prov. viii. 27). Now, the identity of the terms (חוג) demonstrates the comparison (between these three objects).

It has been taught: The tree of life[1] was of such a length that it would have taken five hundred years to go over it; R. Juda, in the name of R. Elae, said: It is not by adding the extent of the branch, but the trunk itself is of this length; and all the rivers of the Creation spring from its feet. Allusion is made to this by the verse, "And he shall be like a tree planted by the rivers of water" (Ps. i. 3). It is further taught[2]: The tree of life represents the sixtieth part of the garden, and the garden the sixtieth part of Eden; it is also said: "And a river went out of Eden to water the garden" (Gen. ii. 10); the garden therefore represents only a part of Eden.

The bottom or overflow of a *coor* (*κόρος*, measure) may be put into another

[a] It must not be forgotten that astronomy had not made great progress at this epoch, and it was still thought that in the morning the sun issued from the firmament. See B., tr. *Pesahim*, fol. 95 *b*.

[1] See *Bereshith Rabba*, chap. iv.; *Debarim Rabba*, chap. ii.; *Medrash Ḥazith*, or on Canticus vi. 2; Medr. *Shoḥar tob*, chap. i.

[2] See B., tr. *Taanith*, fol. 10 *a*.

measure called a *tirkab*[3]," in the same way as the residue of Ethiopia is received by Egypt; that is equivalent to saying that: If it requires forty days to traverse Egypt, it would require more than six years for Ethiopia[4]. The Rabbis say: "The length of life of the Patriarchs gives the sum of the distance of heaven from the earth[5]." As there is between heaven and earth a journey of five hundred years, so there is the same distance between one heaven and another[6], and its breadth is the equivalent of it. And who is it who tells us that this is the breadth of heaven? R. Aboon says: It is written (in Gen. i. 6): "And God said, Let there be a firmament in the midst of the waters; let it be exactly in the middle of them." Rab said: The heavens were humid the first day, and they were dried on the second. Rab also says: The words, *let the heavens be*, mean "let the heavens be solid," as they congeal, let them be hard and let them extend. R. Juda ben Pazi thus explains the word רקע: "Let the heaven be like a garment spread over the earth;" this is similar to what is said (in Exod. xxxix. 3): "And they did beat the gold into thin plates" (which has the same meaning as "extend").

It has been taught, in the name of R. Joshua, that the thickness of the heavens is of two fingers. It is, then, R. Ḥanina's opinion which is under discussion; R. Aḥa thus explains, in the name of R. Ḥanina, the following verse: "Hast thou with him spread out the sky, which is strong, and as a molten looking-glass?" (Job xxxvii. 18). The term "spread out" indicates that they are made like a plate. One might have thought the sky was not thus formed (but was primitive); that is why the word *consolidated* is used. To show that they (the heavens) are unalterable, they are said to be like a molten looking-glass, that is to say, that at all times they seem to be newly molten. R. Yoḥanan and R. Simon ben Lakish conversed on this subject. The one said: Man spreads his tent on stakes

[3] This contains 3 *kab*: a *coor* contains 30 *sâd*, each *sâd* containing 6 *kab*; therefore a *tirkab* = $\frac{1}{60}$ of a *coor*.

[4] The forgoing note of the measures: *cour* and *tirkab* form the proportion 1 to 60, which is applied to the relation of Ethiopia to Egypt. If, therefore, it requires 40 days to travel through Egypt, it would require, to travel through Ethiopia, 40×60, or 2400 days, or 6 lunar years and 276 days (1 lunar year = 354 days), or 6 years 210 days (solar years of 365 days): the Talmud calls this 6 years *and more*. Therefore those editions of the Talmud which fix it at 7 years are erroneous.

[5] In allusion to Deut. xi. 21: "That your days may be multiplied, and the days of your children in the land which the Lord sware unto your fathers to give them, as the days of heaven upon the earth." There is in the term "as the days of heaven" (כימי), a combination of words, which it is impossible to translate. The said sum is composed thus: Abraham 173 years, Isaac 180, Jacob 147—total, 500. Cf. *Bereshith Rabba*, sect. xv. (fol. 13, col. 2); B., tr. *Ḥaghiga*, fol. 13 *b*.

[6] There are supposed to be seven higher heavens.

which end by falling asunder; whilst of the heavens it is said: "He spreadeth them out as a tent" (Isa. xl. 22); and they are said to be *consolidated*[7]. R. Simon ben Lakish said: Usually, when things are made of molten iron, they later on attach themselves by rust; but here it is not so; the heavens always appear to be newly molten. Referring to this last remark, R. Azaria interprets the verse: "Thus, the heavens and the earth were finished, and all the host of them. On the seventh day, God ended his work which he had made;" "and God blessed the seventh day" (Gen. ii. 1 and 3). What follows? "These are the generations of the heavens" (Gen. ii. 4). What relation is there between these two points? It means that the days, weeks, months, and years pass without changing; as it is written: "These are the generations of the heavens and of the earth when they were created, in the day that the Lord God made the earth and the heavens" (that is to say, that nothing was changed).

Rabbi says: There are four watches in the day and four in the night[8]; the time called *ōné* is $\frac{1}{24}$ of the hour; the moment $\frac{1}{24}$ of the *ōné*; and the instant $\frac{1}{24}$ of this last. Its length is, according to R. Berakhia, in the name of R. Ḥelbo, the time it takes to utter it; according to the wise men, it is the twinkling of an eye. According to Samuel, it is the 56,848th part of an hour[9]. R. Nathan says: There are three watches, for it is said "In the middle watch" (Judges vii. 12), and there can be no middle watch excepting there are three. R. Zerikan and R. Amé, in the name of R. Simon ben Lakish, say that Rabbi has, in confirmation of his opinion, the verse: "At midnight I will rise to give thanks unto thee, because of thy righteous judgments" (Ps. cxix. 62); and it is also written: "My eyes prevent the night watches" (Ps. cxix. 148). This proves that at midnight two watches at least have yet to run, say four in all. R. Ḥiskia, or R. Zerikan, and R. Aba were conversing; the one explained the origin of Rabbi's opinion, and the other the origin of R. Nathan's. According to the former, it is based on the word "midnight" (being the hour at which at least two watches have yet to run); the latter rests on the expression "*middle* watch" (which only admits of there being three). How does R. Nathan explain R. Rabbi's interpretation of the first verse? Sometimes, said he, David was up at midnight, and sometimes also "*his eyes prevented the night watches*," in the following manner: When David had supped royally (protractedly), he rose only at midnight; but when he supped alone (without ceremony), "*his eyes prevented the night watches*," i.e. he rose before the second of the three watches (at ten o'clock); the morning, however, never found David in bed. He says so himself: "Awake

[7] See *Bereshith Rabba*, sect. xii. (fol. 15, col. 3).

[8] See *Babli*, the same tr., fol. 3 *b* and 7 *a*, and '*Aboda Zara*, fol. 4.

[9] As an hour contains 60 minutes, or 3600 seconds, or 216,000 tierces, the fraction $\frac{56,848}{216,000}$ is equal to at least 4 tierces, or nearly $\frac{1}{13}$ second.

up, my glory; awake, psaltery and harp: I myself will wake early" (at daybreak) (Ps. lvii. 9). In other words: Let my glory awake to sing that of the Most High; my glory is nothing before His majesty; I awake the dawn, and it is not the dawn that awakes me. His weakness prevented him, by saying: Kings are accustomed to let the dawn wake them, and thou gettest up before it, or to sleep until the third hour (nine o'clock), and thou risest at midnight. It is, he says, *to praise the decisions of His mercy*. What did David do? R. Pinchas, on the authority of R. Éliézer bar R. Menahem, said: He took the harp and psaltery, and placed them under his head; at midnight he rose and played on these instruments, so that those of students should hear him. What did they say of it? This: If the king occupies himself at this hour with the laws and religion, how much more should we do so. R. Levi said: A harp was suspended at David's window in order to wake him; the north wind blew on it [1], and caused it to play of its own accord. It is written: "As the minstrel sings" (2 Kings iii. 15), not *with* him, but *sings* spontaneously, i.e. the instrument. How does Rabbi [2] answer Nathan, who rests his opinion on the words *middle watch?* R. Hoona said: According to Rabbi, the end of the second and the commencement of the third form, together, the night. But, said R. Manu, is that an answer? Is it written, *the* middle hours (towards the middle watch), or *a* middle [3] hour? It has been answered that the first watch does not count; for, people in general are still awake.

"The wise men say: until midnight."

R. Yossa, on the authority of R. Yohanan, says: This opinion serves for a rule. This Rabbi ordered the students of the Law to come and recite the Shema' before midnight, and then to proceed to study (for fear of missing the proper hour whilst arguing). This proves two things: 1st, that this opinion serves for a rule; 2nd, we may conclude that some words are added after the blessing which follows the Shema' [4]. It has been taught that: he who reads the Shema' in the Temple in the morning has fulfilled his duty; but not so he who does so in the evening. Why this difference? According to R. Hoonâ, by the authority of R. Joseph, the evening Shema' should be said at home, in order to drive out

[1] Is this not analogous to the Eolian harp? See B., tr. *Synhedrin*, fol. 16; *Tanhuma*, sect. *Behaalothekha; Rabba* on Num. xv.; *Ruth Rabba*, chap. v.; *Ekha Rabbati;* or on Lam. ii. 18.

[2] Who states that there are four watches and not three.

[3] Midnight is therefore in the middle of the second watch, between ten and two o'clock.

[4] According to him it is not necessary to bring together the formula of the *deliverance* and the *'Amida*. We shall speak of this further on.

the bad spirits (demons); this proves that nothing is added after the first blessing (contrary to the preceding opinion, and the formula which follows refers to the nocturnal demons). This is the opinion of R. Samuel bar-Naḥmani; when he proceeded to calculate the embolismic year, he paid a visit to R. Jacob Gerosa. R. Zeira hid himself then in the garret, and he heard the Rabbi repeating the Shema' until he fell asleep. Why so? R. Aḥa and his son-in-law R. Taḥelifta, on the authority of R. Samuel bar-Naḥman, say: It is in virtue of the verse, "Stand in awe, and sin not; commune with your own heart upon your bed, and be still. Selah." (Ps. iv. 4.) It is the opinion of R. Joshua bar-Levi which is under discussion, for he read psalms after the prayers (as is done now, in our time). It has, however, been taught that nothing is said after the blessing[5]. That is so for the morning blessing. And indeed R. Zeira, on the authority of R. Jeremiah, says: In three cases[6], the ceremonies should follow on without interruption; the slaughtering (of the sacrifice) after the imposing of the hands; the blessing after the ablution; the Prayer (*'Amida*) after the section recalling the Deliverance of Israel[7]. 1st, After the imposing of the hands, the slaughter: "And he shall put his hand upon;" and "he shall kill it" (Lev. i. 4, 5). 2nd, After the ablution, the benediction: "Lift up your hands (when they are clean) in the sanctuary, and bless the Lord" (Ps. cxxxiv. 2). 3rd, After the *Deliverance* comes the *Prayer*: "Let the words of my mouth, and the meditation of my heart, be acceptable in thy sight, O Lord, my strength, and my Redeemer" (Ps. xix. 14). And again: "The Lord hear thee[8] in the day of trouble" (Ps. xx. 2). R. Yosse bar-Aboon said: He who slaughters the sacrifice immediately after imposing the hands on it, does not run risk of the sacrifice becoming unworthy of service; he who pronounces the formula of the blessing immediately after the ablution is certain of escaping Satan during meals[9]; and he who recites the *'Amida* immediately after the formula of the *Deliverance*, has nothing to fear from Satan for the whole day. R. Zeira gives an example which is contrary to the assertion: Having stopped immediately after the *Deliverance*, to recite the 'Amida, he was taken into the king's service and commissioned to carry myrtle to the palace. Rabbi! said the others to him, it is a great favour; many people pay to visit the interior of the palace. R. Ame says: Who does he resemble, who does not recite the 'Amida immediately after the *Deliverance?* He resembles a favourite who knocks at the king's door; the king opens to see what he

[5] How then could this Rabbi allow himself to break this prohibition?

[6] See *Debarim Rabba*, chap. ii.; *Toledoth Aron*, chap. xxi.; Midrash on the Psalms, chap. i.; B., tr. *Menaḥoth*, fol. 93.

[7] See B., on the same treatise, fol. 42.

[8] As we shall see, the *'Amida* includes prayers of supplication.

[9] He shall come to no harm in eating.

wants, and if the solicitor goes away, the king withdraws his friendship from him.

"R. Gamaliel says: until dawn, &c."

His opinion is conformable to that of R. Simon, who taught as follows: Sometimes the Shema' is said twice running, once before dawn and once after, and therefore both the day and night's duty are accomplished. If R. Gamaliel is of R. Simon's opinion, as regards the evening, is it so with regard to the morning? Or is he of the same opinion as R. Zeira, brother of R. Ḥiya bar-Ashia and of R. Abba bar-Hanna, according to whom, if a person recites the Shema' with the priests on duty at the Temple, the prescription is not fulfilled, because it is said too early? (The question is not decided.)

2. (1.) [The following is a case in support of R. Gamaliel's opinion:] It happened that his sons came from a feast (potatio [1]) after midnight. They said to him: "We have not yet recited the *Shema'*." He answered them: "If the pillar of the morn has not yet risen, you are bound (obliged) to say it."

Has R. Gamaliel, who questions the opinion of the (other) Rabbis, acted upon his own opinion? Has he not questioned the opinion of the Rabbis, in doing, however, as they did? Has not R. Akiba acted in the same manner? And R. Simon ben Yoḥai, is he not in the same case? When did R. Meir, whilst acting in the same way as the Rabbis, differ from their opinion? Where has he been inconsistent? In the following case, viz.: It has been said [2] that in case of sickness, a compress may be made of old wine and oil perfumed and mixed with water, when the mixture of the oil and wine has been made on the previous day, but not if the mixture has not been made beforehand. R. Simon ben Éliézer says that R. Meir allowed the mixture to be made on the Sabbath, to be applied to the patient afterwards. When, subsequently, he fell ill himself, he would not permit this to be done. Master! said his pupils; living, thou now annullest thine own opinion. Although, he replied, I am not severe towards others, I am so to myself, as other Rabbis dispute my opinions. On what occasion did R. Akiba, although questioning the opinion of others, still conform to them? On the following occasion [3]: A house is rendered impure [4] by the presence of the

[1] On the word משתה (which Lebrecht translates as *Hochzeitmahl*, wedding feast), see Fränkel, *Monatschrift*, 1864, p. 265.

[2] These works are forbidden on the Saturday; B., tr. *Shabbath*, fol. 134 *a*; Jer., ibid. chap. xiv. § 3, end.

[3] Mishna, 1st part, tr. *Shebiith*, chap. ix., and *Oholôth* ii. 6; *Tosselta*, ibid. chap. iv. (see following notes, 4 and 5).

[4] I.e. fragments which make a whole.

spine and skull of two distinct corpses; or by the same quantity of bones, or by a member of two corpses [5], or by the flesh of two persons still living, or by a quarter of a measure of the blood of two corpses; this is the opinion of R. Akiba, but not of the wise men. One day, a basket of bones was brought from the village of Tobee, and was exposed in the courtyard of the Temple of Lood [6]. The Doctor Todros entered, followed by all his colleagues, and he said: There is here neither the spine nor skull of *a* corpse (which would cause a defilement); but, as some are of opinion that the united members of two corpses are supposed to render the whole impure, we will take a vote. The vote was commenced by R. Akiba, who declared that it was pure (according to the wise men): "If thou hadst declared it to be a defilement, we should have agreed with you; but since thou sayest there is no defilement, we agree the more readily." When does R. Simon, while adopting the opinion of the Rabbis, still question it? In the following case [7]: R. Simon says that it is allowable to gather all young shoots (at the commencement of the year of repose, *shmetah*, or seventh), excepting those of the Carob tree, for it has not its like among the plants, and those which have grown at the end of the sixth year cannot be distinguished from those of the seventh year: the wise men forbid it. R. Simon was one day, during the sacred year (*Shemita*, seventh), crossing the fields, and he saw some one gathering the young shoots of that year; he said: Is this not forbidden? Are they not young shoots? On the contrary, was the answer; hast not thou allowed it? Yes, replied the Rabbi; but as my condisciples contest my opinion, you must apply here the following verse: "Whoso breaketh a hedge, a serpent shall bite him" (Eccles. x. 8) [8]. In fine, R. Gamaliel also questions the decision of the Rabbis; but at the same time adopts it (with regard to the time of the reading of the Shema'). This discrepancy between theory and practice may be thus explained: When it is read too late, it is only done so by way of study. But it may also be said after dawn (this answer is thus refuted). Another answer may be that, as a rule, the opinion of the wise men may be adopted, i.e. not to

[5] It is known that the presence of a corpse in the house was formerly a cause of defilement, according to Jewish law. See Num. xxxi. 19. Here the question is to know what quantity constitutes a defilement.

[6] The Talmud often confounds Lodkia (Laodiceum), Lydda or Lod (Diospolis), and Lydia, capital Sardes (Neubauer, *Géographie du Talmud*, pp. 80 and 216); but here Lod is evidently a locality in Palestine, as it is said that a basket of bones was brought from Tobee into the Temple yard at Lood. The village of Tobee has beyond all doubt been identified with the existing place *Kefr Tab*, noted by M. de Saulcy on the road from Ramleh to Jerusalem *viâ* Koubeibeh (*Voyage*, vol. i. p. 81).

[7] See tr. *Shebiith*, ibid., and B., tr. *Pesaḥim*, fol. 51 *b*.

[8] I.e. in theory he holds a contrary opinion; but in practice he forbids it as do the other Rabbis.

go beyond midnight; but in the case of R. Gamaliel's sons returning from the feast, it was past midnight, and therefore impossible to follow this rule, so Gamaliel said to them: Act according to my own opinion.

3. Besides that recitation, anything, the performance of which has been limited by the wise men to midnight, may legally be accomplished up till the pillar of morn ascend (till dawn).

4. The combustion of fats[9], or of the parts or members of certain sacrifices, as well as the consummation of everything which has the day for a limit[1], may also be effected up till dawn. If so, why do the Sages say: until midnight? In order to withhold men from transgression (by forestalling the limit).

We have learnt that to this enumeration must be added the consumption of the Paschal lamb; some say that this is wrong. Who are those who make this addition? The Rabbis[2]. Who is it who holds an opposite opinion? R. Éliézer. What is his motive? He says that the word *night* as used (in Exod. xii. 12) on the occasion of the death of the first-born, and which is applied to the Paschal lamb, indicates, analogically, the hour of midnight. R. Hoona says: It would be impossible, even according to the Rabbis, to extend in this case, at Easter, the limit beyond midnight; for this sacrifice, as it has been said, defiles the hands after midnight (as being late, it is with even greater reason forbidden to eat of it after this hour).

"The consummation of anything which has the day for a limit, &c."

This means holy things of a secondary degree (they follow the same rule).

"To withhold men from transgression."

If the limit is extended to dawn, it might occasionally happen that the

[9] Lev. vi. 2, and vii. 2. We know that Mahometanism resembles very closely Judaism in rites and ceremonies; it is therefore curious to know the Mussulman prescriptions with regard to the immolation of sacrifices. According to a Spanish manuscript in the *Bibliothèque Nationale*, containing a *Traité des croyances, des pratiques et de la morale des Musulmans*, No. 91 (see Analysis by Silvestre de Sacy, in the *Notices et Extraits des Manuscrits*, vol. xi. 1st part, p. 324), we read in chap. xii. of this manuscript: "The time at which sacrifice should be offered is, from the time the sun has risen at the hour called *aldhoha* until sunset; the hour called *dhoha* is that at which the sun has already risen a little above the horizon." See *Chrestomathie Arabe*, by this author (2nd edition), vol. i. p. 162.

[1] Lev. vii. 15.

[2] See *Mekhilta*, sect. *Bô*, chap. vi.; B., tr. *Pesahim*, fol. 85 and 120.

presence of dawn had not been observed, and thus these sacred things might be consumed too late (which is forbidden); but in fixing midnight for a limit, there would be no sin in going a little beyond the hour.

5. (2.) From what time do we recite the *Shema'* in the morning? When blue may be distinguished from white. According to R. Éliézer, when one can discern betwixt blue and leek green (which is more difficult). This prayer may be finished until the sun shine forth[3], or until the third hour (nine o'clock), according to R. Joshuah[4], for such is the custom of royal princes to rise at the third hour. He who recites the Shema' after this hour loses nothing. He is like a man reading the Law (it has the same merit as the reading of an ordinary passage of the Law).

It has rightly been taught that it is necessary to be able to distinguish the blue threads of the *tsitsith* (fringes) from the white. What are the Rabbis motives? It is written: "Speak unto the children of Israel, that they make them fringes" (Num. xvi. 38), and "that ye may look upon it" (Num. xvi. 34). R. Éliézer says: The white threads must be distinguishable from the blue. According to R. Meir, it is written: "That ye may look upon it[5];" to show that he who accomplishes the prescription of the fringes, looks as it were to God. Now, the blue threads resemble the sea, and the sea the plants, and the plants Heaven, which itself resembles the Throne of Glory, which has been compared to a sapphire. For it is written: "And above the firmament that was over their heads, was the likeness of a throne, as the appearance of a sapphire stone" (Ezek. i. 26). By others, the words "Thou mayest look upon it" are interpreted: that a man may be able to distinguish his neighbour at a distance of four cubits. According to R. Ḥisda, the latter idea predominates. What is the consequence? A person with whom one is familiar may be recognized at a much greater distance, whilst a stranger cannot be distinguished even close at hand. In what case, therefore, can this interpretation be applied? In the case of a person little known, such as an unfrequent guest, ξένος. Others say: It implies that it must be possible at that distance to distinguish a wolf from a dog, or an ass from an onager; and according to others a friend should be recognized at a distance of four cubits. The theory of the comparison between a dog and a wolf, or the ass and the onager, is propounded by the same person who, as mentioned above, demands as a test the power of

[3] At the moment of the projection of the sun's rays.

[4] See for division of hours, above, p. 1, n. 3.

[5] See Sifri, sect. *Shlaḥ*, on Num. xv. 38; *Med. Rabba* in Num. iv., and B., tr. *Sôta*, fol. 17.

distinguishing blue from green (it is the more difficult one). And again the same person who proposed blue and white as test colours, advocates the theory of the recognition of a friend at four cubits distance (it is the easier test, and requires less light to accomplish it).

The reading of the morning Shema' has been prescribed for the hour at which the sun darts its rays, so that the prayer 'Amida may immediately follow the passage relating to the Deliverance, and be said by daylight. R. Zeira says: I see the motive (it is indicated in Ps. lxxii. 5): "They shall adore thee at the rising of the sun." Mar 'Ookba states that zealous people (εὔθικος) rose at the first hour and recited the Shema', and then the other prayers, so as to finish at the time that the sun darts its rays. R. Juda relates that he was once walking behind R. Eleazar ben Azaria and R. Akiba, who were speaking on religious subjects. R. Juda says: When the time for reciting the morning Shema' arrived, and after I had said it, I thought they had forgotten it in their preoccupation. I recited it a second time; but they did not commence it until the sun's rays touched the summits of the neighbouring hills.

"This prayer may be finished until the sun shine forth."

R. Zabdi, son of R. Jacob bar-Zabdi, on the authority of R. Yona, says that it should be said only when the sun's rays scintillate on the mountain-tops.

"According to R. Joshua: until the third hour (nine o'clock)."

R. Idi, R. Hamnonia, and R. Ada bar-Aḥa, speaking by the authority of Rab, say that the above opinion has regard to those who had forgotten to say it. R. Hoona says: This was the object of a discussion between two *amoraïm*, of whom one quoted the above precept to the other, who had forgotten to say the Shema'. But the other made the following objection, viz: Is it possible to establish a rule for one who forgets to pray? If the opinion of R. Joshua is to serve for a rule, it must be an absolute rule for all. Yes; but this subject has been mentioned, so that every one may take care to recite the Shema' in proper time.

It has been taught[6], that while studying (the Law), the studies must be interrupted in order to say the Shema', but need not be interrupted to say the 'Amida. R. Aḥa says: The Shema' is prescribed by the Pentateuch, but not so the other prayer. R. Aba says: There is a prescribed time for the Shema', but not for the 'Amida. R. Yosse says: The Shema' does not exact such undivided attention as the 'Amida. Rabbi makes an objection with regard to R. Yosse: Admitting, he says, that the Shema' does not exact a very great

[6] Cf. J., tr. *Shabbath*, i. 1 *bis* (fol. 3 *a*).

attention, do not the first three verses of it exact it? Yes, was the reply; but as they are very short, they are read with earnestness[7]. R. Yoḥanan, on the authority of R. Simon ben Yoḥaï, says[8]: When we are studying the Law, we do not interrupt our studies, not even for the *Shema'*; but, adds he, speaking now on his authority: we (I) who are not assiduous in our studies, interrupt them even for the 'Amida. Each of these opinions is in conformity with the several views of the above-mentioned Rabbis; for R. Yoḥanan has said: Please God that man prayed all day[9], for a prayer is never valueless. And R. Simon ben Yoḥaï says: Had I been on Mount Sinai, at the time that the Law was given to Israel, I would have asked God to give man two mouths, one to read the Law, and the other to speak about ordinary affairs. He adds: If with one mouth man has so much difficulty to withstand calumniators, what would be the result if man had two? R. Yosse said, in the presence of R. Jeremiah: R. Yoḥanan's opinion is in conformity with that of R. Ḥanania ben Akabia, for it is said: The writers of the rolls of the Pentateuch[1], of the phylacteries, and of the *mezoozoth* (sign of door-post), must stop to read the Shema', but not the 'Amida. R. Ḥanania ben Akabia says: As they interrupt their labours for the one, they ought also to do so for the other commandments of the Law. Does not R. Simon admit that the studies should be interrupted to perform the *Soocca* or the *Loolab* (two ceremonies of the Feast of Tents)? Is he not of opinion that one should not study if there is no desire to execute[2]? (i.e. What is the use of studying the Law and the religious ceremonies, if one does not fulfil them?) For, in that case, it were better not to be created. And R. Yoḥanan, does he not say, regarding those who study the Law without acting accordingly, that it would be better for him that his mother's womb had closed on him, and he had never been born? R. Simon ben Yoḥaï replies, that both precepts[3] are of the same order, and one cannot annul the other. Has it not, however, been said that he who reads too late, does so without regard to its liturgical value? Does this not show that, at an opportune moment, the prayer should precede study? This is quite true; but, says R. Juda: As R. Simon ben Yoḥaï gave himself up continually to study, this was preferred. R. Aba Mare says that a late reading of it has only the same value as a Biblical study; but read at a seasonable

[7] And their contents require attention.

[8] Babli, tr. *Shabbath*, fol. 11 *a*.

[9] See above, § 1 (p. 2).

[1] J., tr. *Biccurim*, iii. 3.

[2] They derive from the word, ושננתם, as says the Grand Rabbi Trénel (*Univers Israélite*, 1872, p. 373). The question is whether the study of the Law is to be interrupted in order to read the *Shema'*. Raschi explains it thus: Should he on that account rebel against the destructive implements, shears and knives?

[3] See *Wayyikra Rabba*, chap. xxv.

moment, it has the same value as the Mishnâ. R. Simon ben Yoḥaï is consistent in his opinions: To read the Bible, says he, is a secondary merit. According to the Rabbis, it has the same value as the Mishnâ [4].

6. (3.) The Shammaï school says: In the evening all men are to recline when they recite the Shema', and in the morning they are to stand up, for it is written (Deut. vi. 7): "*When thou liest down and when thou risest up.*" But the Hillel school says: Any one may read it in his own way (in whatsoever position he prefers), for it is written: "*in going thy way*" (Deut. vi. 7). If so, why is it said: "When thou liest down and when thou risest up" [5]? That means: When mankind usually lie down, and when mankind usually rise up.

We have seen that Hillel explains the two verses. How does Shammaï explain the verse on which his adversary bases his opinion? His opinion is that it serves to exclude him who occupies himself with religious subjects and the bridegroom [6]. One day, R. Elazar ben Azariah and R. Ismael were staying in a house together; the former was in bed, and the other still up. When the moment to recite the evening Shema' arrived, the one rose (according to Shammaï), and the other bowed down. R. Elazar ben Azariah said to the other: We are acting like the man who, being complimented on his long beard, replied that he grew it in opposition to those who shave themselves; in the same manner, I who was lying down rose up to say the Shema', and thou who wast standing up didst bow thyself down. Thou, answered the other, didst rise in conformity with the opinion of Shammaï, and I have done the contrary, as permitted by Hillel; or, also I acted thus so that the disciples should not think, by my example, to follow and make a rule of Shammaï's opinion.

7. (4.) R. Tarphon said: I was travelling, and having bent down to recite the *Shema'* according to the words of the school of Shammaï, I was in danger of robbers, ληστής (not having seen them soon enough). The Sages said to him: Thou wast guilty against thyself (didst deserve to be in danger), because thou didst transgress the words of the school of Hillel.

The wise men say, on the responsibility of R. Yoḥanan [7], that the words of the

[4] For fear of forgetting the Mishnâ, which was learnt by heart, it was made to prevail. Cf. J., tr. *Sabbat*, xvi. 1 (fol. 15 *c*); *Horaïoth*, iii. 5 (fol. 43 *c*).

[5] Motion is incompatible with standing still or lying down.

[6] Both are dispensed.

[7] J., tr. *Synhedrin*, chap. xi. § 4 (6); tr. *'Aboda zara*, chap. ii. § 8.

Rabbis compare favourably with those of the Law, and are as agreeable as they are: "*Thy taste is like unto that of good wine*" (Canticles viii. 10). According to Simon bar-Aba[8], speaking on the authority of R. Yoḥanan, they resemble those of the Law and are preferable to them, for "*thy loves are better than wine*" (Canticles viii. 10)[9]. Here is the proof of it, says R. Abba bar-Cohen, on the authority of R. Juda bar-Pazi: If R. Tarphon had not read the Shema', he would only have transgressed an affirmative prescription, punishable by a slight penalty; whilst in reading it as he did, contrary to Hillel's judgment, he rendered himself liable to be punished by death, in virtue of the verse, "*He who breaketh a hedge* (the Law), *a serpent shall bite him*" (Eccles. x. 8). R. Ismael teaches that: The orders of the Pentateuch contain either prohibitions or permissions, the first are of importance (solemn), the latter are not; but the words of the Doctors are always so. We will prove this: We have learnt that the negation of the precept of the phylacteries, which is an opposition to the Law, is not a sin (for it is only necessary to consult the text to know that it exists); but he who would put five sections to it (instead of four), and thus add to the orders of the Doctors, would be condemnable. R. Ḥanania, son of R. Ada, on the authority of R. Tanḥoom bar R. Ḥiya, says: The decisions of the elders have more value than those of the Prophets; it is written: "They shall prophesy[1]; but they shall not prophesy for those whom shame doth not quit;" and: "I shall predict for thee wine and drink." To what may be compared the Prophets and the wise men? To two couriers[2] sent by a king to a distant province; with regard to one, he writes that: If he presents himself without my seal and stamp, σμαντήριον, he is not to be trusted; but with regard to the other, he writes: That he may be trusted without producing these tokens. Also is it said with regard to the Prophets: "And he giveth thee a sign or a wonder" (Deut. xiii. 2); whilst on the other hand it is written: "*According to the sentence of the law which they shall teach thee*" (this is their superiority), "*thou shalt do*" (Deut. xvii. 11). This, however, is not decided until after a *bath-kol*[3] has been held; before that, if any one wishes to act severely, and to adopt as rules the solemn opinions of Shammaï and Hillel, he merits to have applied to him the verse, "*The fool walketh in darkness*" (Eccles. ii. 14) (for these

[8] The text has אוו. The ו and the י are doubled when these two letters are to be pronounced as consonants (*w* and *y*), not as vowels (*oo*, *i*); so says M. Jos. Derenbourg, *Revue Critique*, 1872, p. 114, note.

[9] By the words "*thy tastes*" and "*thy loves*" are meant the Rabbis.

[1] That is to say, the wise men; they will expound the Law.

[2] Literally (according to J. Lévy, *Neuh. Wörterbuch*, s.v.), two notaries of the army (πόλεμος and νοτάριος, *notarius*, for the Aramæan term in the Talmudic text).

[3] Literally, "a daughter of voice" (echo from the Heaven). See *General Introduction*.

opinions sometimes differ). It would be impious, on the other hand, to adopt the opinions of one or the other, choosing those which are the easiest. It would have been right to follow sometimes the easiest, and sometimes the most difficult decisions of one or the other school. This applies only in so far as the *bath-kol* had not spoken [4]; but since it has declared for Hillel, the decisions of Hillel are law, and the transgressor of them merits death.

It has been reported that the *bath-kol* has said: The decisions of all of them are the words of the living God; but Hillel's opinion predominates. Where has this been revealed? At Yabne, as says R. Bivi, on the authority of R. Yoḥanan.

8. (4.) In the morning, two benedictions are said before the *Shema'* and one after it; in the evening, two blessings before and two after it, one long and one short [5]. Where the Sages have said to lengthen (that a long prayer is ordered), it is not allowed to shorten, and to shorten, none is allowed to lengthen; when it is to be terminated by the closing formula (*Be thou praised, Lord*), it is not allowed not to close (to suppress this formula), and *vice versâ*.

R. Simon, on the authority of R. Samuel bar-Naḥman, says: This arrangement of the prayers is made in virtue of the verse, "*and in his law doth he meditate day and night*" (Ps. i. 2); the meditation of the day and of the night should be equal [6].

R. Yosse bar-Abin, on the authority of R. Joshuah ben Levi, says: That it is in virtue of the verse, "*Seven times a day do I praise Thee, because of Thy righteous judgments*" (Ps. cxix. 164). R. Naḥman adds: He who accomplishes this precept of praising God *seven times*, does as well as if he *meditated on the law day and night*. Why are the two sections of the *Shema'* read every day? R. Levi and R. Simon have both replied. R. Simon says: Because each section recalls the precept to read it going to bed and at rising. R. Levi says: "Because in them the Decalogue (Exod. xx.) is recapitulated. Thus: 1st, "*I am the Lord thy God*" corresponds to "*Hear, O Israel, the Lord is our God.*" 2nd, "*Thou shalt have no other gods before Me,*" to "*The Eternal is one.*" 3rd, "*Thou shalt not take the name of the Lord thy God in vain,*" to "*Thou shalt love the Lord thy God;*" *for, if you love the King, you will not take a false oath in His name.* 4th, "*Remember the Sabbath and sanctify it,*" to the words "*that thou mayest remember.*"

[4] I.e. before Hillel's opinion had definitely prevailed.

[5] A long blessing begins and ends with the words, "Blessed art thou, O Lord;" a short blessing only ends with these words.

[6] I.e. As in the evening the third section of the Shema', devoted to the *sight* of the *Tsitsith*, cannot be applied in the evening, it is replaced by another benediction.

Rabbi adds: It is this precept about the Sabbath which is equivalent to all the others, for it is written: "*Thou hast made known unto them Thy holy Sabbath, Thou hast given them commandments and laws,*" &c. That shows that it is worth all the religious prescriptions. 5th, "*Honour thy father and thy mother,*" to the words "*so that thy days and those of thy children be multiplied*[7]." 6th, "*Thou shalt not kill,*" to the words "*Thou shalt soon perish;*" for he who kills shall be killed. 7th, "*Thou shalt not commit adultery,*" to the words "*You shall not follow the desires of your hearts or of your eyes;*" for, says R. Levi, the heart and the eyes are the seducers[8] which draw men towards sin (being the organs of covetousness), for it is written (Prov. xxiii. 26): "*My son, give Me thy heart, and thy eyes shall follow My ways;*" the Most Holy (may He be blessed!) says: "If thou givest Me thy heart and thine eyes, I know that thou art Mine." 8th, "*Thou shalt not steal,*" corresponds to the words "*Thou shalt reap thy wheat,* and not thy neighbour's." 9th, "*Thou shalt not bear false witness against thy neighbour,*" to the words "*I am the Eternal Lord thy God;*" and it is said, "*the Eternal God of truth.*" And what is the meaning of this last word? R. Aboon says: That he is the living God and the King of the universe. R. Levi says: The Most Holy has said that to bear false witness against one's neighbour is equivalent to the blasphemy of denying God as the Creator of heaven and earth. 10th, "*Thou shalt not covet thy neighbour's house,*" to the words "*And thou shalt write them upon the posts of thy house*" (and not of the house of thy neighbour).

It has been taught[9]: The head of the section of the Temple told the priests to give a benediction, and the assistants answered. What benediction did they give? According to R. Matna, on the authority of Samuel, it is the benediction of the Law; then, the Decalogue was read and the three sections of the Shema'. R. Ame, on the authority of R. Lakish, says: That shows that omitting the benedictions (which accompany the Shema') does not hinder the recitation. R. Aḥa says: That proves nothing; for the Decalogue is like the integral part of the Shema' through its contents (and constitutes no interruption). And R. Matna and R. Samuel bar-Naḥman say: The Decalogue should be recited every day as a prayer; why is it not done so? It is not to give the enemies of religion cause to suppose that the Decalogue alone has been revealed to Moses on Mount Sinai. R. Samuel bar-Naḥman, on the authority of R. Juda bar-Zebda, says: It would be well if the chapters of Balak and of Bileam were read every day by the faithful; it is not done, for fear of fatiguing them. And indeed in this chapter, according to R. Hoona, is found the mention of the setting and the rising of the sun (Num. xxiii. 24); and according to R. Yosse bar-Aboon, the

[7] That is, the reward spoken of in the Decalogue, about the respect towards parents.

[8] See Matt. xv. 19; Mark vii. 21. Cf. *Bamidbar Rabba*, chap. x.

[9] Mishna, v., tr. *Tamid*, v. 1.

coming out of Egypt and the Royalty (Num. xxiii. 22). According to R. Eliezer, this episode should be said, because it is found in the Pentateuch, in Prophets (Micah vi. 5), and in the Hagiographs (Neh. xiii. 2).

It was therefore the master of ceremonies who ordered the benedictions, that the assistants repeated: first, the benediction of the Law, *Ahaba* (second of morning prayers); but the first blessing had not yet been said? R. Samuel, brother of R. Barakhia, answers that the light of the sun not having appeared just then, one could not, in praising God, call him "Creator of the lights" (so its place is changed). On the Saturday, a blessing is added for the company of guards who go out (in their turn). What is this prayer? According to R. Ḥelbo, it is the following: "May He who resides in this house (God), place in the midst of you fraternity, friendship, peace, and good intercourse."

Samuel says: If any one has risen early to study the Law before the recitation of the Shema', he must say the formula of the benediction (of the Law); after the Shema', it is no longer necessary (for the benediction of the Shema' is an exemption). On condition, adds R. Aḥa, that the study takes place immediately after the prayer. R. Hoona says that: If the subject be of the Exegesis, the formula must be said; but if it be a legal subject, it is useless. R. Simon says: It must be recited in any case. R. Ḥiya bar-Ashe relates this: When we were studying before Rab, either Exegesis or Jurisprudence, we used to say the formula of prayer. If the Shema' is read with the other persons, on service in the Temple, the duty has not been accomplished, for the priests said it at a late hour (on account of their labours). R. Zeira, in the name of R. Ame, says: In the time of R. Yoḥanan, we would go out on the days of fast, and read the Shema' after the third hour (9 h.), without any one forbidding us to do so. R. Yosse and R. Aḥa also came out on those days, and the Shema' was read in public after the third hour. R. Aḥa wished to oppose himself to this custom. R. Yosse said to him: They have already read it at the proper time, and they only repeat it to recite the 'Amida afterwards. It is because of the people, answered R. Aḥa, that I oppose myself to it, so that they may not suppose it is the proper hour for this reading.

These are the offices that may be lengthened: those of the New Year, of the great pardon or public fasting. It is when he prays that the learned man may be distinguished from the ignorant. Here are the short prayers: those of the precepts concerning the enjoyment of fruit, the counsel about the thanksgiving after meals, and the end of these thanksgivings. Does that mean that all the others may be lengthened? No, says Ḥiskia: From what has been said about prolongation being a bad quality and abbreviation a good one, it may be concluded that there are no fixed rules (the category for short ones is, then, unlimited). On a fast day, the formula for the Deliverance of Israel in the 'Amida must be lengthened (by adding *'Anénoo*, &c.). Does that mean that,

for the other six medial prayers, the addition does not take place (contrary to the rules)? R. Yosse answers: So that it might not be supposed that this prayer, which forms part of the 'Amida, should not be prolonged, it has been necessary to proclaim the precept of this prolongation (on fast days). The following are the formulæ of the blessings, during the reading of which the people bend down: at the commencement and the end of the first blessing of the 'Amida, and at the last but one, which is the blessing of thanksgiving. Those who bow down at each blessing are informed not to do so. R. Isaac bar-Naḥman, on the authority of R. Joshuah bar-Levy, says: The high priest bows down at the end of each blessing; the king at the beginning and end. R. Simon says, on the same authority, that the people bend a little, and do not stand erect again until the prayer is ended. Why? Because it is written: "*When Solomon had made an end of praying all this prayer and supplication unto the Lord, he arose from before the altar of the Lord from kneeling on his knees*" (1 Kings viii. 54). There is a difference between genuflection[1] and prostration. R. Ḥiya the Great, in demonstrating to Rabbi the first way of bending down, became lame, but was afterwards cured. On the other hand, R. Levi bar-Sissi, whilst demonstrating the second style, became incurably lame. "*With his hands spread up to heaven*" (1 Kings viii. 54) is said there. R. Aïbo adds that he held himself like a gouty person (i.e. a little bent forward). This proves, says R. Abina, that his hands had not at all benefited by the construction of the Temple. R. Ḥalaphta ben Shaul taught that every one should bend forward with the officiating priest, when the end of the thanksgiving is being said. R. Zeira said: No, they should only bow at the word *Mŏdim;* he followed the officiating priest word by word, so as to prostrate himself at the same time as he did, at the beginning and end of the sections. When R. Yossa went to Palestine, he noticed them bowing down and reciting certain words in a low voice, and asked what they were saying. Why should he have been astonished? Did he not know what had been said by R. Ḥelbo, on the authority of R. Yoḥanan and of R. Jeremiah, by R. Ḥanina on the authority of R. Maysha, and by R. Ḥiya on the authority of R. Simai; or as others say, the condisciples on the authority of R. Simai? The following is the formula: "We acknowledge ourselves (humbly) before Thee, Master of all creatures, God worthy of praise[2], Rock of the world, living Being of the universe, Author of creation, Thou who raisest the dead to life, that Thou wouldst preserve the life Thou hast given us, that Thou wouldst pardon us our sins, support us, and permit unto us to render thanks to Thy name; be praised, O God, worthy of praise." R. Aba bar-Zabdi pronounced, on the authority of Rab, a different formula: "We humbly acknowledge that we must give thanks

[1] J., tr. *Soucca*, v. 4.

[2] See the Jewish Prayer Book, '*Amida*, sect. 17 (18).

unto Thy name; *my lips shall greatly rejoice when I sing unto Thee, and my soul which Thou hast redeemed* (Ps. lxxi. 23); be praised, O Lord, worthy of praise." R. Samuel bar-Mena, on the authority of R. Aḥa, said: "Praises and thanks unto Thy name; Thine is the greatness, Thine is the power, Thine is the majesty; may it please Thee, O Lord our God, and God of our forefathers, to support us in our fall, and to lift us up out of our humiliation, for Thou supportest those who fall, and Thou straightenest those who are bowed down[3], Thou art full of mercy, and there is no other but Thee; be praised, O Lord, who art worthy of praise." Bar-Kapara said: "We must kneel, bow, and prostrate ourselves before Thee; before Thee all must bend the knee, and every tongue shall invoke Thee. *Thine, O Lord, is the greatness, and the power, and the glory, and the victory, and the majesty; for all that is in the heaven and the earth is Thine; Thine is the kingdom, O Lord, and Thou art exalted as head above all. Both riches and honour come of Thee, and Thou reignest over all; and in Thine hand is power and might; and in Thine hand it is to make great, and to give strength unto all* (1 Chron. xxix. 11, 12). With all our heart and soul we prostrate ourselves. *All my senses say: O God, who is like unto Thee?* Thou deliverest the poor from out of the hands of him who is stronger than him, and Thou defendest the needy from him who useth violence to him. Be Thou praised, O Lord, who art worthy of praise." R. Judan said: The Rabbis have the habit of saying all these (which they said in a low voice); but other Rabbis say: they recite sometimes a formula, and sometimes another of these formulas (i.e. only one).

It is not right, as a rule, to bend down too low. R. Jeremiah says that it is not right to do as some do[4], but all parts of the body should be bent, so that *all our organs* should adore him. On this point, the opinion of R. Ḥanan bar-Aba is contested. He said to his colleagues: I am going to tell you of a beautiful thing; it is to have seen that Rab bowed down in this manner, and I told Samuel of it. He thereupon got up and embraced me. One should bow in saying *Be Thou praised,* and stand up straight again when arriving at the name of the *Lord.* Samuel said that the reason of it is that it is written: "*The Lord raiseth them that are bowed down*" (Ps. cxlvi. 8). R. Ame said: That does not seem right to me; should we not bow in uttering this name, for it is written: "*and was afraid* (was bowed down) *before My name*" (Mal. ii. 5)? No, said R. Abin; if it had been written, *at My name,* it would have been right to bow down in uttering it; but as it is written "*before*" *My name,* we must bow before uttering it. R. Samuel bar-Nathan, and R. Ḥama bar-Ḥanina relate that a certain priest, whilst officiating, bowed down too low, and was in consequence

[3] Allusion to 1 Chron. xxix. 11.

[4] For when they bow, they do not bend their necks.

interdicted by order of Rabbi. R. Yoḥanan says that he was made to come down, and R. Ḥiya bar-Aha says that he was only reprimanded.

The blessings which commence by the formula *Praised be God,* are as a general rule those terminating by *barookh,* &c. If two blessings follow one another, as for example in the Shema' and 'Amida, this formula is not used. But, objected R. Jeremiah : Why is this formula used in the blessing of the Deliverance (called Easter evening), although another blessing follows? That is different, for R. Yoḥanan says: If the reading of the *Hallel*[5] has been heard at the Temple, it may be dispensed with (for in this case, the *Hallel* not being repeated, the formula would be isolated). R. Eliezer objected to R. Yossa: How does the end of this same benediction also contain this formula, although it follows the other so nearly? R. Yossa answered that these two parts are distinct, one bears reference to the future, the other to the past. May not the same objection be made for the *habdalla* (prayer that separates the Saturday, or festivals, from the week)? It is also different, for R. Aba bar-Zabdi said that Rabbi recited them separately, and afterwards together with his glass in his hand[6]. R. Ḥiya Rabba said them (at once) together. The invitation to the blessing for the meal (which presents the same difficulty) is also explained, for if only two persons are eating together, they do not say what precedes the thanksgiving. As for the end of the first section of this thanksgiving (which wrongly contains the formula referred to), it is a question not yet decided. In the same manner for the benediction of the fourth section of the meal, it is thus expressed, because, according to R. Hoona, it was composed (alone) at the time of the burying of the warriors of Beṭhar: The word *tôb* (*good,* therein contained) is recalled there, because these bodies had no bad smell[7],—and by the word *hametib* (benefactor), thanksgivings are offered to God because they have been interred. The formula of sanctification (*kiddoosh*) of Saturdays and festivals begins in the same manner (although it is very close to other benedictions); it is so because it sometimes happens that whilst sitting drinking on the preceding evening before night, the festival has been sanctified without interruption, and, consequently, without reciting the formula of the benediction of the wine (that is to say, alone). As for the formula of the end, if it seems to be in contradiction with the above rule, it is because, according to R. Mena, it represents the general rule (*typus*) of the benedictions. R. Judan says: If the benediction is short, it begins by the words, *Praised be Thy name, O Lord;* but it does not finish thus. If it is long, it begins and finishes in the same manner. All the blessings proceed according to their terminations,

[5] The rest of the Psalms, from cxiii. to cxviii., is recited at the service of the festivals and of the new moons.

[6] To say the *habdallah.*

[7] Though they had remained some time without a sepulture. See hereafter, vii. 1.

but not according to the intercalated verses[8]. R. Isaac bar R. Eliezer objected to R. Yosse: If it is agreed that the benediction should be regulated according to its termination, why not say that it should refer to the verse? This is what is meant by the words, "according to the end." If in the morning one had by mistake read a benediction for the evening, and that on finishing one say the exact end of the morning prayer, the duty is accomplished[9]. R. Aḥa says: All the benedictions take a direction agreeing with the termination of the prayer, and those who add (in the third section of the thanksgiving at the meal) the verse (Isa. xii. 6): "*Cry out and shout, thou inhabitant of Zion,*" do not do so for the sake of the benediction, but optionally.

9. (5.) In the evening prayer, the *deliverance of the Israelites out of Egypt* is commemorated (Num. xv. 37). R. Eleazar ben Azaria says[1]: I am almost seventy, and I was never certain that the deliverance out of Egypt should be said at night, until Ben Zoma had expounded it from these words (Deut. xvi. 3): "*That thou mayest remember the day when thou camest forth out of the land of Egypt all the days of thy life.*" "*The days of thy life*" (generally) represent the day; the addition of the word *all* also means (includes) the nights. But the Sages say: The days of *thy life* represent this world (actual life), and the word "*all*" means the days of the Messiah.

Although invested with high authority, Eleazar lived many years; but according to the general rule, honours shorten life. At Babylon, it was taught that the third section of the Shema' must not be said at night (Num. xv.); however, if it has been begun, it must be continued (according to the wish of Ben Zoma). But the Rabbis of this place (Jerusalem) say that from the outset, the first verses of this section are begun to be read without finishing them[2]. The Mishnâ is in contradiction with the opinion of the Rabbis of Jerusalem, since it says that at night, the coming out of Egypt is recalled (which seems to imply the reading of

[8] That is to say, in the benedictions the recitation is regulated by the end of them. In the morning, when making the ordinary recitation, a benediction of the evening had been read by mistake, and that on finishing one finds out the mistake, if the last words of the morning's benediction are said, that is sufficient. It is useless, in this case, to recite the Bible verses that refer to the subject developed in the benediction, and to use at the end the final expression: *Praised be God!* &c. Cf. J., tr. *Taanith*, ii. 3.

[9] See B., tr. *Pesahim*, fol. 104.

[1] See *Sifri*, sect. *Reëh*, chap. cxxx., end; *Mekhilta*, sect. *Bô*, chap. xvi.

[2] That is to say, the verses relating to the *Tsitsith* are omitted, the precept not being applicable to the night, and they pass to the verses relating to the Deliverance out of Egypt.

all the chapter). R. Aba or R. Juda, in the name of Rab, say that the words of the *Mishnâ* only refer to the following formula: "We thank Thee that Thou hast brought us out of Egypt, and that Thou hast delivered us out of bondage, that we may praise Thy name."

Does not the Mishnâ also seem to contradict the opinion of the Rabbis of Babylon[3], when it gives us to understand that the third section is only applicable to the day? And, indeed, the entire section is only applicable to the day (because of the verses relating to the *tsitsith*, but the others are also said in the evening). R. Aba bar-Aḥa went to Babylon, and he saw that this reading was begun and entirely finished, and he has not heard it said that the beginning of the third section should not be read, and it is only necessary to finish it if the reading has been begun by mistake. The Rabbis of Jerusalem say that this section should be begun but not ended (that is to say, the particulars relating to the *tsitsith*, not applicable to the night, are left out). It has been asked of R. Aḥa bar R. Zeira: How his father did? Did he act up to the opinion of the Rabbis of Palestine, or those of Babylon? R. Ezechias says: He followed the opinion of those of Jerusalem, and R. Yose followed that of the Rabbis of Palestine. R. Ḥanina says: This last opinion seems to be the right one; for R. Zeira acted with great severity, as also did those Rabbis (of Babylon); it proves that he was of their opinion. It has been taught that he who reads the Shema' in the morning must, in the blessing that follows, recall the Deliverance out of Egypt, according to Rabbi; the almighty power of God must be recalled; and finally, according to others, the passage of the Red Sea, and the death of all the first-born must be called to mind. R. Joshua ben Levi says: All these facts must be mentioned, and the words "Rock of Israël and its deliverer." He also says: If the gift of the Law has not been mentioned in the second section of the blessing of the meal, it must be repeated. Why? Because it is said (Ps. cv. 44): "He gave them the lands of the heathen." To what end? "That they might observe His statutes, and keep His laws[4]." R. Aba bar R. Aḥa, on the authority of Rab, says: If in this section the marriage of Abraham has not been recalled, or if in the third section the mention of the reign of David has been omitted, it must be repeated. R. Ila has said: If the words "consoler of Jerusalem" have been said, that is sufficient. Bar-Kappara says: He who (in the prayer) says *Abram* instead of *Abraham*, transgresses an affirmative prescription[5]. According to R. Levi, it is also a negative prescription; this opinion is taken from the verse (Gen. xvii. 5), "Neither shall thy name be called Abram." The positive order

[3] They say, as it has just been mentioned, that if the reading of the first verses has been begun, it must be continued, contrary to the rule formerly in use, according to the Mishnâ, not to say them again in the evening.

[4] It is therefore inseparable.

[5] See *Med. Rabba* on Gen. xlvi. and Num. iii.

is contained in these words: "But thy name shall be Abraham." But, it was objected, Have not the men of the great Synagogue called him Abram? Is it not said (Neh. iv. 7): "Thou art the Lord God, who didst choose Abram"? This is different, and means that when he was only *Abram* (before the divine revelation), "thou didst choose him." And likewise, if Sarah is called by the name of Saraï, do they transgress a commandment? Yes, it was prescribed to Abraham. If that is so, why, when one calls Israel by the name of Jacob, is not the prohibition violated? Because this second name has been added without suppressing the first. Why, after changing the names of Abraham and of Jacob, was not the name of Isaac also changed? Because the names of these two patriarchs was given them by their family, whereas that of Isaac was given by God; for it is said (Gen. xvii. 19): "Thou shalt call his name Isaac." Four persons have received their names[1] before their birth, viz.: Isaac, Ismael, Josias, and Salomon. It was said of Isaac: "Thou shalt call him Isaac;" of Ismael: "Thou shalt call him Ismael" (Gen. xvi. 11); of Josias: "Behold, a child shall be born unto the house of David, Josiah by name" (1 Kings xiii. 2); of Salomon: "And he called his name Salomon" (2 Sam. xii. 24). Up to the present we have spoken of godly people; but of the ungodly it is said: "For the wicked are estranged from the womb" (Ps. lviii. 3). Ben Zoma says: In the future, it will not be necessary for Israël to recall the departure from Egypt. Why? Because it is said: Therefore, behold the days come, saith the Lord, that they shall no more say: The Lord liveth, which brought up the children of Israël out of the land of Egypt; but they will say: The Lord liveth, which brought up and which led the seed of the house of Israël out of the North Country. The Doctors answered: That does not mean that the fact of leaving Egypt will be set at nought; but it will be secondary with regard to future events. It is said (Isa. xliii. 18): "Remember ye not the former things," that is to say, of the Egyptians; "neither consider the things of old," that is to say, the (inimical) kingdoms. It is also said: "Thou shalt not be called Jacob, but thy name shall be Israel." The Doctors observed: That does not mean that the name of Jacob will be annihilated, but it will be added to that of Israel, which will be the principal, whereas that of Jacob will only be accessory. The following verse: "I will do a new thing, now it shall spring forth" (Isa. xliii. 19), alludes to the war of Gog. To explain the subject better, it is given as a fable. What is it like? To a person who meets a wolf on his way; he escapes, and begins a tale about a wolf. Then he meets a lion, from which he escapes, whereupon he forgets the tale about the wolf, to relate his adventures with the lion. Finally he meets a serpent, and escapes; he then forgets the first two adventures to tell a tale about the serpent. It is thus for Israel; the two last misfortunes have caused the first to be forgotten.

[1] See *Medrash Mekhilta*, sect. *Bô*, chap. xvi.; *Pirké R. Eliezer*, chap. xxxii.

CHAPTER II.

1. If any one is reading in the Law (studies the passage of the *Shema'* in the Pentateuch) when the time for the recitation arrives, it will be sufficient if one's attention is given to the reading (in a devotional manner); but if not (in the contrary case), he is not free (this reading is not sufficient). At the end of the sections one may be the first to salute the persons out of respect, and one can answer their bow; but in the middle of a section one must neither give nor answer a salute, except from fear (in a case of danger[1]). It is the opinion of R. Meir. R. Juda says: If one is in the middle, he salutes from fear; and, to honour any one, it is only allowed to answer; but at the ends of the sections he salutes out of respect, and repeats peace to every man.

R. Aba says: This assertion of the Mishnâ (that it is sufficient to apply one's attention if by chance one is reading the Pentateuch) proves that the want of the blessing is not an obstacle to the accomplishment of this duty[2]. R. Yossa says: "If it is admitted that the blessings are indispensable, if they have been said (before or after), you must apply yourself to all; if it was not understood, it would have been necessary to say also that in the Mishnâ it is forbidden to interrupt oneself between the sections of the Shema' (and that is difficult in an accidental reading, because of the interval which separates them), and yet nothing has been said of that; in the same way, although nothing has been said about the blessings, they must be recited with attention. The contrary opinion of R. Aba is proved by what follows: R. Aba says, in the name of R. Juda: It

[1] The interruption of a prayer, unless it be unavoidable and indispensable, constitutes an irreverence to God, that a feeling of respect easily explains; and on the other hand, it must not be forgotten what an importance the Orientals attach to a salutation, and to what danger it exposed the Jews in the midst of the Romans.

[2] Since, in the hypothesis of the Mishnâ, it is only supposed that reading the Pentateuch one arrives at the time for prayer at the Shema', without having made the preparatory prayers.

is sufficient to apply oneself to the reading of the first section, without having done so for the second section (it is the same, with more reason, for the benedictions). What difference is there on that account between these two sections? It is, says R. Ḥanina, because all that is written in one section is also contained in the other. If it is so, why read more than one? The first, says R. Ila, is applied to the individual alone, the second to the community (because it is written in the plural, as an address to the people); the first contains the theory, the second the practice [3]. Bar-Kapara says: It is sufficient to apply one's attention to the three first verses. In fact, it has been taught that one's attention must be applied in this recitation as far as the words "*you will inculcate them*" (my precepts); after which the simple reading is sufficient [4]. R. Hoona, R. Oori, R. Joseph, R. Juda, in the name of Samuel, say: You must during this reading assume the celestial sovereignty by remaining standing (as a sign of respect). What! if one is sitting, must one rise? (Is it not contrary to the opinion of Hillel?) However, if one is walking, one should stop still for a time (to give more solemnity to one's expression).

It has been taught that the sound of the word אחד (*one*, in the first verse of the *Shema'*) should be lengthened. R. Naḥman bar-Jacob says that one should only lengthen the pronunciation of the end of this word. Somkhos bar-Joseph says: He who lengthens the pronunciation of this word shall see his days and his years prolonged in happiness. R. Jeremie lengthened this sound far too much: Thou needst not insist so much, said R. Zeira; it is sufficient to give it the necessary time to acknowledge (mentally) the reign of God in Heaven, on the Earth, and the four cardinal points. Rab asked R. Ḥiya the Great: How is it that I do not see Rabbi assume upon himself the celestial sovereignty? He answered: When thou shalt see him put his hands on his face, he will be accomplishing this act of submission to God. But, asked Rab, must he not recall the departure from Egypt (which I do not see him do at present)? It is not possible, answered he, that he should not say a few words (and that suffices). R. Tabiome asked of R. Ḥiskia: Can you not conclude from Rabbi's manner (putting his hand on his face at the beginning of the Shema'), that it is sufficient to apply one's attention during the first verse? No, answered Adda; it has been taught that the attention must be applied as far as the words "you will inculcate them." R. Meira says, in the name of R. Juda, or in the name of R. Yosse the Galilean [5]: If one has interrupted oneself during this recitation long enough to finish it all,

[3] Because therein these words are found: *You shall practise them* (the divine precepts).

[4] There is a play upon the word ושננתם, which signifies at the same time *to inculcate* and *to repeat*, or read again.

[5] Cf. J., tr. *Meghilla*, chap. ii. § 1 (fol. 73).

the duty is no longer accomplished entirely (and you must begin again). R. Aba and R. Jeremie, in the name of Rab, said: This opinion has been adopted as a rule, for it was stated in the name of R. Juda, who had it from R. José the Galilean. R. Yoḥanan, on the authority of R. Simon ben Yehozadak, adds that it is the same thing concerning the reading of the *Hallel*[6] and of the *Meghilla* (history of Esther read on that festival). Aba bar R. Hoona and R. Ḥisda were sitting together; and they said concerning this same subject, that it is so when the *Shophar* is rung (at the New Year). They went to Rab's study, and they heard R. Hoona say in the name of Rabbi, that even if one has heard the nine peals of the Shophar in the space of nine hours of the day (say each peal at an hour's interval), the duty of listening is considered accomplished. R. Zeira says: When I was at Babylon, I inquired about it, and I learnt it on arriving here (at Jerusalem). R. Yosse, in the name of R. Yoḥanan, says: It is even allowed to have heard these sounds at any time in the day, as long as the order of the peals has been observed[7]. R. Yosse asks: If there are, says he, two listeners, one of whom should hear (according to his order) a single short note at the beginning, and the other listener a similar note at the end, can the same sound serve at once for the two persons who are listening? (The Talmud has not answered the question).

In like manner R. Elazar ben Ḥanania[8] asks: If in the reading of the Shema' and its benedictions, or of the Shema' without its benedictions, or of the benedictions without the Shema', one has interrupted oneself a quarter of an hour; then after having resumed the reading, if there has been a second interruption as long, is it judged after the time this person takes to read it[9], or is it considered according to the time others might take? Is the reading null, or should it be resumed? R. Matna answers: It seems that they count according to the time this man would take. R. Abahoo asked R. Yoḥanan: If, whilst I am reciting the Shema', I happen to pass near an impure place, and that I interrupt myself on that account, can I, without failing in my duty, content myself by continuing? My son, answered Abahoo, if thou interruptest thyself during a space of time sufficiently long to read it all, thy duty is not accomplished. R. Eliezer went to see R. Simon bar-Abba, who was ill. The latter addressed him a question: If, because of my weakness, I happen to sleep in the midst of my reading of the

[6] See above, p. 25, note 5.

[7] Here is this order: 1st, *Teqia'* (a single, short note); 2nd, *Trooa'* (a quavering, longer note); 3rd, a new *Teqia'*. Cf. J., tr. *Rosh Hashana*, iv. 10; Gr. R. Wogue, *Traduction du Pentateuque*, Lev. xxiii. 23 (t. iii. p. 297, note 2).

[8] For his genealogy, see Derenbourg, *Essai, &c.*, note x., p. 472.

[9] According to the Mishnâ at the head of this chapter, the interruption does not annul the accomplished duty.

Shema', am I exempted from reading it again? Yes, answered he. R. Jeremie asked of R. Zeira: Has R. Eliezer decided this case in this way, because he knows that R. Simon bar-Aba observes scrupulously the divine prescriptions, and that he applies his attention thereto (even in his delicate state of health), or else did he think he ought to make an exception in favour of his particular weakness? It is in a peremptory manner that R. Eliezer judged this case, answered he (therefore, even if it should happen that a healthy man should fall asleep, he need not begin again). It is a question that has been discussed: R. Eliezer says that this reading is sufficient; R. Yoḥanan is of a contrary opinion. However, the discussion only relates to the reading of the Shema', for which the interruption is allowable, because it is composed of sections (which do not follow in the Pentateuch). But, for the reading of the *Hallel* and the Story of Esther, R. Eliezer submits to the opinion of his contradictor.

It has been taught: He who interrupts himself to ask after the health of his master, or of any one who is more learned than himself, may act as he pleases. That proves that one must render homage to those who are superior in science. It is again seen by the following: If any one tears his clothes at the news of a decease (according to the lawful prescription), and that the person who was thought dead comes back an instant to life, then finally dies, it is not necessary to operate a second laceration, if the definitive death took place immediately; but a second one is necessary if an interval of time has elapsed since the false announcement. What do you call "at once"? The time necessary to say a word. But what is its duration? R. Simon, in the name of R. Joshua ben Levi, says: It is the time that elapses when you present (short) salutations to your neighbour. Abba bar-bar-Ḥana says, in the name of R. Yoḥanan: It is the time that a disciple would take to present his salutations to his master, saying (in three words), "I bow, to thee, my master[1]." R. Yoḥanan leant on Jacob bar-Idi whilst they were walking; as soon as R. Eliezer saw them, he hid himself[2]. There are two offences, said R. Yoḥanan, on the part of this Babylonian: first, he does not bow to me; and then he cites one of my opinions without naming me. Such, was answered, is the custom with them, that the inferior does not bow to the superior; thus they apply the verse: "*The young men saw me, and hid themselves*" (Job xxix. 8). As these two rabbis continued on their way, they saw a schoolroom. Here, said R. Jacob (to console him), R. Meir sat when he explained the subject of study; he expounded a doctrine in the name of R. Ismaël, but he repeated another in the name of R. Akiba, without naming him. It is because, said R. Yoḥanan, every one knows that R. Meir was his disciple. The same for thee, answered he; every one knows that R. Eliezer is thy disciple. Is it allowed to walk before a cursed

[1] J., tr. *Moëd qaton*, iii. 7 (fol. 83 *c*, *d*).
[2] J., tr. *Sheqalim*, chap. ii. § 7 (fol. 47).

idol? What! answered R. Yoḥanan, will you render him that honour (of turning aside)? Pass before, and shut your eyes. So, R. Jacob adds (if it is rendering honour to turn aside), R. Eliezer has done well not to pass before thee. O Jacob bar-Idi, replied R. Yoḥanan, thou art an adept at soothing all vexations. But R. Yoḥanan wished that what he had taught should be proclaimed on his authority. It is also the favour that David begged for: "*I will abide in Thy tabernacles for ever*" (Ps. lxi. 4). R. Pinḥas and R. Jeremie, in the name of R. Yoḥanan, added this explanation: Did it ever enter the mind of David to live eternally? Certainly not. David only asked as a future honour that his words should be repeated as in his name in the synagogues and schools. What enjoyment will that procure him? Levi bar-Nezira says: When after his death the sayings of a man are repeated, his lips move at the same time in the tomb. Where do they learn that? From a verse that says: "*He causes the lips of those that sleep to move*" (Cant. viii. 10); as, in the vat, the wine flows all alone from the grapes. R. Ḥanina bar-Papai and R. Simon also explain it: one says that it seems to him as if he drank spiced (*conditum*) wines; the other, as if he drank old wine, the good taste of which still remains in the mouth long after it has been drunk[3].

There is no generation which has not its scoffers. What did they do in David's time? They went before his windows, and cried out ironically: David! at what epoch will the Temple be built[4]? When shall we go into the house of the Lord? And the king answered: Although you intend to irritate me, I swear that my heart is full of joy. It is also what is said: "*I was glad when they said unto me, Let us go into the house of the Lord*" (Ps. cxxii. 1).

On the words "*And when thy days be fulfilled*" (2 Sam. vii. 12), R. Samuel bar-Naḥmeni thus expressed himself[5]: The Most High said to David: I will accord thee a complete life, and not a mutilated and uncompleted life; verily, it is thy son Solomon who shall build my house. Is it not to offer sacrifices therein? I prefer to them that which thou doest: the exercise of justice and equity. And what proves it is the verse: "*To do justice and judgment is more acceptable to the Lord than sacrifice*" (Prov. xxi. 3).

"At the end of the sections."

For what causes (insufficiently determined in the *Mishnâ*) ought one to reply to the salutations[6]? Is it only in case of danger, or to render honour to

[3] Cf. B., tr. *Synhédrin*, fol. 90 *b*.

[4] See *Medr. Rabba* on Deut. v.

[5] J., tr. *Rosh Hashana*, i. 1.

[6] This question of the Talmud is addressed to the two suppositions given by the Mishnâ: that of an interruption between the sections of the Shema' or of the blessings accompanying it, or of an interruption in the middle of the prayers themselves.

any one. It can be decided from this: At the end of the sections, it is said, one may be the first to give the salute in case of danger, and one should also answer a salutation, according to R. Meir; that proves that in the interval between the sections, one can bow, and the more so if it is to render honour (if it was not so, the second hypothesis need not be expressed). The second supposition is explained by the reverse: In the middle (of a section), it is said, the salutation may be expressed in case of fear, and he can also answer to a salutation. And in what case may one answer? Is it only in a case of danger, or to render an honour? What follows solves the doubt: R. Juda says: In the middle, one addresses the salutation in a case of danger, but one can answer if only to render an honour (it is understood that one answers in a case of danger, since in that case one may begin to give the bow). That proves that, for the hypothesis of R. Meir (in the middle), one addresses the salutation in a case of danger, and one only answers for the same reason (for if one were allowed to answer in the middle, even to render honour, his opinion would be the same as that of R. Juda). Until now, we have only spoken of the middle of the sections (supposing that means between the verses). But is it the same thing for the middle of the verses? R. Jeremie made signs in this case (but did not speak). R. Yona answered verbally, because, according to R. Hoona and R. Joseph, this permission is expressed in these words: *thou shall speak*, בם, contained in the *Shema'*; these words mean that even in the middle of a verse one may *speak* (when it is indispensable).

2. This is what is called the intervals of the chapters: between the first and the second benediction, between the second and the words of the *Shema'* (Hear, O Israel), between each of the three sections of the *Shema'*, between that and the blessing after it. According to R. Juda, between the last section of the *Shema'*[7] and the benediction that follows, none is to pause[8].

R. Levi says that R. Juda intends to bring together in this way the last words of this section: "*I am the Eternal, thy God,*" with the first word following, *truth*, according to the verse: "*The Eternal God of truth*" (Jer. x. 10).

3. (2.) R. Joshua ben Korḥa asks: Why are the sections disposed thus[9]? That one may first take on himself the kingdom of Heaven,

[7] Num. xv. 37-41.

[8] He forbids the interruption there.

[9] Literally: Why does the (section) "Hear" precede "and it shall come to pass"? Why not say at the last those which, in the Bible, are the last?

before he take on himself the yoke of the commandments (express one's faith, then one's adhesion to the precepts of the Law). The passage (of Num. xv.) which forms the third section (although coming first in the Bible) is placed the last because it is only adapted to the day [1], whereas the second (Deut. xi. 13-21) has no limit (may be practised by day and by night).

R. Ḥanina says, on the authority of R. Yoḥanan: Why is it prescribed that the men should wear phylacteries, read the Shema' and pray (the 'Amida)? It is in order that he should entirely accept the divine yoke [2]. Rab points out another order: One should read the Shema', wear the phylacteries, and pray. Does not the next Braïtha seem to be in opposition to the opinion of Rab in the following case: If any one is in the act of burying a corpse when the hour for the reading of the Shema' arrives, he must retire into a pure place, put on the phylacteries (first), read the Shema' and pray (therefore, the order is not the same)? No; Rab (in opposition to the Braïtha) agrees with the Mishnâ; it only says that man should, before anything else, make a profession of faith, and then an act of adhesion to the precepts of the Law (contained in the second section of the Shema'). R. Yanaï says: When one puts on the phylacteries, one should be pure in body [3]; and why does one not keep them on (all day)? Because of the hypocrisy (of those who, wearing them all day [4], wished to make believe in their piety). Here is an example: A man entrusted his neighbour with a deposit, but he denied having received it. "It is not in thee, the robbed man exclaimed, that I put my faith, but in these objects (the phylacteries) that thou wearest on thy head." R. Yanaï, after an illness, wore them three days consecutively [5], meaning thereby that illness effaces sin. What is the proof of that? This verse: "*He forgiveth all thine iniquities, and healeth all thy diseases*" (Ps. ciii. 3). R. Yoḥanan ben-Zaccaï removed the phylacteries neither summer nor winter, and

[1] It contains the precept to wear and to "*look* upon it," i.e. the fringes (Num. xv. 39).

[2] That is to say, when he is clothed in the insignia of Religion, תפילין, then only he will say his prayers. These phylacteries contain, in a leathern case, four sections of the Pentateuch written on parchment, meaning: Exod. xii. 1-10; xii. 11-16; Deut. vi. 4-9; xi. 13-21. To these divisions are attached, according to traditional prescriptions, straps of leather dyed black. One of these divisions, called "that of the head," is fixed on the forehead by a knot formed beforehand by these straps. The other division, called "of the hand," is attached by a running knot to the left arm, above the elbow, and one rolls the strap round the arm seven times, and then round the fingers.

[3] B., tr. *Shabbath*, fol. 130 *a*.

[4] Idea exposed in the Gospel (Matt. xxiii. 5).

[5] See Midrasch *Shoḥar Tob* on Psalm c.

his disciple R. Eliezer followed his example. In summer, as R. Yoḥanan did not bind his head with a turban, he wore both; whereas in winter, as he wore a turban to protect himself from the cold, he only wore those of the arm. Was it not forbidden him to wear phylacteries (because of the state of nakedness to which R. Yoḥanan reduced himself in summer, on account of his excessive corpulency)? R. Ḥiya bar-Abba says: In his home (upon him) he wore a tunic. When he went to the bath, on arriving near the attendant, he took off the phylacteries. R. Isaac says that he put them on again at the house of R. Jacob Tarmossra (far from the baths, at a servant's); they were brought to him as he left the bath, and then he would say to those persons [6]: Two holy arks accompanied Israel in the Desert; that of the Lord and that of the remains of Joseph. The nations of the world were astonished and said: Is it possible that the ark of a deceased mortal should be carried along with the ark of the Eternal Being? It is because, answered Israël, the one obeyed the precepts of the other. Why did he relate this? It was, said R. Ḥanina, because he wished to speak of the Bible as soon as he left the bath (where it is forbidden). But, objected R. Mana, had he no other Bible story to relate except that one? Yes, and it was with a private intention that he related this fact (to reprove those persons who only wore the phylacteries during their prayers). Joseph, said he, only became a king because he observed the divine precepts, and we only obtained this honour (that conferred by the Law of Moses) because we followed the precepts of God; and you would neglect his commandments!

How [7] is the formula for the blessing of the phylacteries pronounced? R. Zerikan, on the authority of R. Jacob bar-Idi, says that for those of the hands, the following words are said: "May He be blessed, who sanctified us by His commandments, and who bade us wear the phylacteries." When they are taken off, one says: "May He be blessed," &c., "to observe his laws." This last formula is said according to the opinion of him who thought that the verse (of Exodus) which recommends the observing of the law relates to our subject. But, as for the opinion of him who admits that same verse refers to the Passover, there is not (for the phylacteries) any precise decision. And so R. Abahoo, on the authority of R. Eliezer, says [8]: He who puts on the phylacteries during the night, transgresses a positive order contained in this verse (Exod. xiii. 10): "*Thou shalt therefore keep this ordinance in its season, from year to year*" (literally, from *day to day*); it says: "*the day*" and not the *night*, or on *ordinary days*, excepting the Sabbaths and festivals. Did not R. Abahoo, however, sit during the night, studying the Law, with the phylacteries on his head? No, he had them next to him, as if he had to guard a sacred trust. One may also admit that the verse

[6] B., tr. *Sôta*, fol. 13.

[7] B., tr. *Menahoth*, fol. 36 *a*.

[8] J., tr. *'Erooben*, x. 1.

contains the prohibition of wearing the phylacteries in the night, but not the order to take them off in case they had been worn all the day. It is also said that the duty (of wearing them only on ordinary days) is also deduced from this verse: "*And it shall be for a sign unto thee upon thine hand*" (Exod. xiii. 9), excluding the Sabbaths and festivals, which are in themselves a religious mark. But does it not appear clearly enough from the words "from one day" (ordinary) to another[9]? Certainly that would suffice; but, as R. Yoḥanan observes, for every rule that is not expressed in a positive manner, it is right to confirm it by two texts. Elsewhere[1], it has been taught: "Women and slaves shall be exempted from reading the Shema', and wearing the phylacteries." The women because it is said: "*And ye shall teach them unto your sons*" (Deut. xi. 19), and consequently not to your *daughters;* and as the men receive special orders to study the religious prescriptions, they must also submit to the duty of wearing the phylacteries, whereas it is not so for the women. To this rule it has been objected that Michal, daughter of Saül, wore the phylacteries, and that the wife of Jonas went to Jerusalem on festivals (without being obliged); and yet the wise men did not oppose themselves to either case. (Is not that in contradiction with the former rule? For, if these two examples were forbidden cases, the wise men ought to have opposed themselves to them, according to the principle that forbids to add anything to the Law.) That is true, says R. Ḥiskia bar-Abahoo; therefore, Michal, daughter of Saül, was advised by the wise men to refrain in future, and the wife of Jonas was brought back home.

This has been taught: At the entry of the baths and at the place where every one remains dressed, one can read the Shema' and the 'Amida, and with more reason, one can bow to one's neighbours[2]; one can wear the phylacteries, and one need not take them off. In the room where the greater number are in a state of nudity, one gives no salutation, and cannot say any prayer; it is necessary to take off the phylacteries (that one might be wearing). In the intermediate room, where some are dressed and others are not, one may bow, but recite no prayer; it is not necessary to take off the phylacteries (if one wears them), but one ought not to put them on before being entirely out of the establishment[3]. This approves the behaviour of R. Yoḥanan, exposed by R. Isaac, who only put the phylacteries on again when he was far from there, at the servant's (Jacob Tarmossra). R. Jeremie asked of R. Zeira: Is it the same thing for an establishment that only opens in summer? It is always a bath, was the answer, and considered as an

[9] That is to say: Why seek for a second text to prove this rule?

[1] 3rd chap. of this same treatise, § 2.

[2] The salutation implied the pronunciation of a divine name, and had to be made properly.

[3] Out of respect, one ought not to expose them in a profane place.

unclean place, though there is nothing unclean. Mar-'Ookba says: It is like the snout of a pig, which is a moving uncleanliness. R. Youna asked: What is to be said of the uncleanliness which is near the seaside (which being continually washed by the waves, has no bad smell)? R. Ame answered that Assaï has taught R. Jeremie's opinion, and it is best to try and avoid the dirt without paying any attention.

R. Zeira says, on the authority of R. Aba: One may, having the phylacteries on the head, eat something unthinkingly, but not make a meal; one may doze, but not give way to complete sleep. According to the teaching of some, one single blessing is sufficient when one puts on the phylacteries (that means, that if one has only eaten a little, it is not considered an interruption which obliges one to begin again). According to others, one must say the blessing a second time (after having eaten anything, one's attention being apt to wander). One understands the opinion of him who admits that the first benediction is sufficient, because one supposes that he bears in mind what he wears on him. But how must one explain the opinion of him who says it is necessary to say another prayer? Does not the fact of having eaten with phylacteries on still exist (it would then be necessarily a want of respect towards the religious duty)? R. Zeira answers that Aba bar-Jeremie does not speak of a meal, but of any one who tastes anything (and who, however, blesses it; in that case he does not forget).

R. Zeira says, on the authority of R. Aba: One ought not to enter an urinal with holy books or phylacteries in one's hand. When (in such a case) R. Yoḥanan had a book of homilies in his hand, he would pass it to his pupils; whereas, when he had on the *tephilin*, he did not take them off. Is not this teaching of R. Aba contradicted by a *baraïtha*, which declares the reverse and allows the entrance? No; when it says they must be taken off, it proves that there still remains (afterwards) time enough to put them on again by daylight; in the other case, they should not be taken off; otherwise, one would not accomplish a religious duty by putting them on again (for, at night it is useless to put on the *tephilin*). Then why be wanting in respect (by not taking them off)? Therefore, R. Aba commands to take them off. As a rule, they were to be confided to a companion; but as one day one of these ran away with them, the custom has been established of putting them in a hole devoted to that use. When through this custom a lamentable accident occurred[4], it was decided they should be held in one's hand when entering these places. R. Jacob bar R. Aḥa adds, in the name of R. Zeira: On condition that it is still daylight (on coming out), that they may be put on again;

[4] A prostitute carried them off one day, and bringing them to the Temple, accused a student of having given them to her; when the student heard this he killed himself in his despair. See Babli, same treatise, fol. 23 *a*.

in a contrary case, it is forbidden to keep them on, for, far from thus observing a religious precept, one would seem to despise it. Mesha, grandson of R. Joshua bar-Levi, says: He who wishes to act well, places them in his heart on a little bag, according to this text (Ps. xvi. 8): "*I have set the Lord always before me.*" There (at Babylon) it has been taught: that one must not put on the *tephilin* if one is not like Elisha, the man with wings (that is to say, in a case of danger, as at the time of that celebrated event. A Roman order once interdicted wearing them; a magistrate passed; the Rabbi who had on the *tephilin* saw him, and took them in his hand; and when the Roman asked him what he was carrying, he answered that they were the wings of a pigeon[5]; and a miracle took place, which metamorphosed them into wings and saved the pious Rabbi, who was near becoming a victim to his religion).

R. Zeira, on the authority of R. Abba bar-Jeremie, says: It is forbidden to commit any impropriety in a cemetery, and to him who could act so this text is applied (Prov. xvii. 5): "*Who mocketh the poor, mocketh his Creator.*" R. Ḥiya Raba (great) and R. Yonathan were walking before the bier of R. Simon bar-Yossi bar-Lekonia[6], and R. Yonathan jumped over some tombs. R. Ḥiya Raba said to him: The dead must say to each other that to-morrow those men will be with us, and yet, to-day they inflict suffering upon us. But, answered he, have these dead any understanding? Is it not written (Eccles. ix. 5): "*The dead have no understanding*"? Thou knowest how to read the Bible, was the answer, but not to interpret it. "*For the living know that they shall die*" (says the same verse). The wise, even after their death, are still considered as living; and "*the dead that know not anything,*" are the wicked, who during life are already considered as dead. How is that known? By this verse (Ezek. xviii. 32): "*For I have no pleasure in the death of him that dieth.*" Can one say that he who is dead dies again? No, it refers to the wicked, who during life are called dead[7]. And how is it known that the just are called living, even when they are dead? By this text (Deut. i. 6, 8): "*The Lord our God spake: Go in and possess the land which the Lord sware unto your fathers Abraham, Isaac, and Jacob,*" *saying*. Why add: לאמר (saying)? Because God ordered him to go and "*say*[8]" to the Patriarchs (in Paradise): "All the conditions I have made with you, I will fulfil them after you, towards your sons."

If a copy of the Pentateuch has its letters mixed or joined[9], it is, however,

[5] B., tr. *Shabbath*, fol. 130 *a*.

[6] Cf. Medrash on Eccles. ix. 5, and on Gen. xxxix.

[7] This passage recalls a passage of the Gospel (Matt. viii. 22). Maïmoni and Spinoza understood the words of the Ecclesiastes in another way, observes Mr. Ad. Franck (*Journal des Savants*, Feb., 1872, p. 557).

[8] So, they do speak after their death.

[9] J., tr. *Meghilla*, i. 9 (11), fol. 71 *c*; tr. *Soférim*, ii., end.

sufficient according to some (for the duty of reading), and not according to others. R. Idi, in the name of R. Simon or R. Yoḥanan, says: He who says it is sufficient, supposes the letters are attached at the bottom (which is not a great inconvenience), and he who declares the joined writing inexact, speaks of the case where the letters would be joined at the top; there is only a doubt and discussion in the case where the letters are joined in the middle of the finals (which are long, it would then be impossible to read it).

The same Rabbi teaches that one should not pray on a high place, because it is written, according to R. Abba, son of R. Papi: "Out of the *depths* have I cried unto thee, O Lord!" (Ps. cxxx. 1). He says again: One should not commence praying whilst experiencing a natural want, because it is said: "*Prepare to meet thy God, O Israel*" (Amos xv. 12). R. Alexander says that this text: "*Keep thy foot when thou goest to the house of God*" (Eccles. iv. 17), means that one should take care to be in a state of complete cleanliness. According to R. Jacob bar-Abai, this text means that one must be clean and pure when going to the Temple. R. Abai thus interprets the verse: *Let thy fountain be blessed* (Prov. v. 18). "When thou approachest a tomb, be not defiled." R. Berakhia thus explains the verse: *A time to be born and a time to die*. "Happy is he who when he dies is as pure as at his birth, for then he dies undefiled [1]."

4. (3.) If any one recites the *Shema'* so low as not to be audible to his own ears (that he cannot hear himself) [2], he is legally free (and has nevertheless accomplished his duty); but, according to R. Yosse, it is not sufficient. If he recites it inaccurately [3], he is free (it is not necessary to begin again), according to R. Yosse, and it is (necessary) according to R. Juda. He who recites it backwards (irregularly) is not free (not dispensed from a second reading); and he who makes a mistake in his recitation, must begin again at the place where he made the mistake.

Rab says that custom adopts as a rule the opinion of any of the above in their easiest meaning. If it were not so, what does your Master Rab wish to teach by that? Is it not a fixed rule that if an anonymous person is not of the opinion of R. Yosse, the former's opinion has the preference? Or else, if R. Yosse discusses the opinion of R. Juda, has the opinion of the latter more weight? Why, then, does Rab say that the opinion of each of them is adopted in its least grave aspect? Because, having heard that R. Ḥiya had taught this opinion on the

[1] Rabba on Deut. vii. and Eccles. viii.
[2] Sifri on Deut. vi. 4.
[3] Literally: without a good pronunciation.

authority of R. Meir (so that it was no longer anonymous), it was necessary to state precisely what rule was to be followed in a contested case.

It has been taught: "If any one says the prayer (*'Amida*) too low to hear himself, the duty is nevertheless considered as accomplished." Whose opinion decided that point? That of R. Yosse[4]. And who is this R. Yosse? He who professes in the Mishnâ an opinion contrary to the anonymous opinion.

R. Matna also says: It is this doctor's opinion. And indeed R. Yossah (a namesake of R. Yossah, who came long after him) says: It is not to be believed that the word Shema', which means *listen, hear,* is the subject which forms the discussion between R. Yosse and the Rabbis, and that for all the other commandments it is not necessary; we are told, on the contrary, that the author of this opinion, according to R. Matna, is R. Yosse; that shows that it is the same thing for the Shema' as for all the other commandments. Why? Because R. Yosse proves it by this verse (Exod. xv. 26): "*and wilt give ear to his commandments*" (all); thy ears should hearken to the words thy mouth pronounceth. But then, said R. Ḥisda, what will a deaf person do when he is reciting? He speaks after his fashion. The opinion expressed in the Mishnâ by R. Juda is in his favour. R. Yossa says it may therefore be concluded that R. Ḥisda admits that the anonymous opinion which forbids a deaf man to perform the oblations, is R. Yosse's. And indeed R. Ḥanina, on the authority of R. Ḥisda, says it is his opinion. R. Yosse bar R. Hoona says: It must be so, for when the enumeration of the first five persons who are not to share in the oblations is made, the deaf are not included therein[5]. So, failing a contrary opinion, they suppose it is allowed him. It is R. Yosse who forbids it. But (it will be said) that is natural, since the oblation, even if it be already deducted, cannot be made use of. No, that is not natural, for the deaf do not come in the enumeration of the five last persons for whom it is forbidden; finally it must be said that the prohibition for the deaf was made by R. Yosse.

[4] Since in the opinion of the *Mishnâ* it is a duty which even suffices for the reading of the Shema', it is needless to say that it is the same thing, in his opinion, for the *'Amida*, which is less serious.

[5] In order to understand this deduction well, the following Mishnâ must be seen, it is in the treatise *Trumoth* (oblations which belong to the priests, chap. i. § 1): "There are five persons who cannot deduct anything from the tithe, for fear of fulfilling the duty insufficiently; these are: the deaf, the mad, children, he who deducts what does not belong to him, and the stranger who takes the oblation from an Israelite's property, even with the owner's permission. The deaf, speaking without hearing, should not partake; but if he has done so, it is valid. Everywhere else, when the deaf are mentioned, the deaf and dumb are alluded to." This opinion does not bear the name of its author, and it may be applied to R. Yosse. Cf. J., *Trumoth*, i. 1 (fol. 41 *c*); tr. *Meghilla*, ii. 5 (fol. 73 *b*).

This is the list of the words of the Shema' to the reading of which one must apply one's attention (so as not to mistake them, because of the concordance of the last letter of the first word with the initial letter of the following word): for instance, על לבבך, *on thy heart*;—"on your heart;"—"the grass in thy field;"—"you will soon perish;"—"at the corner of the raiment, a thread;"—"you of the Earth." R. Ḥanina, on the authority of R. Aḥa, adds the expression נשבע ה', "*that God has promised by oath*[6]," to this list. R. Samuel bar-Ḥanina also adds, on the authority of R. Oschia (the formula of the first benediction of the morning): "Who made the light, and created the darkness[7]," so that it should not be said: "Who made the light, and created the brightness of the day." R. Ḥaggai, on the authority of Aba bar-Zabda, also adds these words: "There have they *sung* Thy name," that it may not be said: "They have praised Thy name there[8]." R. Levi R. Abdima from Ḥipa, on the authority of R. Levi bar-Sisi, says: A stress must be put on the ז of the word תזכרו[9]: "*so that ye may remember*" (in the third section of the Shema'). R. Yona, on the authority of R. Ḥisda, says: the words "*His grace is eternal*," must be pronounced in the same manner (Ps. cxxxvi.).

It has been taught[1] that the ceremonies must not be performed by the people of Ḥipa, Baizan, or Tebon, for they pronounce the letter ח like ה, and the ע like א (the same philological observation as above); it is only allowed if their pronunciation is correct.

"He who reads backwards has not accomplished his duty."

R. Yona says, on the authority of R. Naḥman bar-Ada, or according to R. Yosse on the authority of Naḥman Saba: The Bible expression: והיו, "*let them be*" (Deut. iv. 6), shows that the words must remain in that order. It is the same thing for the reading of the *Hallel*[2], and the Story of Esther. For this last it is easily understood, for it is expressly stated: "*according to the writing*" (Esther viii. 9); but what is the proof for the *Hallel*? It is therein said (Ps. cxiii. 3): "*From the rising of the sun until sunset, the name of the Eternal God is praised*" (in the same manner as the reverse cannot take place for the sun, so also the order of the words must not be changed). What consequence may be deduced from that? R. Aban answered: That the sequel also plainly contains an order; the chapter "*When Israel came out of Egypt*" (Ps. cxiv.), refers to the past; and

[6] A curious philological observation; already the sound of א and ע could be confounded.

[7] Imitation of Isa. xlv. 7. Compare for the details, Babli, same treatise, fol. 11 *b*.

[8] To avoid the confusion of the two ל in the word הלל, *to praise*.

[9] So as not to read: תשכרו, "you will (or shall) be paid."

[1] Cf. J., tr. *Meghilla*, ii. 1.

[2] See above, p. 25, note 5.

"*It is not in our favour, O Lord!*" (Ps. cxv.) is applicable to the present generation; and "*I love the Lord, because He hath heard my voice*" (Ps. cxvi.), refers to the time of the Messiah. The verse: "*Bring forth the victim crowned with myrtle*" (Ps. cxvi. 27), refers to the wars of Gog and Magog (commotions which were to precede the coming of the Messiah); and the following, "*Thou art my God, and I will offer Thee thanksgiving,*" bears reference to the future.

R. Aḥa, on the authority of R. Joshua ben Levi, says that: He who established this prayer (the 'Amida) has regulated it in this manner [3]: The three first benedictions and the three last are in the honour of God. The medial benedictions refer to the wants of man: "May we be favoured with the gift of wisdom," or "Thou hast favoured us with this gift;" "Accept our repentance," or "Thou hast accepted our repentance;" "Forgive us," or "Thou hast forgiven us;" "Deliver us," or "Thou hast delivered us;" "Heal our diseases," or "Thou hast healed our diseases;" "Bless our days," or "Thou hast blessed our days;" "Unite us," or "Thou hast united us;" "Judge us with equity," or "Thou hast judged us with equity;" "Confound our enemies," or "Thou hast confounded our adversaries;" "Confer upon us Thy justice," or "Thou hast conferred upon us Thy justice;" "Build up Thy house, listen to the voice of our prayer, and be favourable to us." This last prayer is not the expression of a necessity; but it has been rendered in this manner, according to the ideas expressed in this verse (Isa. lvi. 7): "*Even then will I bring them to my holy mountain, and make them joyful in my house of prayer.*"

R. Jeremie says [4]: The hundred and twenty members of which the Grand Assembly was formed, comprising more than eighty prophets [5], have arranged that prayer and put it in order. Why has the prayer "Most Holy God" been compared to that which contains the prayer for wisdom? Because after the verse (Isa. xxix. 23), "*They shall sanctify the holy One of Jacob,*" it is said, "*They also that erred in spirit shall come to understanding*" (Isa. xxix. 23). *Wisdom* is followed by *repentance*: "*Make the heart of this people fat, and make their ears heavy, and shut their eyes,*" &c., as far as the words: "understand with their heart, and repent." *Repentance* is followed by *pardon*: "*Let him return unto the Lord, and He will have mercy upon him, and to our God, for He will abundantly pardon*" (Isa. lv. 7). The Pardon follows the Redemption (Ps. ciii. 3, 4): "*Who forgiveth all thine iniquities, who healeth all thy diseases, who redeemeth thy life from destruction;*" and he will say first: "He healeth the sick." R. Aḥa says: Why has the Deliverance out of Egypt been fixed upon for the seventh benediction? To show that in future Israel will only be delivered in a seventh year of peace

[3] And this order should be observed.

[4] B., tr. *Meghila*, fol. 17 *a*.

[5] M. Derenbourg, in his *Essay*, p. 35, note, reads this number as meaning thirty.

(agrarian, *shometa*). R. Yona explains, on the authority of R. Aḥa, the verse: "*A song of degrees, When the Lord turned again the captivity of Zion*" (Ps. cxxvi. 1); it is the seventh song, to show that Israel will not have been brought back until the seventh year. R. Ḥiya bar-Aba says: Why has that of the healing of the sick been fixed upon as the eighth benediction? Because of the circumcision which takes place on the eighth day, according to the verse (Mal. ii. 9): "*My covenant was with him of life and peace.*" R. Ḥiya bar-Aba says, on the authority of R. Alexandria: Why is the benediction for the fruits of the year the ninth? It is according to the verse (Ps. xxix. 5): "*The voice of the Lord breaketh the cedars.*" For one day He will destroy those who augment the prices on the markets[6]. R. Levi, on the authority of R. Aḥa bar-Ḥanina, says: Why, after this last benediction, does follow that which concerns the reunion of the dispersion of the children of Israel? Because of this verse (Ezek. xxxvi. 8): "*And ye, O mountains of Israel, ye shall shoot forth your branches, and yield your fruit to my people of Israel.*" Why? "Because they are at hand to come;" that is to say: When the captives will be united, then the proud shall be humbled, and the righteous shall be happy. On this subject it has been said: The heterodox and the irreligious are included in the prayer, that the proud may be humbled; the proselytes and the elders in the one demanding protection for the righteous; and prayers are offered for David's family in that which refers to the building of Jerusalem (Hosea iii. 5): "*Afterward shall the children of Israel return, and seek the Lord their God, David their king.*"

The Rabbis say: As for the King Messiah, whether he be among the living or the dead, He shall be called David (meaning whether he exist or no, he will be of a royal stock). According to R. Tanhooma, the reason would be this (Ps. xviii. 50): "*Great deliverance giveth He to His king, to David His anointed*[7]." R. Joshua ben Levi says: His name shall be *Tsemaḥ;* and according to R. Judan, son of R. Aïbo: It shall be *Menaḥem* (comforter). R. Ḥanina, son of Abahoo, says: You must not conclude that these two opinions contradict each other, for in fact these two names are the same[8]. The following tale which we have from R. Judan, son of R. Aïbo, proves it: One day, an Israelite, whilst cultivating his field, heard his cow cry out; an Arab, who was passing, also heard her: Son of Juda, cried he, son of Juda! quit thy cow, quit thy plough, for the Temple is destroyed (and thou shalt either mourn or flee, instead of till the earth). The cow bellowed a second time. Son of Juda, said the Arab, son of Juda! take back thy cow and thy plough, for the King, the Messiah, has just been born.

[6] They stood in the markets, whose doors were made of cedar.

[7] Therefore the *Anointed* (Messiah) will be of the Royal family of David.

[8] Numerically they resemble each other; for the letters of the word צמח, like those of the מנחם, added together, make in each group: 1 3 8.

What is his name? Menaḥem. And what is his father's name? Ezechias. And from whence does he come? From the royal town of Bethlem in Judea[*]. The Hebrew sold his cow and his plough, and bought some baby's clothes. He went from town to town; when he arrived at the town mentioned, he saw that all the women were buying clothes, excepting Menaḥem's mother. And he heard the women say: Mother of Menaḥem, come and buy clothes for thy child. Oh, said she, I should like to see the enemies of Israel strangled[1], for on the day of the infant's birth, the Temple of Jerusalem is destroyed. We are certain, answered the traveller, that if, because of his advent, the Temple is destroyed, it will also be rebuilt by him (therefore, be comforted, and make thy purchases). But, said she, I have not a groat. Never mind, said he, come, buy what thou needest; if to-day thou hast not the necessary money before thee, I will come to be paid another day. Two days afterwards, he came back into the town. "What hast thou done with thy child? he asked of the woman. I know not, answered she; since thou wast here there has been storm and tempest, and my child has been taken from me[2]." R. Aboon says: Why all that from a tale concerning the Arab? A verse of the Bible sanctions it (Isa. x. 33): "*Behold the Lord, the Lord of Hosts, shall lop the bough with terror;*" and the following: "*And there shall come forth a rod out of the stem of Jesse*" (meaning, that the birth of a Messiah of the line of David shall make up for the destruction of the Temple).

R. Tanḥooma teaches in answer to the question: Why has the benediction in which we beseech God to answer our prayers been placed the fifteenth[3]? Because of the verse (Ps. xxix. 10): "*The Lord sitteth upon the flood,*" that is to say: He forbids such a plague to reappear upon this earth. The benediction which calls to mind God's worship serves as a thanksgiving, according to this verse (Ps. l. 23): "*Whoso offereth praise glorifieth me, and to him will I show the salvation of God.*" We must end by the word *peace* (for all the benedictions end by this word). R. Simon ben Ḥalaphta says: Nothing contains more benedictions than *peace*. Therefore it is said (Ps. xxix. 11): "*The Lord will bless His people with peace.*"

"If a mistake has been made, it is necessary to begin again where the mistake is committed."

[*] Mark ii. 7-19.

[1] The mother's curse is directed to the child, and she curses the enemies of Israel, in order not to curse the child.

[2] In the *Medrash Rabba* on Lamentations, chap. i. § 16 (fol. 68, col. 3), this passage is repeated in almost the same words, but rather "arameens," with a few insignificant additions.

[3] The explanation of the order of the eighteen benedictions of the 'Amida, interrupted by a digression, is here resumed.

Supposing the word וכתבתם, *you will write*, of the second section, has been put in the place of the first, it is necessary to begin again at the first. If the place where the mistake has been made is forgotten, the prayer must be resumed where there is a certainty of its being correct. One day, R. Ḥiya, R. Yossa, and R. Ama went out to erect a nuptial canopy to R. Eliezer: they heard R. Yoḥanan interpreting religious subjects. Which of us, said they, shall go near to him to hear what he says? Let R. Eliezer go, said they, for he is used to that voice. He went, and on coming back he said: This is what he is teaching. If, whilst you are reading, you arrive at the words "*so that*" (second section of the Shema', last verse), it is a certain proof that so far the perusal has been conscientious. R. Illia and R. Yossa say, on the authority of R. Aḥa: If the greater part of the 'Amida has been recited, and the reader is at the fifteenth benediction, it is a certainty that so far the reading has been attentive. R. Jeremie says, on the authority of R. Eliezer: If any one has recited the 'Amida without attention, and thinks that he will apply himself better on a second recital, he must begin again; but if it is the reverse, it is useless. R. Ḥiya the Great says: I have never been able to fix my attention; I wished to do so once, but my mind wandered all the time, and I kept on asking myself who should enter first into the presence of the king: Is it the chief of the captives or the governor[4]? Samuel says: I began counting the birds (through distraction). R. Aboon bar-Ḥiya counted the stones in the wall (domus). As for me, said R. Mathne: I render thanks to my head, because it bows of its own accord at the moment of thanksgiving (I am so absorbed).

5. (4.) Workmen may read the *Shema'* on the top of a tree or of a wall (which is being erected[5]); but they are not allowed to do so for the Prayer (or 'Amida).

This is exactly what was taught (in a *beraitha*): "The workmen read this on the top of a tree, and the masons on the top of a wall." It has also been said that the workmen say the prayer of the 'Amidâ on the top of an olive-tree, or on top of a fig-tree. So, for the other trees, it would be necessary to come down before praying, whereas the master of a house (who is not prejudiced by the time he might lose if he interrupts his work) must always get down before he prays.

[4] For the etymology of the Persian word *Arkafta*, see Fleischer in *Neuhebr. Wörterbuch*, i. 280 *a*.

[5] Literally: on the coping-stones of the wall; layer stones. Maimoni says: טאפיה, "that which emerges;" which J. Levy, *Neuhebr. Worterbuch*, s.v., changes into טפיא (? מפו); see Dozy, *Supplément aux Dictionnaires Arabes*, ii. 65, 66.

Why, then, is the exception made only for those who are in the olive-trees, or the fig-trees? Because, answered R. Aba and R. Simon, the fatigue of getting down from these trees is very great (because of the branches).

The street porter may read the Shema' with a load on his back; but he must not begin its recitation when loading or unloading, because then he is absorbed in his work. He must by no means recite the 'Amida before he has unloaded, unless the weight does not exceed a measure of four *cab* (which is not heavy). R. Yonathan imposes as a condition to equilibrate the load, placing two-thirds in front and one-third behind. Finally it has been taught that it is wrong to wink the eye[6] during this reading (making signs to any one, thereby drawing away one's attention).

The workmen who are busy working near the master of a house (and who eat in his house), recite the first of the four benedictions for meals, only making a summary of the third and fourth, and finishing by the final formula of the second; but if the salary of their work consists of the meal alone (as day labourers), or if they are at the master's table, they recite the four blessings entirely. This proves, says R. Mena, that work is forbidden whilst this blessing is being said; if not, it would not be commanded to shorten the thanksgiving if one is working, and it would have been sufficient to say that work may be done during the recital of entire blessings (so it is forbidden). R. Samuel bar R. Isaac, on the authority of R. Hoona, says: A prayer should never be recited with pieces of money in the hands (for one is absorbed). It is forbidden to place them before oneself, but not to put them behind; because then they are not thought of so much. R. Yosse wrapped his money in a piece of cloth (so as not to come into immediate contact with it), and held it in his hand. It is like this that the man should act who is entrusted with a charge (in a judicial sense), according to the rule[7] established by R. Isaac: "*And bind up the money in thine hand*" (Deut. xiv. 25); this shows that it should be kept in the hand. R. Yosse bar-Aben taught the same principle to R. Hillel, his son-in-law. R. Ezechias and R. Jacob bar-Aḥa were sitting down, and the latter had some money before him. At the moment of praying, he took it out of the purse and gave it to mind to R. Ezechias' servant; he then tied his own and the servant's raiment together (so as to avoid any chance of robbery). The servant, however, undid the knot, and tried to run away, which R. Jacob perceiving, he called out: "My money!" (this joke proves that it was not kept in the hand).

R. Ḥanina says: The Shema' may be recited and prayers said even with a pail of water on the head (which is very embarrassing). R. Hoona says: These prayers do not require a very strict attention. R. Mena said: I made this the subject of an observation to R. Pinchas; and admitting that the Shema' does

[6] B., tr. *Yoma*, fol. 19 *b*.

[7] B., tr. *Baba Metsia*, fol. 42 *a*.

require a strict attention, the 'Amida does not. R. Yosse declares that R. Ḥanina's opinion (about the pail of water) is conformable to what was said by R. Jacob bar-Aḥa, on the authority of R. Yoḥanan: It may finally be concluded that this question of work during prayer has not been clearly proved by Law (it is not known which are allowed and which forbidden).

6. (5.) A bridegroom is exempted from reading the Shema' on the night of the wedding, and even until the following Saturday evening, as long he has not accomplished the conjugal right. It happened that R. Gamaliel was reading the *Shema'* on the first night of his marriage. Master, said his disciples to him, hast thou not taught us that bridegrooms are dispensed from reading it on the first night? It is true, he replied; but I will not hear you to deprive myself of the yoke of the kingdom of Heaven even one hour (I could not for a moment forget the profession of the Jewish faith).

7. (6.) Again, R. Gamaliel went to bathe on the night after his wife had died. Hast thou not taught us, said his disciples to him, that it is forbidden for the mourners (the relatives of the dead) to bathe during the first days of mourning? Yes, he answered; but I am not like all other men (in such good health as others), and have a feeble constitution (ἀσθενής).

Who is it who taught[a] that it is forbidden for a person mourning to bathe during the first week following the death? R. Nathan. When R. Ame happened to be thus situated, he asked R. Ḥiya bar-Aba what he should do, and R. Ḥiya bar-Aba was of the same opinion as R. Nathan: that a week must elapse before bathing. When R. Yosse was in mourning, he asked advice of R. Aba bar-Cohen, and received a contrary answer. R. Ame consulted Resh Lakesh, who was also of R. Nathan's opinion. Are there not two points, he was asked? No, was the reply; we attribute it to R. Ḥiya bar-Aba, and you attribute it to Resh Lakesh (in the main it is the same thing). It may also be proved by this: R. Ḥama, father of R. Oschia, to whom the same thing happened, asked advice of the Rabbis, who told him that the bath was forbidden. R. Yosse said: Who are the Rabbis who have been consulted? Are they of this place (Jerusalem), or of the south (Babylon)? If they are of this place, it is easy to understand that they have been consulted; but if they are of the south, how is it to be understood that having great men *here*, their inferiors should have been consulted? And also, if they are of the south, how can we explain the difference of their opinions?

[a] J., tr. *Moëd qaton*, iii. 5.

for some allow the bath, and others forbid it, as in the present case? Has it not been taught that in places where the bath is customary after the burial of a relative, it may be taken as it is in the south? It is because they consider the bath as necessary as food and drink: some forbid because they fear it will be made a subject of pleasure; but it is permitted if it is not made a pleasure. Thus, when Samuel bar-Abba was afflicted with a skin disease, R. Yosse was asked if it was allowed him to take a bath. What! he said, you ask the question when a life is in danger? There can be no doubt that it is permissible, if even it were on the ninth of month Ab, or the Day of Atonement. R. Yosse bar-Ḥanina said: If a person is seen making an ablution, it cannot be forbidden him, for it would not be known whether he was washing to purify himself, or to refresh the body, for a cold bath is not considered a bath. R. Aba was also of this opinion [9]. R. Aḥa said: After returning from a long journey, and having sore feet, it is permissible to bathe them.

People who are mourning and those who have been anathematized may, if they have a journey to make, wear sandals (ordinarily forbidden), and take them off on entering a town. It is the same with the Fast of Ab and all other public fasts [1]. It has also been taught that in places where it is customary to inquire after the health of mourners on Saturdays, it may be done, as it is in the south. R. Oshia the Great was in a certain place, and seeing on Saturday some people in mourning, he saluted them: I do not know, said he, what the custom is in your country; but I salute you according to our custom.

R. Yosse bar R. Ḥalaphta was praising R. Meir before one of the people of Sephori, and called him, "A great man, a holy man, and a modest man." One Saturday, seeing some persons in mourning, he saluted them: he was asked whether he praised him because he was of his opinion? What harm, said he, is there in that? He saw on Saturday some people in mourning, and he saluted them. You may thereby, continued he, understand the strength of his reasoning (and make your conclusions); he came to teach that the signs of mourning are laid aside on Saturdays. According to this verse (Prov. x. 22), "*The blessing of God maketh rich*" (which refers to the Saturday blessing), and "they shall mourn no longer" (refers to the mourning); as it is said of David (2 Sam. xix. 3): "*Behold, the king weepeth and mourneth for Absalom his son*" (this verse also refers to mourners); therefore, on Saturday the mourning is suspended.

8. (7.) When Toby, slave of R. Gamaliel, died, he received visits of condolence (accepted marks of sympathy). Hast thou not taught us, said his disciples to him, that condolence should not be accepted for

[9] J., tr. *Taanith*, iii. 6.

[1] We know that in these days ablutions and the wearing of sandals are forbidden.

the death of a slave? He answered: My slave Toby was not like other slaves, for he was honest and pious.

Is it to be concluded from these words that for others (free people) consolation is acceptable? Yes; and therefore it has been taught precisely: Condolence[2] should not be accepted for the death of a slave[3]. When the servant of R. Eliezer died, his disciples came to express their sympathy; but he would not listen to them. To avoid them, he went into the interior court, and they followed him; he went into the house, where they still followed him. "I should have thought, said he, that lukewarm water was sufficient for you, whereas even hot water would not burn you (I mean that you do not pay attention to my most severe recommendations). Has it not been said that consolation should not be accepted for the loss of a slave? It is not that they are considered equal to beasts of burden; but, if consolation should not be accepted for free people who, however, are not of the family, so much the more would it be so for slaves. Therefore, if any one loses his slave or a beast of burden, he must be told that God will make up for his loss." When R. Ḥiya bar-Ada, the nephew of Bar-Kapara, died[4], R. Eliezer accepted condolence and wept over him, because R. Ḥiya bar-Ada had been his disciple. That proves that a pupil should be as dear as a son to you And he made this funeral speech in his honour: It is said (Solomon's Song vi. 2): "*My beloved is gone down into his garden, to the beds of spices, to feed* (*his flocks*) *in the gardens and to gather lilies.*" How is it that after speaking of one garden, it afterwards mentions several? This is the interpretation of this verse: *My beloved*, means the Almighty; *is gone down into his garden*, that is to say the Universe; *to the beds of spices*, meaning Israel; *to feed* (*his flocks*) *in the gardens*, this means the other nations of the earth; *and to gather lilies*, these words represent the holy people that the Almighty calls away to place them with his chosen people. Let us take an example and make a comparison: What is our subject like? It is like a king who would love his son too much. What does the king do? He makes his son a garden: as long as the son obeys his father's injunctions, the latter visits all the universe to find the most beautiful flowers and have them transplanted into the son's garden. But, if he is vexed by his son's behaviour, he pulls up all the flowers. It is the same thing for the Israelites when they do God's will. He goes over all the world and seeks amongst the other nations for a wise man, and he brings him to the Israelites and unites him to their nation, as, for instance, Jethro and Rahab. But when they vex the Lord, he takes from them even the just men who are among them.

[2] For formula of Consolation and its ceremonies, see chap. iii.

[3] See Gr. Rab. Zadoc Kahn, *De l'Esclavage selon la Bible et le Talmud*, pp. 67, 68; *Inscriptions grecques au Musée du Louvre*, Catalogue Froehner, No. 192.

[4] See *Rabba* on Eccles. v. 11, on Cant. vi. 2; *Bereshith Rabba*, chap. lxii.

One day R. Ḥiya bar-Aba and his companions, or according to others, R. Yosse bar R. Ḥalaphta and his companions, or else R. Akiba and his companions, were sitting under a fig-tree, studying the Law. The master of the fig-tree came and examined it early in the morning, and picked the fruit. The doctors, fearing he might suspect them, went to another place. The next day, the master (grieved at their departure) came to them and said: Masters, why are you depriving me of the pleasure of seeing this commandment (the study of the Law) fulfilled at my house? We were afraid, answered they, that thou mightest suspect us. The owner explained the reason of his behaving thus. He said, he came to uncover the fruit to the freshness of the morning, and to pluck the fruit which the sun's rays would have rotted. This proves, said they, that the master knew the right moment for plucking the fruit, and he did so immediately pick the fruit. So, also, does the Most Holy know the moment when it is good for the just to retire from the world, and he takes them.

When R. Aboon bar R. Ḥiya died, R. Zeira wept for him. It is said (Eccles. v. 11): "*The sleep of a labouring man is sweet, whether he eat little or much;*" it is not written: *whether he sleep little or much*, but, *whether he eat little or much* [5]. Of what does the death of R. Aboon bar R. Ḥiya make us think (he died young)? Of a king who, having hired many workmen in his service, perceives that one of them shows more ardour in the work than the others. When he sees this, what does the king do? He calls him and walks up and down with him. In the evening the workmen come to be paid: he gives also a full day's pay to the man he had walked with. When his comrades see this, they complain and say: We have been working hard all the day, and this one who only laboured two hours receives as much salary as we do. It is, answered the king, because he has done more in two hours than you in the entire day [6]. In the same manner R. Aboon, although he had only studied the Law up to the age of twenty-eight, knew it better than a learned man or a pious man who would have studied it up to the age of a hundred years.

At the death of R. Simon bar-Zebid [7], R. Ilia came to make a funereal panegyric: There are four things, said he, which are in daily use with us, and all of them, were they lost, could be replaced (Job xxviii. 1, 2): "*Surely there is a vein for silver, and a place for gold where they fine it. Iron is taken out of the earth, and brass is molten out of the stone.*" Supposing these things were lost, they could all be replaced. But if a learned man should die, who will give us another in his stead? Who will take his place? "*Where shall wisdom be found, and where is the place for understanding? Neither is it found in the land of the living*" (said

[5] Sleep is similar to death, and eating is similar to life.

[6] Compare the parable of the eleventh hour's workman in Matt. xx. 1-17.

[7] J., tr. *Horaïoth*, iii. 5.

Job, xxvii. 12). R. Levi says: If the brothers of Joseph felt their hearts fail them when they found the money in their bags, as it is written (Gen. xlii. 28): '*and their hearts failed them, and they were afraid,*"—how much more should we feel, having lost R. Simon bar-Zebid!

When R. Levi bar-Zizi died, Samuel's father came and made his panygeric; he said (Eccles. xii. 13): "*Fear God and keep His commandments, for this is the whole duty of man.*" To whom shall we compare R. Levi bar-Zizi? To a king who has a vineyard in which there are a hundred vines, which give him every year a hundred barrels of wine. He first chose fifty, then forty, then thirty, then twenty, then ten, and at last a single one which produced a hundred barrels of wine, and whose taste was preferable to that of all the vineyard. It was thus for R. Levi bar-Zizi, whom God preferred to all other men. Therefore it is written, "*the whole* (*duty*) *of man*" (Eccles. xii. 13), meaning that R. Levi is worth all the other men put together.

Cahana was very young, and when he arrived there (in Palestine), a worthless man [8] saw him and asked him (scoffing at his piety): What sin is there at this moment in heaven? (What is being said up there?) It has just been decided, said he, that this man is condemned to death. And the prediction was realized. Another saw him and made the same question. The answer was the same, with the same result. Alas! said Cahana, why, having left my country with good intentions (to study the Law), have I come here to sin? Why have I come here to foretell the death of the children of Israël? I will go, and return to the country whence I came. So he went to R. Yoḥanan and said: If a man is despised by his mother (Palestine), but honoured and cared for by another wife of his father (Babylon), ought he to go to the latter? Yes, answered R. Yoḥanan; and Cahana returned to Babylon. When he was gone, people came to R. Yoḥanan and told him which way he had gone. How is this? said the Rabbi; he is setting forth without saying Good-bye. The question he asked you, they answered, was his way of saying Good-bye (for when he spoke of his mother and stepmother, he wished to describe the two countries which treated him so differently).

When R. Zeira arrived in Palestine, he had himself bled; then he went to buy a pound of meat from a butcher (to get back his strength during his convalescence). He asked: What is the price of this measure? Fifty pieces of money, and a blow which you must receive. I will give you sixty, but spare me the blow. The other refused. Here are seventy pieces. Another refusal. Here are eighty! here are ninety! here are a hundred! Well, then, said he, do according to thy custom. Towards evening he went to the house of prayer.

[8] The term ב׳ פירחה is translated "a worthless man" (not a personage) by Lattes, *Giunte al Lessico Talmudico*, s. v. Cf. J., tr. *Beça*, iv. 3.

Rabbis, said he, what strange customs there are here! A man cannot eat a measure of food without receiving a blow. What makes you believe that? A certain butcher. He was sent for that he might explain his behaviour, but the messengers only found a coffin (he was dead). How is this? said he. Rabbi, thou wast so irritated that thou didst wish for his death? I swear, said R. Zeira, that I felt no anger towards him, and that I submitted to what I thought was a local custom.

When R. Yassa arrived here (in Palestine), he had himself shaved, and went to the warm waters (δημοσία) of Tiberias. A rough fellow met him and gave him a blow on the back of the neck. "Oh, said he, laughingly, how soft is the neck of this man (thine)" (he is very sensitive to a blow). Thereupon the Archon (ἄρχων, a Roman magistrate) came up to judge a robber. The afore-mentioned scoffer assisted at the trial, and began jeering at the culprit. The judge asked the latter if he had any accomplice. The culprit looked up and said: The man who is scoffing at me helped me. He was seized and judged, and it was proved that he had killed a man. They were both led out loaded with two beams (they were to be either crucified[9] or hanged). Just then R. Yassa was leaving the bath; the convict saw him and said: The neck that was soft has become very hard (for me). It is thy evil fate (and not the affront which thou didst offer me). Is it not written (Isa. xxviii. 22): "*Now therefore, be ye not mockers, lest your bands be made strong.*" R. Pinḥas and R. Jeremie say, on the authority of R. Samuel bar R. Isaac: Raillery produces bad results; it begins by causing suffering, and ends by causing destruction, as it is written further on: "*For I have heard from the Lord of hosts a consumption, even determined upon the whole earth*" (Isa. xxviii. 22).

9. (8.) A bridegroom who wishes to recite the Shema' on the marriage night may recite it. R. Simon bar-Gamaliel said: It is not permitted to every one to claim a pious reputation.

It has been taught that: In all cases in which privations or sufferings are imposed (as for example, fasting), each person may consider himself either as a particular person, or as a well-educated man (the latter generally sacrificing more for the sake of religion); and we shall then obtain blessings from Heaven. But the same line of action cannot be pursued, with the exception of the scientific man, when the question is one of luxury or honours (in which vanity might arise), unless one has been appointed an administrator of the community (in which case the dignity of the function is maintained by keeping up an appearance of importance). In order to avoid the mud on the high road, it is allowable to

[9] A Roman judgment.

walk along the edges of cultivated fields, and even on saffron plantations (which would cause considerable loss); but it is allowed to go on them if the high road[1] is completely broken up (in such a manner as to render it impossible to take a few steps). R. Abahoo narrates that R. Gamaliel and R. Joshuah were once obliged to walk alongside the fields, on account of the sodden state of the road; they perceived R. Juda ben-Paphos wading through the mud to get to them. Who, said R. Gamaliel to R. Joshuah, is this man who makes such a parade of his scruples to cross the fields? It is, answered his companion, R. Juda ben-Paphos, whose every action has a pious object in view. But, objected the first, is it not taught that an ordinary person has not the right to go beyond the legal prescriptions, by courting praises for exaggerated scruples, unless one is an administrator of a community? It is true, replied the other; but it is also taught that, in cases of self-imposed suffering, every one has a right to be scrupulous; and he will draw down upon himself the blessings of heaven (such was the case of R. Juda ben-Paphos). However, adds R. Zeira, it must not be made an occasion of despising others (and he does us an injury by acting thus).

On a certain occasion[2], R. Yassa and R. Samuel bar R. Isaac were seated together at meals, in one of the upper rooms of the meeting-house. When the moment for saying the Prayer arrived, R. Samuel bar R. Isaac rose. R. Mishe said to him: That is not according to what Rabbi teaches us; he says: If the repast has been commenced, there is no necessity to interrupt it. Also Ezekia taught, that he who has a dispensation from a certain work, and accomplishes the work nevertheless, deserves to be called a simple man. "Have we not learnt, however (§ 8), was the answer, that the bridegroom is exempted from reading the Shema', and yet, if he wishes to read it, he may do so? It may be supposed, was the answer, that he may apply himself to it as well as R. Gamaliel." And indeed the latter went beyond his own opinion one day, by reciting the Shema' when he was dispensed; and when his disciples pointed out to him that he was acting contrarily to his own teaching, he replied: I will not hear you if you intend that I should authorize myself for one moment to turn away from adoring God.

[1] See J., tr. *Bava Kama*, v. 1; B., ib. fol. 81 *a*.

[2] See J., tr. *Sabbath*, i. 1 *bis* (fol. 3 *a*).

CHAPTER III.[1]

He whose dead lies before him is exempted from reciting the Shema' and the Prayer ('Amida), and from wearing the phylacteries. Those who carry the bier and those who relieve them, and their assistants, those who go before the bier, and those who follow it[2], who are required for the bier, are exempted from reciting the Shema'. But those not required for the bier are bound to recite it. All these (parties) are exempted from saying the Prayer ('Amida).

We have taught[3] that on the first day of mourning, they (the near relatives) do not wear the phylacteries; the second day they are obliged to do so. But, when strangers come (to console them), they must take them off, no matter on what day of the week; this is the opinion of R. Eleazar.

R. Yoshua says that, on the first and second days the phylacteries are not worn, and that, on the third day they are put on, not to be taken off again. If this is so (that on the second day they are still left off), to what good does the Mishnâ teach that: one is only dispensed from wearing the phylacteries as long as the dead is not interred? That is so; but, in the same manner as it was mentioned that the Shema' was dispensed with (before the dead), so also was it with the phylacteries, although the dispensation extends to the second day.

R. Zeira and R. Jeremiah hold, on the authority of Rab, that the R. Eleazar's rule is adopted, concerning the phylacteries (on the second day), and R. Yehoshuah's rule (if they are on, they are not to be taken off before strangers). R. Zeira asks them: When the phylacteries have been put on the second day, as R. Eleazar wishes, ought they not to be kept on (when strangers arrive), as R. Yehoshuah wishes? Yes, said R. Jose, son of R. Aboon; if the phylacteries have been put on, on the second day, according to R. Eleazar's opinion, they must not be taken off (when strangers arrive), as says R. Yehoshuah. Since this is so, we may conclude that R. Eleazar's opinion, for the putting of them on, is the rule.

R. Aboon explains the Mishnâ (the reason why one is dispensed from the

[1] Translated by the late L. Hollaenderski.

[2] Groups of men posted themselves along the way, and they undertook to carry it by turns, considering it an act of piety.

[3] See J., tr. *Moëd Qaton*, iii. 5.

Shema' and the *thephilins*), and he says: It is written (in the Pentateuch): "*That thou mayest remember* (in putting on the *thephilins* and reciting the Shema') *the day when thou camest forth, out of the land of Egypt, all the days of thy life;*" that means, says he, that on the days that one attends to the living (worldly matters), the *thephilins* must be put on and the Shema' recited; but on the days when one attends to the dead (the burial), one is dispensed. He who wishes to be severe towards himself in this matter (and to pray even on the first day of mourning), should be prevented from doing so. Is it in honour of the dead (who are still present), or in order that he should himself attend to the arrangements for the burial? What matters? What difference is there between these two motives? If persons could be procured to undertake the duties of burial, the relatives might then say their prayers; therefore, it is better to admit that the rule is made in honour of the dead. It is therefore forbidden under any pretext. It is not intended that the motive should be understood to be that the person should himself attend to the burial arrangements, for even on festivals, when burials do not take place, one is exempted from the precepts, such as the Loolab[4] and the Shophar (therefore the motive of the prohibition must be the respect due to the dead). In the same manner, according to R. Ḥanina, it is allowed on Saturdays and festivals to exceed the limits of the Sabbath, in attending on the dead or a bridegroom, such as bringing the coffin, the grave-clothes, as on working days, also to bring the weepers (this proves again, that even on days when the dead are not buried, due respect must be shown to them).

When[5] ought they (the near relatives) to overturn the chairs (as a sign of mourning)? According to R. Eleazar, as soon as the body has been carried out of the house. R. Yehoshuah holds that it should be done when the coffin is being closed. When R. Gamaliel died, and was being carried away, R. Eleazar ordered his disciples to overturn the chairs, and when the coffin had been closed, R. Yehoshuah gave the same order. The disciples thereupon replied: We have already done so by order of R. Eleazar.

On Saturday eve the chairs are stood up, and on Saturday evening again overturned. We have taught: The Sophas (or camp bedsteads) may be left upright and not overturned. R. Simon, son of Eleazar, says that it suffices untie the cords (*κλιντήριων*), because then they are not so comfortable, and the sign of mourning is established. R. Jose, on the authority of R. Yehoshuah, son of Levi, supports R. Simon's opinion. R. Jacob, son of R. Aḥa, on the authority of R. Jose, says: For a bedstead fitted with long stems[6], it is enough to take

[4] See above, p. 17, and further on, v. 2.

[5] See J., tr. *Moëd Qaton*, iii. 5 (fol. 83 *d*).

[6] **Τὰ ἀνάκλιτα**: four supports at the corners, on which a board was put to support the bedding.

them out (because then one is on the bare boards). These two sorts of bedsteads are slightly different. R. Jeremiah thus explains them: That which has the leather bands tied from above[7] is called a *mitta;* whilst the *dargash* has its thongs attached underneath (at the bottom). Have we not learnt[8] that the *mitta* and the *'arssé* (another sort of bedstead) are liable to become unclean when they are polished with fish-skin (to soften them)? If these bedsteads have leather bands underneath, why polish them (therefore the *mitta* has leather bands)? R. Eleazar replies that the Mishnâ speaks of Caesarean bedsteads, which must be polished, as they have holes (to put the straps through).

Why are the chairs overturned? R. Krispa explains it, on the authority of R. Yoḥanan, by recalling a verse of Job (ii. 13): *"So they sat down with him 'upon' the ground,"* and not *on* the ground, which proves that the chairs were overturned. Bar-Kapara gives another explanation: God, said he, has given you a form to His own likeness[9], *εἰκόνιον,* now overthrown (dead) in punishment of your sins; let your couch also be overthrown. According to others, bar-Kapara says this: You ought to overturn your couch (bed) on which you have been born. R. Jonas and R. Jose, in the name of R. Simon, son of Lakesh, also explain: the one says that a man in mourning should repose on an overturned bed, because this unusual position would, on waking, remind him of his affliction; the other says that his own change of position (inconvenience) keeps him awake, as a matter of course, and reminds him that he is in mourning.

The mourner must, as long as the dead is not interred, take his meals at a neighbour's; if he has no neighbours, he will eat in another room of his house, failing which he will put a screen between him and the dead; but if this is not possible, he must while eating turn his face towards the wall. In any case he must be frugal. He must not eat meat or drink wine, nor recline on a Sopha whilst eating. He is excluded from the general blessing after meals, and if he says this blessing (aloud), which he should not do, the others should not answer *Amen;* and should they do so, he must not answer *Amen.*

All these provisions are not applicable to Saturdays, but only to week-days. R. Simon, son of Gamaliel, says: Since it is permitted (for a man in mourning) to take his meals on Saturdays (as usual), he is therefore obliged to fulfil all the religious duties of that day; for if this exception is made in favour of his temporal existence, it should with greater reason apply to his religious life. R. Yehuda, son of Pazzi, on the authority of R. Yehoshuah, son of Levi, is of the same opinion.

[7] Or, which is fastened from above, from the outside, according to J. Lévy, *Neuhebr. Wörterbuch,* s.v.

[8] Mishnâ, vi., tr. *Kelîm,* chap. xvi. § 1.

[9] Gen. i. 26.

After having entrusted the body to the funeral assembly, or even to the coffin-bearers, the mourners are allowed to eat and drink. For example, when R. Yosse died, R. Yeḥia, son of Aba, provided the first meal for the mourners; he gave them meat and wine. At the death of R. Ḥaia bar-Abba, R. Samuel, son of R. Isaac, did the same; and on the death of the latter, it was R. Zeira who provided the first meal for the *abelim* (afflicted ones), by giving them lentils, and he said to them: I do as is the custom[1]. R. Zeira, before his death, ordered that the mourners should not eat at all on the first day; but on the morrow they could accept the repast of mourning[2]. When R. Isaac, son of R. Ḥiya the writer (or commentator[3]), was at Tuba, he suffered a bereavement. R. Mane and R. Judan came to render him a visit of condolence, and they drank good wine at his house, which made them gay. On the morrow, when they renewed their visit, R. Isaac said to them, Was it proper to drink so much wine in the house of an *abel?* It only remained for you to set yourselves to dancing! At an *abel's* house, ten glasses of wine are drunk: two before the meal, five during the meal, and three after. The last three are drunk as follows: one at the benediction, one for a sign of charity (friendship), and one for a sign of consolation of the afflicted. When R. Gamaliel died, three more glasses were added, one in honour of the *Hazan* (officiating priest), the second in honour of the chief of the Synagogue, and the third to the memory of the defunct[4]. But, when the *Beth-Dine* (Synod) saw that drunkenness increased more and more, it forbade the three additional glasses, and maintained only the old custom (of ten glasses).

Should a disciple, who is a *Cohen* (descendant of the family of the grand high priest Aaron), profane himself[5] by attending to the funeral arrangements of his master, in order to honour his memory? The following example may serve for a reply: When the father-in-law and master of R. Yanai Zeiri died, the latter (who was a Cohen) asked R. Yose the above question, and received a negative reply. R. Aḥe heard it, and maintained the contrary. When R. Yose died, his disciples attended to the funeral arrangements, eat meat and drank wine. R. Mane reproached them for it, telling them that they had broken one of these two rules: If you are of the number of mourners, you should not have eaten

[1] In the treatise *Bava Bathra* we find the explanation of this custom: as the lentil, unlike other beans, has no cotyledon, the mourner is silent.

[2] According to an old custom, the friends and near neighbours invited the mourners to a repast, and sent them meats. The sending of meats is still practised by pious Jews.

[3] See Brüll, *Jahrbücher*, i. 227-8, on *Moëd Qaton*, i. 9 (according to Eleazar Alaskari).

[4] A custom which has fallen into desuetude amongst the Jews, but practised by others.

[5] Lev. xxi. 1.

meat or drunk wine (while the dead was still present); but, if you do not consider yourselves as near relatives of the defunct, why have you profaned yourselves? You were wrong.

When a Cohen (priest) is studying Law in the Synagogue, and a body is brought in, should he interrupt his studies and leave the Synagogue, or should he stay? The following fact is an answer: A dead man was once brought into the Synagogue whilst R. Yose was studying the Law, and he made no remark to the Cohanim, neither to those who went out, nor to those who stayed in. R. Neḥemia, son of R. Ḥiya, son of Abba, related that his father (who was a Cohen), in going to the rooms where the studies were made, never went through the Cæsarean Arcades; he always went another way round (the dead were buried under these Arcades). R. Ami, R. Ḥiski, R. Cohen, and R. Jacob, son of Aḥe, were walking in the streets (public places, *palatia*) of Sephoris, when they arrived at a cemetery; R. Cohen turned aside. He rejoined them at the other end of the passage and said: On what have you deliberated during my absence? R. Ḥiski forbade R. Jacob to tell him; it is not known why: either because R. Ḥiski was cross at R. Cohen's absence (for he, R. Cohen, must have known that the study of the *thora* must not be interrupted, even at the risk of profaning oneself), or else he was cross because R. Cohen had taken a walk.

We have taught[6] that a Cohen may go to foreign parts (outside of Palestine) to judge a pecuniary or criminal case, to note the new moon, to establish (to make good) the leap-year, to reclaim (by means of justice) a field from a non-Israelite, to protest against an illegal landlord or owner, to study the Law, or to marry. R. Juda adds: If there is a master (in Palestine), he should not cross the frontier. R. Jose holds the contrary: A Cohen may do so even when he can find a master (for his studies) in Palestine; for, he adds, one must be able to choose one's master. This same Rabbi relates (to strengthen his decision) that Joseph Cohen followed his master to Sidon (outside of Palestine), and yet a Cohen is only allowed to leave Palestine to fetch a wife who has been promised to him.

At the moment of the Sacerdotal blessing in the Synagogue, should a dead body be brought in, must the Cohanim who pronounce this blessing go out or not? Magbila, brother of R. Abba, son of Cohen, maintained, in presence of R. Jose, and in the name of R. Aḥa, that they must not leave their places in presence of the dead. R. Aḥa, on hearing this, denied having expressed this opinion, and he added: Magbila may have misunderstood the sense of my words, which I repeated according to R. Juda, son of Pazzi, who taught, on the authority of R. Eleazar, that a Cohen who, being in the Synagogue at the moment of the Sacerdotal blessing, does not take part in it, breaks a positive commandment

[6] See J., tr. *Nazir*, vii. 1.

(which the Cohen should practise). Magbila may have thought that a positive commandment may be subordinated to a negative one[7]. But I do not think that Magbila could have heard me express even this opinion; bring him, therefore, before me, that I may inflict on him the punishment of the *malkoth* (strokes with a thong, for his untruth).

In the Synagogue called "the Synagogue of revolt[8]," in the town of Kissrie, just at the moment of the Sacerdotal blessing, and whilst a dead body was exposed, the Cohanims, who were studying the Law, did not ask (their master) R. Abooha whether they should join with the other Cohanim to give the blessing (and they continued their studies). When the hour for the repast arrived, they told him the hour, and asked to go out (on account of the presence of the dead). R. Abooha replied: You did not consult me in the matter of the blessing (which is a positive commandment), and you now consult me as to whether you should make your repast (which is legitimately allowed)? Hearing this the Cohanim hastened out.

R. Yanai says that a Cohen may go to see a royal personage even in a profane locality. When Diocletian came to Tyre, R. Ḥiya, son of Abba (a Cohen), was seen traversing the cemetery to meet him. R. Ḥiski and R. Jeremiah said, in the name of R. Yoḥanan, that it is almost a religious honour to contemplate the great personages of the kingdom, so that we may distinguish the Israelite princes of the house of David.

May a Cohen profane himself (attend the burial) of a *nassi* (patriarch)? Certainly. When R. Juda the Nassi died, R. Yanai made a proclamation that, in honour of the Nassi, the sacerdotal laws were suspended for that day. When R. Juda the Nassi, the grandson of R. Juda the patriarch, died, R. Ḥiya, son of Abba, called R. Zeira (who was a Cohen) into the Synagogue named *Gouffna*[9], at Siphori, where the body was exposed. On the day of the death of Nehorai (Lucia), sister of R. Juda Nassi, R. Ḥanina sent for R. Mane (to assist at the funeral

[7] To perform the sacerdotal blessing is a *positive* commandment, since God ordered Aaron and his two sons to do so. That one must not profane oneself with the dead is a *negative* commandment.

[8] According to Josephus (*Ant.* XX. viii. 7) there was a fight, before this Synagogue, between Greeks and Jews; no doubt on account of this it received the name of the "Synagogue of the revolt." The same denomination is found again in the Talmud, *Nazir*, vii. 3 (fol. 56 *a*), and the same root מרד, in the expression "resistance money;" tr. *Maasser shéni*, i. 2 (fol. 52 *b*). See Derenbourg, *Essay*, p. 156; Neubauer, p. 95. In our passage the text is faulty, and is marked דמדרתא (Krotoshin edition), or דמרותא (Amsterdam edition). J. Levy translates: *Am Abhange*.

[9] According to Eusebius, it is a town situated fifteen miles from Jerusalem in the direction of Neapolis. It had a certain prominence during the wars against Rome. See Raumer, *Palestina*, p. 99; Neubauer, ib. p. 158.

ceremony); but instead of coming, R. Mane answered: Since, when the Nassi is alive, and is in a profane place, a Cohen must not go to him (to render him honour); with much less reason should a Cohen require to profane himself when the Nassi is dead (especially at the death of a sister of a Nassi). To this R. Nassi replied: This is an exceptional case, in which the religious obligation incumbent on every Israelite must be accomplished in his brother's honour. May a Cohen profane himself for his father's or mother's honour (and go beyond the limits of Palestine to see them)? R. Yosse also, on the news of his mother's arrival at Bozzera, asked R. Yoḥanan whether he might go there? The latter replied that: If there is any danger (for his mother, and his presence could get her out of it), he should not hesitate; but if it is simply for the sake of doing honour to his parents, there might be a doubt on the subject. But, as R. Yosse persisted, R. Yoḥanan said: Since thou art decided to go, go and return in peace. R. Samuel bar-Isaac heard this, and thought that it was not a sincere decision. R. Eleazar thereupon added that there was no necessity to have a more formal authorization (than that of R. Yoḥanan).

Does a Cohen become defiled in joining a funeral procession in honour of the community? Yes, in presence of two routes, one long, but undefiled, and the other short, but defiled (where the dead have been buried); if the public follow the long route, the Cohen must not undeceive them and follow the same route; but if the public follow the short route, the Cohen must not quit it, since he is acting for the honour of the public. This rule only applies to the cases considered as unclean, according to the Doctors; but in all cases which are forbidden by the Law (Pentateuch), the decision of R. Zeïra should be acted upon. He said: The respect due to the public is such that for the moment it takes precedence of a negative commandment.

R. Jonas and R. Jose Galilee, on the authority of R. Jose, son of Ḥanina, say that the Law must not be discussed in presence of the dead. We find, however, that R. Yoḥanan, in presence of the body of R. Samuel, son of Zadoc, asked R. Yani his opinion on this question, viz.: May the revenues realized by an holocaust be applied to the reparations of the Temple? And R. Yani gave the desired solution (this proves that the Law may be discussed in presence of the dead). But it has been supposed that this conversation (between the two Rabbis) took place at a certain distance from the body, or after the funeral ceremony. We find also that R. Jeremiah propounded several questions, for solution, to R. Zeïra, in the presence of the dead body of R. Samuel, son of Isaac, before the completion of the ceremony (which proves again that the Law may be discussed in presence of the dead); but it was answered that this took place away from the body (aside), and not close to it.

It has been taught that the carriers of the dead (of the coffin) should remain barefooted (during the passage), for it might happen that the shoe of one of them

would become torn on the way, and thus interrupt him in the exercise of this religious duty.

R. Zeïra fell down during a conversation, and it was seen that he had fainted. When he came to, he was asked the cause of his fainting; he replied: It happened in consequence of our conversation regarding the verse: "*And the living will lay it to his heart*" (Eccles. vii. 2).

2. After the burial, and during the return, the Shema' should be recited, if there is time enough to begin and end it before arriving at the circle (formed round the mourners to console them); if there is not sufficient time, it must not be begun. Those standing inside the circle (the mourners) are dispensed from saying it; but those outside must recite it.

We teach that[1]: The dead must not be carried away for one hour before, or one hour after the time prescribed for the reading of the Shema', so that it may be said and prayed with the public. We read, however (in the Mishnâ as above), that after the burial, and on the return, the Shema' should be said, if there is time to begin and end it before arriving at the circle. Therefore what we have just said about leaving an hour before or after (the burial), is it not superfluous? No, this latitude is accorded to those who may have made a mistake, or missed (involuntarily) the hour indicated (for the prayers).

We teach that those in mourning, and the assistants (at the funeral ceremony), if they cannot terminate the ceremonies in time, should interrupt them to recite the Shema' only, but not to say the Prayer[2] (this being longer). But it has already happened that the Doctors have stopped the ceremonies, not only to recite the Shema', but also to say the Prayer. We read in the Mishnâ that the Shema' may be commenced (before arriving at the circle), if there is time to finish it (if not, it must not be begun); if we maintain that the ceremony must be stopped in order to recite the Shema', does it not follow that it may be commenced before arriving at the circle? In the one case, it refers to the first day of mourning; but in the other, to the second day.

R. Samuel, son of Âbdooma, says: If he who enters into the Synagogue (at the hour of office) thinks he can finish his Prayer before the *Ḥazan* (officiating priest) commences to repeat (the 'Amida), so as to be able to join in the *Amen*, he may begin and finish it (the Prayer[3]). One of the Doctors held that: This means that there must be enough time to finish his prayer and say the ***Amen*** after the third section of the 'Amida; another Doctor said that this applies to the

[1] J., tr. *Synhedrin*, ii. 2. [2] J., tr. ***Biccurim***, iii. 3.
[3] See further on, chap. iv. § 8.

case where the person thinks he can say his prayer before the *Ḥazan* has finished the sixteenth section, so as to say the *Amen*. R. Pinḥas says that these two Doctors are not at variance, for the former speaks of Saturday prayers, and the latter of ordinary week-day prayers.

We teach that R. Juda said: If there is only one circle, all those forming it must pray, if they are present in honour of the mourners; but the relatives (who take part in the mourning) are exempted. Those (of the assistants) who have arrived at the place where the mourning ceremony takes place, and who have their faces turned towards the mourners (are close to them), are exempted from reciting the Shema'; the others (those who cannot see the mourners) are not exempted. It is in accordance with the subsequent decision (according to the text of the Mishnâ), that those who form or who are inside the circle are exempted from reciting the Shema', but not those who are on the outside. And what we have just taught, of the obligation attaching to those who have only come to do honour, and the exemption of those who have come to console the afflicted, is according to an anterior decision.

We have learnt[4] that when the High Priest has consoled the mourners, the Segan (assisting priest) places them between the High Priest and the assistants; these, then, come (one after the other) to offer their consolations. R. Ḥanina relates that formerly the assistants (the friends, &c.) remained in their places, and that the mourners passed along the rows of the assistants; but, as there arose quarrels between the assistants at the city of Siphoris, R. Jose ben-Ḥalaphta decided that the mourners should keep their places, and the assistants come to them, one by one, to offer their consolations. R. Simon of Tossephta says that the old custom has been again re-established.

3. Women, slaves, and children are exempted from reciting the Shema', and from wearing the phylacteries; but they are bound in the matter of the Prayer, the sign on the door-post (*mezuza*[5]), and the blessing after meals.

The exemption of women (from reciting the Shema' and wearing the phylacteries) is based on the following verse: "*And ye shall teach them your children* (sons and not daughters)" (Deut. xi. 19). And why is the same exemption applied to slaves? Because it is written: "*Hear, O Israel: The Lord our God is one God*" (Deut. vi. 4); which means that we have no other superior but God, whilst the slave is subservient to his master. And why are children exempted?

[4] See B., tr. *Synhedrin*, fol. 18.

[5] *Mezuza:* the parchment which contains verses 4-9 of chap. vi., and verses 12-20 of chap. xi. of Deuteronomy, and which is affixed to the door-posts, as ordered in these verses.

Because it is written: "*That the Lord's Law may be in thy mouth*" (Exod. xiii. 9), meaning, that thou be assiduous in the study of this Law (and a child is not so); but they are all (woman, slave, and child) obliged to recite the Prayer (*'Amida*), because everybody must endeavour to draw down upon himself the Divine mercy. As regards the *mezuza*, it is written (Deut. vi. 19): "*and thou shalt write them upon the posts of thy house*" (the Law). All are obliged to say the blessing after meals, because it is written: "*When thou hast eaten, and art full, then thou shalt bless the Lord thy God*" (Deut. viii. 10).

We are taught that[6] all positive commandments, for the accomplishment of which there is a fixed time, are only obligatory for men, and that women are dispensed; but the commandments, for the accomplishment of which the time is not fixed (i.e. which may be accomplished at any time), are obligatory for men and women. Which are the commandments having a fixed time? They are: the *Sukka* (tabernacles), the *Shoffar* (trumpets of the *Rosh Hashana*), and the *Tephilin* (phylacteries). And which are the commandments not having a fixed time? They are: the restitution of things found to their owners, the taking of young birds by sending their mother back to the nest[7], the erection of a balustrade on the roof (for the safety of the inhabitants), and the precept of the *tzitziths*[8].

R. Simon exempts women from the *tzitziths* because, to accomplish this commandment, the time is prescribed, since any garment for night use need not have *tzitziths*. R. Abina, explaining the decisions of the Doctors (who class the *tzitziths* with the commandments that have no fixed time), says: The garments that are used by day as well as by night must have *tzitziths*.

We teach that: A man may accomplish on his neighbour's behalf (at the prescribed time) any positive commandment, excepting the blessing after meals. We teach that: With regard to religious duties, a person not bound by them, may not exempt his neighbour (by performing them for him). But with regard to those duties which are binding, the same duties may be repeated on behalf of others (neighbours), and thus exempt them. R. Elaia adds, that in this case the blessing at meals is excepted (it cannot be said for one's neighbour), for it is written: "*When thou hast eaten, and art full, then thou shalt bless the Lord thy God*," which means that each one must recite the blessing after his meal. R. Jose and R. Juda ben-Pazzi except also the Shema' and the prayers which each person should say for himself, in order to draw down upon him the Divine mercy.

What difference is there between *Sukka* and Lulab? That is to say: Why

[6] See J., tr. *Kiddoushin*, i. 7; B., ib. fol. 29.

[7] See further, chap. v. § 3.

[8] The *tzitzith* (fringes on the clothes). With regard to these fringes, it is said: "And it shall be unto you for a fringe, that ye may look upon it, and remember all the commandments of the Lord" (Num. xv. 39).

is the blessing of the Sukka said on the evening (preceding) the first day of the Feast of Tabernacles (only once), whilst the Lulab must be said on each of the seven days (every morning of the Feast of Tabernacles)? R. Jose and R. Aḥa asked, at an assembly, this same question, and the answer was: Because it is a duty to remain in the Sukkôths (tabernacles) all the seven days (of the solemnity), nights included; whilst on the other hand, the Lulab is only obligatory during the day (each day separately). R. Jacob Deromi[9] protested that: The study of the Law is also obligatory at night, as well as during the day (and yet the benediction must be said every time one sits down to study); a man may, said he, abstain from eating, during the festival, of things not requiring a blessing, as, for example, fruit which may be eaten outside of the tabernacles (and in this case one is not obliged to spend one's time there, nor to recite the blessing every day); the Lulab, on the other hand, is a positive commandment (for each one of the seven days of the festival), as for the blessing to be said before commencing the study of the Law, it is said in accordance with the verse: "*And in his Law doth he meditate day and night*" (Ps. i. 2).

We teach[1] that a man may have the blessing after meals recited for him by his wife, child, or servant. Did not R. Aḥa, in R. Nearaï's house, say, on the authority of R. Jose, that a child is allowed to say the blessing after meals, in order to accustom him to accomplish that duty? On the other hand, since a child is not obliged to practise the commandments (as we have said previously), can he exempt his father? There is no question here of exemption, the child says the blessing, and the father (if he is ignorant) repeats it (word by word) as we have taught with regard to the Feast of Tabernacles. It is said there that if a slave, a woman, or a child recite the *Hallel* (divers chapters of the Psalms) in order to exempt others, these latter must also repeat it (word by word). The Doctors, however, blame him (the ignorant man, who has the blessing said for him by his son). It is not seemly that a man of twenty should repeat what a child of ten says.

4. A man in his legal uncleanness[2] is to meditate in his heart on the Shema'; but he is not to bless before or after it. After he has eaten he blesses, but not before doing so. R. Juda says: He blesses both before and after it (in his heart).

A mental recitation is made in places where there is no water (to wash oneself). According to R. Meir, a *baal-keri* (a man in his uncleanness), not having

[9] From Darom (South). See above, p. 3, note 2.
[1] See J., tr. *Succa*, iii. 9; *Rosh Hashana*, iii. 3.
[2] *Baal qeri*, who has had an accident (qui fluxum pollutionis senserit).

sufficient water to take a *Tebila* (bath of purification), must recite the Shema' in such a manner as not to be able to hear himself; but he must not say the blessing at the commencement or end of it. The Doctors, however, allow him to recite the Shema' aloud, and say the blessing both before and after it. We teach that: A *baal-keri* who is ill, and on whom nine measures (*cab*) of water have been poured, and another *baal-keri* who is not ill, and who has had three *lug* (small measures) of water poured over him, become clean, and may then occupy themselves with their religious duties; but they may not replace others in these duties, they may only do so after having plunged into forty measures of water[3]. R. Juda is also of this opinion. According to R. Jacob bar-Aḥa, who maintained it on the authority of R. Jose, who himself spoke in the name of R. Yehoshua ben-Levi, a man only became unclean through knowing a woman. R. Hoona says that even he who becomes *keri* (polluted) in dreaming is unclean; but according to R. Jonas and R. Jose, one can become *baal-keri* (when not dreaming) as soon as one notices anything (ejection) from whatever cause.

We have learnt[4] that on the day of *kippur* (pardon) it is forbidden to eat, drink, wash (bathe), to perfume oneself, put on shoes, and to know one's wife. On this head we have also learnt (from a *baraitha*) that a *baal-keri* (remarking his uncleanness on the day of *kippur*) may plunge into water to cleanse himself; but must do so secretly. This is not contrary to the decision of R. Juda ben-Levi, according to whom a man becomes unclean through knowing woman, for he may have known his wife on the eve of *kippur*, and have forgotten to take his bath afterwards. R. Jose ben-Ḥalaphta was seen to bathe himself on the day of *kippur*. Can we suppose that this holy man can have forgotten to take his bath the evening before, after having known his wife? R. Jacob bar-Aboon says that the *Tebila* was instituted to distinguish that man who is like an animal (who like a cock approaches his hens, leaves them to take his meals, and goes again to them afterwards). So the *Tebila* is not obligatory for the *baal-keri*, and R. Jose ben-Ḥalaphta might well neglect it on the eve of Kippur. R. Ḥanina was one morning, before daylight, passing the gates of δημόσια (where were the Tiberias baths); he met there some of his pupils, whom he scolded, telling them that they had no necessity to lose their hours of study by taking baths (to purify themselves), for they could take their *Tebila* during the morning. This proves that the *Tebila* is not forced upon the *baal-keri* (even for the study of the Law).

R. Aḥa was once at R. Yeḥiya's house, and he related that in the time of R. Jehoshua ben-Levi it was attempted to abolish the use of the *Tebila* for men

[3] The *Tebila* (bath of purification) must contain at least forty measures of pure water (from a running stream).

[4] See J., tr. *Yôma*, viii. 1.

and women (after intercourse), because some women at Galilee caught a chill, and became sterile. But R. Yehoshuah opposed himself to the change, saying: You wish to abolish a thing which keeps Israel from sin? How does the *Tebila* keep us from sin? The following is an example: There was once a watchman of a garden who was going to commit a sin with a married woman; but before doing so, he wished to assure himself of being able to purify himself immediately afterwards; in the meantime strangers arrived, which prevented them committing the sin. Another man wishing to seduce one of Rabba's slaves, received from her this answer and refusal: I cannot take the *Tebila* excepting when my mistress takes it. Thou (slave) art considered but as an animal, said the seducer, so thou dost not require the *Tebila*. Hast thou forgotten, replied she, that it is written: "*Whosoever lieth with a beast shall surely be put to death*" (Exod. xxii. 18)? (So the sin was not committed.) According to R. Yeḥiya bar-Abba, the *Tebila* was only introduced in the interest of the study of the Law: As there is no limit to a man's intercourse with his wife; this intercourse happens too often, and too much precious time would be lost to the study of the Law[5].

A *baal-keri* may not study the Law before having taken a *Tebila*. R. Juda bar-Titus and R. Aḥa say, on the authority of R. Eleazar, that this prohibition is based on the verse: "*Be ready against the third day: come not at your wives*" (Exod. xix. 15). We teach that any man or woman suffering from an uncleanness (*profluviosus*), as well as a woman with her courses, and a woman in her confinement, may read the *Tora* (Law), study the *midrash*, the *halakha* (legal part of the Talmud), and the *agada* (ethical part); but all this is forbidden to a *baal-keri*. According to R. Abba bar-Aḥa, on the authority of Rabba, they (the *baal-keri*) may study the *halakha*, but not the *agada*; and according to R. Jose, they may study the *halakha*, which they know, but not the *Mishnâ*. According to another explanation of R. Jose's decision, they may study anything; but may not utter God's sacred names.

R. Sera (who was *baal-keri*) asked R. Jose if he would study with him and R. Aboon the Halakha, in which they were well versed; and he received a reply in the affirmative. R. Ḥiya (whilst also *baal-keri*) studied with his son, R. Jeremiah, the Halakha (during the same night in which he had become unclean), and in the morning he sent his son to work, so as to give himself time to take the *Tebila*. (All this proves that a *baal-keri* must not interrupt his studies to take the *Tebila*.) A Doctor who had arrived at the town of Netzibin whilst the *Tora* was being read, stopped at the sacred names (which he would not dare to utter). R. Juda ben-Bethera said to him: Continue, and enlighten us by your words, for the study of the *Tora* is not susceptible to uncleanness. According to

[5] Another reason may be mentioned: the cold water of the *Tebila* (cold baths) cools the ardour of the blood. This is generally known.

R. Jacob bar-Aḥa the principles of R. Elai, with regard to the shearing of sheep, are to be adopted, and the principles of R. Yoshiya relating to *kelaim* (mixed seeds), and those of R. Judah ben-Bethera regarding uncleanness. The first held that the commandment relating to the shearing of sheep is only applicable to Palestine; the second held that the prohibition regarding mixed seed is only infringed when one sows at the same moment wheat, barley, and the seeds (stones) of grapes, mixed together; the third held that the study of the *Tora* is not susceptible of impurity, i.e. a *baal-keri* need not take a *Tebila* before studying the Law. R. Jose ben-Ḥalaphta was travelling at night[6]; a donkey-driver was behind him. On arriving at a cistern, he noticed that his companion wished to plunge in. R. Jose opposed it. But, said the other, I wish to purify myself after the relations I have had with a married woman, and in addition to which she was in her courses. In spite of this R. Jose forbade him to expose himself to danger; but the man would not listen, and was on the point of plunging in; thereupon R. Jose called out to him: Go! and return not, since thou disobeyest me. And so it happened, for the imprudent fellow was drowned.

R. Jose ben-Jose was on board a ship, and saw a sailor who was attaching a rope to his waist to plunge in the sea: Expose not thyself to danger, said the Rabbi. But I am hungry, said the other; I wish to eat[7]. Thou mayest eat without purifying thyself. When arrived in port, λιμὴν, the Rabbi said to him: Here thou must obey thy scruples, take the *Tebila* before thy meal; I only forbade it thee on the sea, where it was dangerous. R. Yanaï says: Some say that the bath may be taken in still water, and others, that it must be in running water. He who wishes to be scrupulous (by using the latter) will see his days prolonged.

5. If any one, whilst reciting the Prayer, recollect that he is in his uncleanness (*baal-keri*), he is not to stop, but to shorten his prayers (at each section). If he has gone down into the water to bathe (Lev. xvi. 16), and can go up, dress, and recite the Shema' before the sun shines forth, he is to go up, dress, and recite it. But he is not to cover himself with foul water, or with water holding matter in solution, unless he has poured clean water to it. How far is he to keep from foul water or excrement (to pray)? Four cubits.

The teaching of the *Mishnâ* (that a *baal-keri* must not interrupt himself in the recitation of the Prayers) only applies to public recitation; but if one is praying alone, and recollect that he is in his uncleanness, he must stop and wash himself.

[6] Following the road: *Semita*.

[7] The Essenians purified themselves with water before meals.

According to R. Juda, if one is praying alone and there is no water to make an ablution, he must not suspend his prayer; but if there is water, he must stop and wash himself (to continue the prayer). R. Meyer, however (as cited above), held the contrary. R. Ame said: If a sick man has known his wife, he must take the *Tebila*, even if he foresees danger for his health. But if he has become unclean without intention (by pollution), he is dispensed. R. Ḥagui, on the authority of R. Abba bar-Zabdi, says, that in neither case is the *Tebila* to be exacted, so as not to expose him to danger. He who designedly becomes *keri*, if he is ill, must take a bath of nine ordinary measures of water, to purify himself; if he is in good health, he will take one of forty ordinary measures. If a sick man becomes unclean involuntarily, he is dispensed from the *Tebila;* but if a man is in good health, he will purify himself in a *Tebila* of nine measures.

R. Zabdi, son of R. Jacob bar-Zabdi, on the authority of R. Jonas, says: In a town which is distant from running water (river or pond), the *baal-keri* may recite the Shema' before purifying himself (so as not to miss the morning hour prescribed for the Shema'); but the prayers must be said after having taken the Tebila. A delicate (weak) man is not obliged to rise at daybreak (even if the water is close to the town), to take his bath (in case of uncleanness). The teaching of the Mishnâ, that a *baal-keri* may recite the Shema' while bathing, by covering himself with water, applies only in case the water is turbid; but if the water is clear, he must not recite it (for he can in that, by looking down, see his private parts); but if he can, with his feet, render the water turbid, he must do so, and recite the Shema'. We teach that in reciting the Shema', one must place himself at a distance of four ells from human excrement and from the dung of dogs (especially), at the time that it is being used for dressing skins (at the tannery). According to the Rabbis Jeremiah, Zeri, Abina, Ama, Shamaï, Mana, Abooha, Jose ben-Ḥanina, Samuel ben-Isaac, Ḥiya bar-Abba, Jose bar-Abbina, and Hona, in order to recite the Shema' and say the prayers, one must not be within four ells of any dirty or fetid water, or of a badly smelling corpse, human excrement, filth, and urine; even that of children who can already eat a piece of bread (of the size of half an egg at one time), or of any dung of beasts or birds, in fine, of anything dirty, filthy, or stinking.

R. Aboon was asked why it was necessary to place oneself at a distance from infants' excrement and urine (which does not smell)? He replied: "*For the imagination of man's heart is evil from his youth*" (Gen. viii. 21). R. Yadan adds that the words "*from his youth*" mean: from the day of his birth. We find that R. Elaiya and his companions, seated one evening in front of an hotel (*fonduq*), smelt a bad odour (without knowing from whence it arose); they asked themselves whether they could speak of the Law in that place? R. Elaiya replied: If it were light, we should be able to see the foul matter (since we can smell it, and it must be close to us), so we must abstain from speaking of the

Tora, or move away a space of four ells. R. Simon bar-Eleazar said: If a room, *triclinium*, be of a size of ten square ells, and there is some filth in it, it is not permitted to pray there without having at least covered it over, or put it under the bed. The Rabbis Zakhaï, Simon ben-Gamaliel, Jacob ben-Aḥa, Yeḥia bar-Aba, and Ḥanina said: If, in a room of four square ells (or larger) there be a urinal (vessel), at least a quarter of a measure of water must be poured into it, and it must be covered up, and hid before the prayers can be said. On a small quantity of filth, it suffices to throw water, according to R. Benjamin bar-Yapheth, on the authority of R. Yoḥanan. R. Jacob bar-Zabdi spat upon a small quantity of filth (thinking that would suffice); but R. Zera reproached him for this insufficiency.

The box full of books must not be placed under the foot of the bed (marriage-bed); it must be at the head. R. Abbin, in the name of R. Hoona, adds: The bed must be raised ten palms, at least, from the floor, and the cords of the bed must not touch the case. R. Jose, replacing R. Samuel, son of R. Isaac, approves R. Hoona's decision.

A man must not approach his wife in a room in which there is a *sepher tora* (roll of the Law), unless it is placed in a cupboard, ten palms higher than the bed, or enveloped in linen; according to R. Jeremiah, in the name of R. Aboon, R. Yehoshuah ben-Levi, in this case, put a curtain before the Tora.

It is not permitted to sit down on a bench on which the Law is placed. It happened to R. Eleazar to perceive that he had sat down on a bench on which was lying a roll of the Law; he became frightened, and got up, trembling like a man who notices a serpent by his side. If the roll is lying on another object (as, for instance, a piece of wood), placed on the bench, one may sit down. Of what size should the object (piece of wood) be? R. Abba, in the name of R. Hoona, replies that it must be as large as the fist. R. Jeremiah, in the name of R. Zera, says that it suffices for the roll to be placed above the level of the seat (of any size or thickness). If, seated on a donkey or horse, one has with one a satchel, *διсάκκιον*, full of books or human bones, it must be attached to one's back (i.e. one must not sit on it). The phylacteries must be placed above the bed, at the head, and not at the feet. R. Samuel, R. Abba, and R. Eleazar say, in the name of R. Ḥanina, that Rabbi hung up his Tephilin in this manner. According to R. Ḥiski, in the name of R. Aboon, they must not be hung up, in the manner that basket-sellers hang up their goods (i.e. hanging down); the phylacteries must be hung up by their cases, leaving the bands to hang down.

R. Ḥalaphta teaches that one must prevent oneself from yawning and hiccuping during prayers. R. Ḥanina relates that Rabbi put his hand on his mouth if he yawned or sneezed, and that he never spat during prayers. According to R. Yoḥanan, one may spit, so as not to have the mouth embarrassed in praying; but one must spit aside, and not to the right, but to the left (the right hand being

held in greater estimation), for it is written: "*A thousand shall fall at thy side* (*left*), *and ten thousand at thy right hand*" (Ps. xci. 7). Everybody admits that it is forbidden to cover the spittle with one's vestment, *stola*. R. Yehoshuah ben-Levi said: He who spits in the Synagogue during the prayers ought to be ashamed of himself. R. Jonas, however, spat in the Synagogue; but he put his foot on it. R. Jeremiah or R. Samuel ben Ḥalaphta say, on the authority of R. Ada b. Aḥwa[8]: One must not spit during prayers excepting one has moved away a space of four ells. According to R. Jose bar-Abbin, a person, after having spat or made water during prayers, must again move four ells away before recommencing. R. Jacob bar-Aḥa says that it is not a question of actually walking away a distance of four ells; but simply to allow the time it would take to do so to elapse. R. Amma, in accordance with the latter opinion, explains it thus: If one were obliged to walk a distance of four ells one might, by doing so, arrive at a still dirtier spot. R. Abba, in the name of Rabba, says: One must not pray in a place where there is filth, or urine which has not been soaked up. Genooba adds: As long as there is still a trace of urine in a certain spot, one must not pray there. According to Samuel, one may say one's prayers there as soon as the filth has commenced to dry up. Simon bar-Aba, in the name of R. Yoḥanan, approves Samuel's decision. R. Jeremiah and R. Zera, on the authority of Rab, say: Even if the filth is dried up as a bone, one must not say prayers near it. Samuel, however, repeats his words and maintains them. R. Simon bar-Aba, on the authority of R. Yoḥanan, agrees with Samuel. Ḥiski then said: Abbe (or Rabbe) was more scrupulous with regard to urine than other filth. R. Manna answered him: Thou referrest to what Genooba said (as above) in his name.

6. A man in his uncleanness[9] with a running issue,[1] a woman in her uncleanness during separation,[2] and a woman who perceives the need of separation (through her courses), all require the bath (before prayers). R. Juda exempts them (the more particularly that, in such cases, cold baths are dangerous).

The dispensation accorded by R. Juda applies to the case of a person who, being unclean, experiences an accidental issue (if preceded by the uncleanness, *profluvium*); but, if the uncleanness (*profluvium*) declares itself subsequently to the issue, is the bath to be exacted in such a case, in view of its serving to purify the former (accidental) case? This question may be resolved on the ground that,

[8] See J., tr. *Meghilla*, iii. 1.

[9] Latin: *Profluviosus* (a gonorrhean) *qui fluxum senserit*. Lev. xv. 2.

[1] In spite of the first state of uncleanness, a bath must be taken for the second one.

[2] After cohabitation in a pure state.

as it is said: The bath is necessary for a woman who, during cohabitation, perceives herself to be in her courses. R. Juda exempts them. Verily, R. Juda bases himself on one or other of the following motives: (1) That in such a case the bath is useless (seeing the general state of impurity); or, (2) that one does not take account of secondary uncleanness, in view of a superior degree of (contemporary) uncleanness. There is a practical divergence between these two motives if an accidental issue precedes the *profluvium,* in which case the first motive (that of the utility of the bath) is applicable (and the accidental uncleanness may be remedied); but, according to the second motive (i.e. not to take into account a secondary uncleanness in presence of one of a superior nature), the bath is not required (therefore the second motive prevails). One knows now R. Juda's opinion in the case of the secondary uncleanness declaring itself last; but what would be his opinion in the event of the graver state of impurity coming after the lesser one (seeing that the lesser one may be remedied)? We may reply to that, that it is said: If a woman, during cohabitation, perceives that she is menstrual, she must attend to herself; R. Juda exempts them. It is because, according to his opinion, there is no difference between uncleanness (*profluvium*), and the courses (in either case, if the graver uncleanness declares itself last, the exemption is maintained).

CHAPTER IV.[1]

1. The morning Prayer may be said until noon; R. Juda says: Until the fourth hour (ten o'clock). The afternoon Prayer, until the evening; according to R. Juda, until the middle[2] of the afternoon. The evening Prayer has no limited time; and the additional Prayer (Mussaph of Sabbath and festival days) may be recited all day. R. Juda says: Until the seventh hour (one o'clock).

It is written: "*To love the Lord your God, and to serve Him with your heart*" (Deut. xi. 13). This service of the *heart* means Prayer; it is also written: "*Thy God, whom thou servest continually, will deliver thee*" (Dan. vi. 11). Since there (at Babylon) were no organized religious ceremonies, it follows that it can only be Prayer that is meant. It cannot be maintained that all these prayers were said at the same time, for it is said: "*He kneeled upon his knees three times a day*" (Dan. vi. 10). In saying these prayers, one must not adopt any position at choice, for we learn that "*there were three windows towards Jerusalem in his chamber*" (Dan. vi. 11). Are we to infer that this practice was only instituted after the captivity? We cannot admit so in presence of the words "*as he did aforetime*" (Dan. vi. 11). Also we learn, by David, that there were ever fixed hours for Prayer: "*Evening and morning and at noon will I pray,*" &c. (Ps. lx. 18).

Through Ḥannah we learn that one must not raise the voice too high: "*Now Hannah she spake in her heart*" (1 Sam. i. 13); on the other hand, one must not reduce prayer to a simple meditation, for it is written: "*her lips moved*" (1 Sam. i. 13). How, then, is one to act? Speak with the lips. R. Jose bar-Ḥanina says: This verse teaches us four things: *Hannah spake in her heart,* therefore prayer requires attention; *her lips moved,* therefore the prayers must be spoken; *her voice was not heard,* therefore one must not raise the voice too high; "*Eli thought she had been drunken,*" these last words prove that it is forbidden to

[1] Translated by the late X. Z. (anonymous), who helped us also to revise the first chapters of this work.

[2] Supposing the day and night equal, i.e. twelve hours each, the Vesper hour would commence at half-past two; therefore one may say the afternoon Prayer until a quarter to four, at which hour the evening Prayer would commence.

say one's prayers while in a state of drunkenness. There was a discussion on the following subject: Ḥanna bar-Aba, one day, said to his condisciples, I am going to tell you of something which I saw Rabe do, and which when I told Samuel of, he was so pleased at, that he kissed me on the mouth (as a mark of satisfaction); this is what I saw: In saying "Be Thou praised" one bows down, and on coming to the word *Lord*, one stands upright again [3]. Samuel adds: I can give the reason for this custom, it is written: "*and he raiseth up all them that be bowed down*" (Ps. cxlv. 14). I cannot admit that, said R. Ami, for is it not written: "and was afraid before My name" (Mal. ii. 5)? That remark would be just, replied R. Aben, were it written, *and was afraid "at" My name*, but it is "*before* My name," i.e. before having uttered My name he is afraid (and there, one bows down). R. Aba bar-Zabdi prayed aloud. R. Jonah prayed in a low voice in the Synagogue; but when at home he prayed in a loud voice, so that the members of his family might learn their prayers through him; indeed, adds R. Ḥanna, they learnt their prayers through hearing their father (R. Jonah).

From where have they (the ancients) obtained the three prayers [4]? R. Samuel bar-Naḥmeni says: They (the prayers) are established upon the three periods of the day affecting all creatures; thus, in the morning, one should say: "I render thanks unto Thee, O Lord my God, and God of my fathers, that Thou hast brought me out of the darkness (of the night) unto the light (of the day)." In the afternoon, one should say: "I render Thee thanks, O Lord my God, and God of my fathers, that Thou hast permitted me to see the sun, at the going, as at the rising thereof." In the evening, one should say: "Let it please Thee, O Lord my God, and God of my fathers, to bring me out from the darkness to the light, as Thou hast done before." R. Yehoshuah ben-Levi says: They have learnt them (the three prayers) from the patriarchs: that of the morning, from Abraham: "*Abraham got up early in the morning to the place where he stood before the Lord*" (Gen. xix. 27); now the expression *he stood* ('Amad) signifies *he prayed*, as it is written: Then stood up (*vayaamod*) Phinehas, &c. (Ps. cvi. 30). The afternoon prayer comes to us from Isaac: "*And Isaac went out to meditate* (שוח, *pray*) *in the field at the eventide*" (Gen. xxiv. 63); this word, *lasouah*, means to pray. So we read (Ps. cii. 1): "*A prayer of the afflicted, when he is overwhelmed, and poureth out his complaint* (שיחו) *before the Lord.*" As for the evening prayer, we have it from Jacob: "*And he lighted* (vayifga') *on a certain place, and tarried there all night.*" The word *vayifga'* signifies to pray [5], as it is said: "*Let them therefore pray* (yifgu'oo) *the Lord God of Sabaoth*" (Jer. xxviii. 28), and again: "*Therefore pray not thou,*" &c. (veal tifga' bi) (Jer. vii. 17).

[3] See above, chap. i. § 8.
[4] See Medrash on Psalms, chap. xxv.; *Tanḥuma*, section *Miqetz*.
[5] See *Sifri*, section *Waethḥannan*, chap. xxvi.; *Bamidbar-Rabba*, chap. ii.

The Rabbis maintain that the prayers were instituted as parallels to the daily sacrifices, the morning prayer conformably to the morning sacrifice: "*The one lamb shalt thou offer in the morning*" (Num. xxviii. 4), and the same for the afternoon (Num. xxviii. 4). As regards the evening prayer they did not know with what to combine it, so they prescribed it without giving the motive; for which reason, we find in the Mishnâ that the evening prayer has no fixed hour. According to R. Tanḥuma, it was instituted in remembrance of the burning of the remains and entrails of the evening sacrifice, which was done during the night, on the altar. R. Juda (who maintains that the evening prayer can only be said up to ten o'clock) relies upon the Tora, for R. Ismael taught that it was written: "*And when the sun waxed hot it melted*" (Exod. xvi. 21), i.e. at the fourth hour (ten o'clock); now if one should wish to say that these words indicate the sixth hour, I would reply that this hour is pointed out by the following words: "*And he sat in the tent door, in the heat* (כחם) *of the day*" (Gen. xviii. 1). The words: *in the heat of the day* (וחם) must mean the fourth hour. And also, as the word *morning*, which is found in the passage relating to Abraham's sacrifice, signifies the fourth hour, the same word used with regard to the *Manna*, must have the same signification; at the fourth hour (ten o'clock), the sun is hot, but the shade is cool; at the sixth hour, however (midday), the sun and shade are both equally hot. According to R. Tanḥuma, the words *the sun being hot*, signify the hour at which no creature finds shade.

R. Jose was praying at the third hour (nine o'clock); R. Ḥiya bar-Aba did the same; R. Berakhiya Hamnonia recited first the Shema', and the other prayers afterwards. But the objection to this is that it has been decided that he who recites the Shema' after the third hour, does not lose the benefit of the prayer, which is reckoned to him as having the same spiritual value as the study of the Law. (Why therefore separate, as R. Berakhiya does, the Shema' from the other prayers?) The reply was that this was only to mean or apply to the case where the Shema' is recited at the fixed hour.

One might suppose that R. Juda, in fixing on the fourth hour (for the Shema'), bases himself on the following story, told by R. Simon, in the name of R. Yehoshuah ben-Levi: Under the Greek domination[6], the Jews, besieged in the Temple, gave every day two vessels of gold, which they passed out through a little window in the walls, and in return they received two lambs (for the daily sacrifice); one day, instead of lambs the Greeks sent two goats; but the Most Holy (praised be His name) opened their eyes, and they found two lambs in the

[6] Yavan; the Talmud styles thus the Seleucides who, after the death of Alexander, occupied the Syrian throne; the incident related by the Talmud took place under the reign of Antiochus Epiphanus. See J., tr. *Taanith*, iv. 5, and *Histoire d'Hérode*, by F. de Saulcy, p. 18.

Temple stables. With regard to this (morning) sacrifice R. Yuda bar-Aba says that it was offered at the fourth hour. R. Levi adds that during the same reign, they (the Jews) passed out two vases of gold for the price of two lambs; one day two pigs were given in return (derisively); but when the pigs had been hoisted about half the height of the wall they became fixed, and the wall was shaken down, and thrown to a distance of more than forty parasanges from the land of Israel; from that time, on account of the sins of Israel, the daily sacrifice was interrupted, and the Temple subsequently destroyed[7].

On what do the Rabbis base their opinion? It is written: "*Two lambs day by day*" (Num. xxviii. 3), thus dividing the day into two parts. R. Juda explains the words "*two every day*" in the following manner: present two offerings each day; or, offer up as daily sacrifices (and not extraordinary sacrifices); or, offer them up during the day. The Mishnâ instructs us[8] as follows: The morning sacrifice is slain at the north-east angle of the altar, near to the second ring, and that of the evening at the south-east angle, near to the second ring; and it says that the morning and evening sacrifices must be chosen beforehand.

R. Ḥiya, in the name of R. Yoḥanan, says: With regard to the prayer Minḥa (of the afternoon) and the prayer Mussaph (supplementary, of festivals), priority is given to the former. It was endeavoured (in the schools) to maintain that this rule only held good in case of there not being time enough to say both before night; but R. Zera, as well as R. Nathan bar-Tubi, affirm, on the authority of R. Yoḥanan, that this rule holds good in the contrary case. But it was objected that by reciting the Minḥa before the Mussaph one accomplishes the religious duty, but that one should not act voluntarily in this manner? It was answered thereto, that the foregoing only applies in case of the hour for saying the Minḥa not having arrived. Thus R. Yehoshuah ben-Levi taught his pupils, saying to them: When you go to a repast (ἄριστον), never sit down at midday without having said the Minḥa, for fear of the repast lasting a long time, and causing you to miss, either on a week-day or on a Saturday, the hour appointed for this prayer. But what is the appointed hour for this prayer? A quarter to eleven[9]. Verily we learn[1], that the evening sacrifice was slain at the middle of the eighth hour (half-past two), and laid on the altar at the middle of the ninth hour (half-past three), excepting on Easter eve, when it was offered an hour

[7] In B., *Bava-Kama*, fol. 82, this incident is supposed to have occurred during the struggle between Hyrcanus and Aristobulus. On this account also was it forbidden to rear pigs in Palestine. See *Histoire d'Hérode*, by F. de Saulcy, p. 18.

[8] Mishna, v.; tr. *Tamid*, chap. iv.; tr. *Edouyoth*, vi. 1.

[9] By dividing the day into two equal parts, commencing at six a.m., the hour for saying the *Minḥa* would be a quarter to five in the evening (or eleventh hour since the morning).

[1] See *Mishnâ*, tr. *Pesaḥim*, v. 1.

earlier (on account of the Paschal lamb). We see, therefore, that the time for saying the Minḥa begins early, and that explains R. Yehoshuah's advice to his pupils, as above. R. Jeremiah said: You say that the time for saying the Minḥa lasts two hours and a half, whilst for the sacrifices you accord three hours and a half? R. Jose replied that the comparison of the Minḥa to the evening sacrifice is not complete: it should only be collated with the offering of the incense, which is made afterwards; he relies on the following verse: "*Let my prayer be set forth before Thee as incense, and the lifting up of my hands as the evening sacrifice*" (Ps. cxli. 3). Take off an hour for the preparation of the sacrifice; there remains two and a half hours [2].

R. Jose ben-Ḥanina said his morning prayer as soon as the sun appeared, and his evening prayer just before it had entirely disappeared, so as to be filled all day with the fear of heaven, according to the verse: "*For this shall every one that is godly pray unto Thee in a time when Thou mayest be found*" (Ps. xxxii. 6), that is to say, at the hour that God reveals himself to the world by the light. R. Ada's uncle (his mother's brother) had Rab's *taleth* (the service mantle) on the day of the great fast; the latter said: When the sun shall be as high as the tops of the palm-trees, thou wilt give me my taleth, that I may recite the *neila* (close of the fast). When the sun is at that height at Babylon, where Rab was, it is still day here (in Palestine), for Babylon is lower than Palestine. This, according to R. Yoḥanan, results from the verse: "*That sayeth to the deep, Be dry*" (Isa. xliv. 27); it is Babylon which is thus called the deep of the world. It has been proved that he who prays much will be heard (God does not hear the prayers of the Israelites, because they are sinful; but if they were not so, the more they pray, the more acceptable they are to God).

A contrary opinion has, however, been expressed [3], on the authority of R. Levi, by R. Aba, son of R. Papi, and R. Yehoshuah of Saḥnin, who explained in that manner the verse: "*In all labour there is profit; but the talk of the lips tendeth only to penury*" (Prov. xiv. 23); they applied this verse to Ḥannah, who, having prayed too much, shortened the days of Samuel's (her son) life; she said: "*And he will there abide for ever*" (olam) (1 Sam. i. 22). But it was objected that the word *olam*, as applied to the Levites, means the fiftieth year, and Samuel lived fifty-two years. R. Yose bar R. Aboon says: The two years during which she suckled him must be deducted (leaving fifty) [4]. There is no contradiction; according to Levi, the former case applies to the particular individual, and the latter to the community (the one is rewarded, whilst the other is punished). R. Ḥiya, on the authority of R. Yoḥanan and R. Simon, son of Ḥalaphta, relied

[2] This shows what relation prayer has to incense.

[3] See J., *Biccurim*, ii. 1; tr. *Taanith*, iv. 1.

[4] How reconcile these two opinions, that prayer is useful, and that it is injurious?

upon this verse: "*And it came to pass thus as she continued praying*" (1 Sam. i. 12), to prove that he who prays much is heard. The prophet thus called the place Babel, because it is the place on the earth which lies the lowest. According to R. Yoḥanan, the name of *tzoula* (depth or abyss) was given to Babel because it was there that the victims of the Deluge were swallowed up (Exod. xv. 10), conformably to this verse: "*As Babylon hath caused the slain of Israel to fall, so at Babylon shall fall the slain of all the earth*" (Jer. li. 49).

It is written: "They found a plain in the land of Shinar, and dwelt there" (Gen. xi. 2). It is called *Shinar*, says Resh-Lakesh, for it is there that were precipitated (*Sheninaroo*) those who died by the Deluge; or else because they died there of epilepsy (*naar*, to writhe), deprived of light and baths (which would have been good for the sick); or else because they are despoiled (same word in Hebrew) of good works (neither offerings nor tithes); or else because its princes die young; or else because it (this country) has raised up an adversary, and an enemy to God, that is Nabuchodonosor the impious. Rab bar-Judah said: If you do as the Rabbis, R. Judah cannot consent to it; but if you do as R. Judah, you act in conformity with all opinions. On what has one relied to establish the *neila*[5] (closing prayer of the long fast)? According to R. Levi, on the following verse: "Yea, when ye make many prayers, I will not hear them" (Isa. i. 15), it is said slowly so as not to arrive at the Neila before night. What is the proper moment for saying the Neila? The Cæsarean Rabbis say that there is a difference of opinion on this subject between Rab and R. Yoḥanan. According to the former, it is at the moment of the shutting of the gates of Heaven (at night); and according to the latter, at the closing of the gates of the Sanctuary. As R. Juda Antordia remarks, the following Mishnâ supports the latter opinion: Thrice during the year, it says, the priests (at the Temple of Jerusalem) give the benediction four times a day, viz. on the fasting days, on the day of the changing of the *Maamad*[6], and on the great fast; once in the morning, again at the additional prayer or Mussaph, at the Minḥa prayer, and, fourthly, at the closing prayer or Neila (as one of the benedictions takes place at the Neila on the day of the great fast, and as this prayer is said during the day, there is no question here of the gates of Heaven, for it cannot be maintained that they are closed during the day). The brother of R. Ada's mother (his maternal uncle) had Rab's *taleth* on, on the day of the great fast; Rab said to him: When the sun

[5] We have seen, above, what is the supposed origin of the other prayers.

[6] By *maamad* is meant a division of the Israelites, corresponding to a division of the priests, called *mishmar;* the entire nation was divided into twenty-four *maamadoth*, just as the priests were formed into an equal number of *mishmoroth*. Whilst the one was attached to the service of the Temple, the other was subjected to certain pious works, of which the most severe was a four days' fast. See *Mishnâ*, ii.; tr. *Taanith*, chap. iv. §§ 1 and 2.

shall be as high as the tops of the palm-trees, thou wilt give me my *taleth* that I may recite my Neila. Does not Rab contradict himself? On the one hand he says that it is at the time of the shutting of the gates of the Sanctuary, and on the other (in his discussion with R. Joḥanan) he says: at the closing of the gates of Heaven? R. Matna replied that, as Rab prayed lengthily, he arrived at the Neila towards night (so that the closing of the doors of the tabernacle, and of the gates of Heaven, coincided). It was asked: Does the Neila dispense one from the evening prayer? R. Aba and R. Ḥiya, in the name of Rab, answer in the affirmative[7]. But, objected R. Aba to the latter, at what part (of the 'Amida) is the prayer of separation (*habdalah*[8]) said? R. Yona objected to R. Aba: Can an 'Amida of seven benedictions dispense you from the duty of saying one of eighteen? But, replied R. Aba, have I not already refuted the opinion of Rab by the first objection? A refutation is not enough, replied the other; this opinion must be annulled. R. Yose said that R. Aba's objection is irrefutable. As regards that of R. Yona, it may be said that on account of the fast it was intended to lighten the burden and that the 'Amida (of the Neila), composed of only seven benedictions, dispenses with that of the evening in which there are eighteen. R. Aba bar-Mamal said to his condisciples: I have heard your masters affirm that the Neila does not dispense with the evening prayer; this opinion has been supported by R. Yosse bar R. Aboon, on the authority of R. Ḥiya, in the following terms: The eighteen benedictions must be recited every day, even also on Saturday evening, on the day of *kippur*, and on public fasts (refutation of the foregoing opinion of R. Yose); and R. Naḥman bar-Isaac, on the authority of R. Yoḥanan ben-Levi, said: If *kippur* falls on a Saturday, although there be no Neila on Saturday, the Sabbat is mentioned in the Neila prayer (this, therefore, forms part of the offices of the day, and cannot dispense with the evening prayer). To the above two rules are added the following: If the Neomenia and a public fast fall on the same day, although the Neila is not effected during the Neomenia, it is mentioned in the Neila prayer; R. Simon, on the authority of R. Yoḥanan ben-Levi, says: On the *Ḥanuka*-sabbat, although there is no Mussaph (supplementary prayer or sacrifice which only exists for solemnities of Biblical institution), the Ḥanuka is nevertheless mentioned in the Mussaph. It is the same with the Neomenia, which takes place during this festival (and which allows a Mussaph).

When the Neomenia falls on a fast day, at what part of the 'Amida is the solemnity mentioned? According to R. Zeira, in the fifteenth blessing; according

[7] B., tr. *Yoma*, fol. 87.

[8] This prayer is said in the fourth of the eighteen blessings of which the 'Amida is composed. On festivals only the three last are recited, and a blessing, special to the solemnity, is intercalated between them. See Appendix II.

to R. Aba bar-Mamal, in the sixteenth; according to R. Abina, in the fourth; and, says R. Aba, since in all circumstances it is inserted in the fourth, it must be the same in this particular case; and indeed the custom is in accordance with R. Aba's opinion.

What chapter (of the *Tora*) is read[9] on this day (Neomenia and fast united)? According to R. Yose, the passage of the benedictions and maledictions (viz. Lev. xxvi. and Deut. xxviii.). But, objected R. Mena, does one not know that it is a fast, since the supplications are said, with the head bowed (this prayer is only said on public fasts)? This prayer, replied R. Yose, is but a reminder that the above chapter must be read.

R. Judan of Cappadocia said before R. Yosse, on the authority of R. Juda ben-Pazi, that on this day, the chapter of the *Tora* which refers to the Neomenia is read; R. Yose, getting up as well as R. Juda ben-Pazi, summoned him in these terms: Is it from thy father that thou hast heard that? My father, replied he, only said that for the town of Ein-Tob, where they knew perfectly well that it was *Rosh-ḥodesh* (new month); it was in this place that, at certain dates, the Neomenia was proclaimed; but in all other places the chapter of blessings and curses is read.

Jeremiah the Scribe asked R. Jeremiah what chapter ought to be read if the Neomenia happened to fall on a Saturday? That of the Neomenia, answered he; R. Ḥelbo said before R. Arni (and the Mishnâ agrees with him on this point) that for every solemnity, whether it be the Ḥanuka or the Purim, the ordinary reading should be interrupted, and the chapter relating to the solemnity read in its stead. Isaac Seḥora asked R. Yitzhaq: Which is the chapter that should be read at the Neomenia which falls during the Ḥanuka? Three persons are called in for the Neomenia, and one for the chapter of the Ḥanuka; R. Pinḥas, R. Simon, and R. Aba bar-Zamina, on the authority of R. Abdoomi from Man-Ḥifia[1], held the contrary opinion, viz.: three for the chapter of Ḥanuka, and one for that of Neomenia, as the fourth is only called on account of Neomenia (for the Ḥanuka only one is called). Bar Shalmaya the Scribe said to R. Mana: Behold, when the Neomenia of Ḥanuka falls on a Saturday, first seven persons are called (settled number for the Saturday), then the others are added for the chapters of the Neomenia and the Ḥanuka (therefore the same thing should take place during the week, and when the Neomenia and the Ḥanuka happen to fall together on a working day, the chapter of the Neomenia must be read first, and the chapter of the Ḥanuka added for the fourth). I have asked the Scribes this question, continued he, but they answered: You should not ask us this question, but rather the Rabbis, who are more learned than we are. Rabbi commanded

[9] See J., tr. *Taanith*, ii. 10 (14).

[1] Ḥeifa is also mentioned in J., tr. *Eroobin*, ii. (fol. 20 *a*).

his orator Abdone[1] to make a public proclamation, announcing that the evening prayer might be said (on a Saturday) before it was quite dark, and R. Ḥiya b. Aba did the same thing. R. Ḥanina says that R. Ismael, son of R. Yose, took him one day to an inn, and said: My father once recited the evening prayer (on a Saturday) before it was quite dark. R. Ame observes that R. Yoḥanan does not approve of that, but (says the Talmud) if the protest of R. Yoḥanan refers to the act of R. Ḥanina, he is wrong; for one may take from the profane hours of a working day to multiply the holier hours (thus anticipating the Sabbath). Moreover, the ass-drivers came (one Friday) from Arabia to Sephoris, and they said: Ḥanina b. Dossa has already begun the feast of the Sabbath in his town. (It is therefore a custom generally accepted, that the Friday evening prayer should be anticipated, and so it is impossible to admit that R. Yoḥanan disputed this point. Therefore, the opinion of R. Ḥanina should be rectified: it relates to the prayer of the Saturday night according to the facts just alluded to, and that is what R. Yoḥanan disputes.) And even on this point, there was no ground for contestation, for Rab (agreeing with R. Ḥanina) commanded his orator to announce publicly that whoever wished to say the Saturday night prayer before night could do so, and R. Ḥiya b. Aba did the same (their several opinions are against that of R. Yoḥanan).

At the school of R. Yanai it was taught that any one who was lying down was not obliged to arise (to say the evening prayer, which is not an obligation); but R. Zeira says: Whenever I did so, I trembled for fear of experiencing nocturnal alarms; therefore (if any one wishes to lie down before night), he should conform to the opinion of Rabbi and R. Ḥiya b. Aba. R. Jacob b. Aḥa says: It has been said that the evening prayer is an obligation, according to R. Gamaliel, and R. Yoshua says it is optional; this discussion may be compared to that which relates to the closing prayer (*Neila*). In R. Gamaliel's opinion, the recitation of the Neila does not dispense with that of the evening prayer, whereas R. Yoshua opines that it does.

A disciple once asked R. Yoshua his opinion about the evening prayer, and he answered that it was optional. Having addressed the same question to R. Gamaliel, he was told it was an obligation; but, said the pupil, R. Yoshua said it was optional. When I enter the Assembly to-morrow, arise, and ask the question again; the next day the disciple did so, and repeated his question regarding the evening prayer. It is an obligation, said R. Gamaliel. But, answered he, R. Yoshua tells me it is optional. R. Gamaliel addressing himself to R. Yoshua, said: Is it true that you expressed this opinion? No. Then

[1] In the large schools of Palestine and Babylon there was first the master or chief, then came the orators, whose business it was to transmit the oral teaching of the master to the pupils, and to discuss it with them, they were called *Amoraims*. See *Bereshith Raba*, chap. vi.

arise, said R. Gamaliel, and let them bear witness against you.[3] R. Gamaliel remained seated and explained the subject, whilst R. Yoshua was standing. The assembly (shocked by this act of authority) murmured and said to R. Ḥootzpith the *turgueman* (drogman) that he must close the lesson.[4] Then all the assembly rising, said to R. Gamaliel: "All have felt the effects of thy pride!" And immediately R. Eleazar b. Azaria was named (Nassi instead of R. Gamaliel); he was then sixteen years old, but (by the effects of a miracle) his head became in that day filled with the wisdom of old age, his hair became white.

R. Akiba grieved sorely (because R. Eleazar b. Azaria had been preferred to him), and to console himself, he said: It is not that he is more learned, but he comes from a more illustrious race than myself. Happy is the man whose right has been made by his ancestors; happy is he who can find his strength in them! R. Eleazar b. Azaria descended from Esra in the tenth generation. How many seats were there in the school (on the day when, for the first time, R. Eleazar held the dignity of Nassi)? There were eighty, according to Jacob b. Sissy, without counting the disciples who were beyond the rails. Three hundred, according to R. Yose b. R. Aboon (R. Gamaliel had been very severe about the admission of the *beth-din* and the school in the enclosure). It is thus the words of the Mishna must be understood (which prove the election of R. Eleazar): This is what was taught by R. Eleazar b. Azaria to the wise men of the vineyard of Yamnie: "Does that mean there was a vineyard at Yamnie? No, it refers to the disciples who were arranged before him as the vine-plants in a vineyard."[5]

Directly after the election of R. Eleazar b. Azaria, R. Gamaliel went to all the members of the tribunal to reconciliate himself with them. He also went to R. Yoshua, and found him making needles. "Is this the work you live on?" said he. "Until the present time you had had no wish to know anything about me; misfortune will befall the generation you are teaching!—I beg your forgiveness," resumed Gamaliel (and R. Yoshua granted it). To R. Eleazar b. Azaria, according to some, a bleacher was sent. Others say it was R. Akiba who said: He who is Cohen, and son of a Cohen (priest) must sprinkle the holy water.[6] May he who is neither Cohen, nor son of Cohen, say to him who is Cohen and son of Cohen: Thy waters are as the waters of a cistern[7]; thy

[3] The accused was obliged to remain standing during the hearing of the witnesses.

[4] Thus dismissing the audience.

[5] See *Rabba* on Canticle viii. 11.

[6] Allusion is here made to the respective situations of R. Gamaliel and R. Eleazar. R. Eleazar descended from a pontifical family, that of Ezra; whereas R. Gamaliel, by what tradition says, descended from a pagan who had been converted to Judaism.

[7] Any person who had a taint of impurity, had to be sprinkled by the priest, and the water was taken from a running stream (see Numbers, ch. xix.).

cinders as those which come from the oven.[8] R. Eleazar answered: You have forgiven him; let us go together to the door of R. Gamaliel, and invite him to take back the dignity of Nassi. However, R. Eleazar was not deprived of all his honours, he was still maintained as *ab-beth-din* (vice-president of the supreme tribunal.[9]

2. When R. Neḥonia-ben-Hakana entered the school, and when he left it, he made a short prayer. They asked him: What was the object of this prayer? When I arrive, answered he, I pray that no offence may happen through my fault; and when I leave I thank God for the graces He has conferred upon me.

What was his prayer when he arrived? "May it please Thee, eternal God, God of my fathers, that I be not irritated against my disciples, nor my disciples against me; that we may not pronounce to be impure that which is pure, nor pure that which is not so; that we may not forbid what is allowed, and that we allow not what is forbidden, so that I may not be despised, neither in this world nor in the next." What was it he said when leaving (the *beth-hamidrasch*)? "I render Thee thanks, Eternal God, God of my fathers, because Thou hast placed my lot amongst those who frequent the schools and synagogues, and not amongst those who visit the theatres and circuses (circenses), for I and they, we all work and watch; I work to deserve Eden, and they work for their destruction, as it is said (Ps. xvi. 10): *For Thou wilt not leave my soul in hell, neither wilt Thou suffer Thine holy one to see corruption.* R. Pedath, on the authority of R. Jacob b. Idi, R. Eleazar, after each of the three obligational prayers of the day, added these words: "May it please Thee, Eternal God, God of my fathers, that no hatred may enter men's hearts against us, nor in our hearts against men, let none be jealous because of us, and let us not be jealous of any one; let the study of Thy law be the study of our life, and may our words be accepted by Thee as supplications." R. Ḥiya b. Aba added these words: "Let our hearts be united in the fear of Thy name, lead us away from whatever is hateful to Thee; bring us near to all that Thou lovest, and show mercy to us because of Thy name." In R. Yani's school it was taught that the following prayer should be said on awaking: "Praised be Thou, O God, Who givest back life to the dead;[1] Lord, I have sinned against Thee. May it please Thee, Eternal, my God, to give me a pure heart, a happy life, good inclinations, a good friend, a

[8] And not from the red cow (see ibid).

[9] B., ib. fol. 28 *a*.

[1] In the opinion of the Rabbis, sleep is a sixtieth part of death (B. same treatise, fol. 57).

good reputation, a bountiful eye,[2] a good and modest soul, an humble spirit; that Thy name be not profaned amongst us, and that we may not become objects of mockery for the world; let not destruction await us, and let not our hope be eternal death; grant we may not be obliged to ask the help of men, and let not our food be dependent on their bounty, for their gifts are small, but the shame they inflict is great; let our life be devoted to the study of Thy law, and passed with those who accomplish Thy will; build up again Thy parvisthy city and Thy tabernacle [3] soon in our days."

R. Ḥiya b. Aba prayed thus: "May it please Thee, Eternal God, God of our fathers, so to dispose our hearts that we may offer Thee sincere penitence, that we may not be ashamed before our ancestors in the next life."[4] According to R. Yudan, of the school of R. Ismael, the *Amorai*[5] was commanded to say this prayer after the explanations. R. Tanḥuma bar Isblustiska's prayer was as follows: "May it please Thee, Eternal God, God of my fathers, to vanquish and take away the yoke of all bad passions that are in our hearts, for Thou hast made us to fulfil Thy will, it is our duty so to do, it is also Thy wish and ours; the ferment that is in the paste[6] turns us from it; it is visible for Thee that we have not strength enough to resist it; may it therefore please Thee, Eternal God, God of our fathers, to cause love, good will, peace and friendship to reside amongst us; let our end be happy, let our hopes be realized, let the number of those who study Thy law be increased; grant we may enjoy happiness in Eden (future life); let us have a good heart and find a good companion; may we find every day when we arise what our heart desires, and may the desires of our souls be directed to Thee in all that is good."

"On going out, I offer up thanks for my lot." According to R. Aboon (these words mean), "I render thanks to God, Who has given me an intelligence and good works to perform.[7]"

3. R. Gamaliel said: The 18 benedictions should be recited every day; R. Yoshua says: It is sufficient to give a summary of the 18 benedictions; R. Akiba says: That he who knows his

[2] It signifies, "That we may be charitable." See Prov. xxii. 9.

[3] The temple and town of Jerusalem.

[4] If our souls were placed before the heavenly throne, on an inferior degree to that which is occupied by our ancestors.

[5] The chief of each school had an *amorai* or orator, who explained to the pupils the teaching of the master, and discussed it with them.

[6] This expression is used to express the passions which reside in the heart.

[7] A sound "intelligence" which does not deceive itself, and does not declare pure what is impure. And "good works," because he is patient with his pupils.

prayers well by heart should recite the 18; if not, it is enough to make a summary of them.[8]

Wherefore 18 benedictions? R. Yoshuah b. Levi says:[9] They are in connection with the 18 psalms, finishing at the 19th: *The Lord hear thee in the day of trouble.* If it be objected that there are nineteen psalms, the answer is that the 1st and 2nd are, properly speaking, but one. It has been said that he who, having prayed, has not seen his prayers answered, ought to fast.[1] R. Mena says that this psalm (The Lord hear thee, &c., which comes directly after the 18 which are the foundation of the 18 blessings) proves to any learned man that he should say to his master:[2] "Let thy prayer be heard." According to R. Simon, these 18 benedictions have been established in reference to the 18 links (of which a man's spine is composed) which enable him to bend during his prayer, as it is written (Ps. cxxxv. 10): *All my bones cry out, saying, O God, who is like unto Thee?*" R. Levi says that the 18 blessings are in accordance with the tetragram which is repeated 18 times in Psalm xxix. R. Hoona says: It will perhaps be objected that the prayer of 18 blessings is composed of nineteen; the answer should be that the prayer of the *minims* (unbelievers) was prescribed later on at Yabne.[3] R. Elazar bar R. Yose objected, however, that in Psalm xxix. (which, it has been previously remarked, served as a foundation for the eighteen blessings) the name of God is mentioned 19 times (therefore, to this prayer they might have given a number corresponding to the names of the Divinity[4])? He answered: Because of that it is said that the prayer for the minims (infidels) is inserted, and the prayer for transgressors in that of the uncharitable (the 12th), the prayer regarding elders and strangers in that of the righteous (13th), and the prayer of David relating to Jerusalem (14th). Is the holy name repeated often enough (in the psalm) for each of these subjects? (No; therefore the 18

[8] In those days this book was rare in Palestine, the prayers were learnt by heart, by the children. There was in each community a man, the *Hazan*, whose special care was to teach them prayers. See Mishna, tr. *Sabbath*, i. 6.

[9] See J., tr. *Taanith*, ii. 2.

[1] The eighteen psalms are followed by the psalm beginning by the word *yaanekha*, which means to grant, and which the Rabbis interpret by to fast; which also gave birth to the above idea.

[2] This psalm is dedicated by Israel to David its master.

[3] Town in which R. Yoḥanan b. Zaccai sought a refuge before the destruction of the temple, and where the principal Rabbis and Pharisees joined him later on. Therefore this blessing has not been inserted in the Ritual by the great Synods, and although it is admitted, the blessings are still numbered as 18.

[4] The name R. Elazar wished to add to form the nineteenth is not a tetragram, that is why it was not counted.

tetragrams[5] only were taken, and it is easy to understand why in the origin the prayer only had 18 blessings). According to R. Ḥanina, on the authority of R. Pinḥas, these 18 benedictions have been published in reference to the same number of times that the names of the three patriarchs are repeated in the Tora;[6] if, again, it be objected that these names are repeated there 19 times, it should be answered that the verse (Genesis xxviii. 13), "*And behold the Lord stood above it*," is not included;[7] if the contrary objection, that there are only seventeen, is made, the answer must be that the verse (Genesis xlviii. 17), "*My name and the name of my fathers*," must be included.[8] R. Samuel b. Naḥmeni, on the authority of R. Yoḥanan, says: It refers to the verb "to ordain" which is repeated 18 times in the second narration of the building of the Temple. Yoshua b. Aba adds that they are only counted from the verse (Exodus xxxviii. 23), "*And with him was Aholiab, son of Ahisamach of the tribe of Dan*," up to the end of the volume.[9]

As for the 7 blessings of the Sabbath, whence do they proceed?[1] R. Isaac says: They refer to the words, "*The voice of God*," which are repeated 7 times in Psalm xxix. According to R. Juda Antouriah, they are in accordance with the tetragram repeated 7 times in the canticle for the Sabbath (Ps. xcii.). The 9 blessings for the *rosh hashana* (new year) were established, according to R. Aba of Carthage, in reference to the tetragram repeated 9 times in Anna's prayer, finishing with these words: "*God will judge the extremities of the earth*" (1 Samuel ii. 10).[2] According to R. Ḥelbo and R. Simon b. R. Naḥman, the 24 blessings for days of fast[3] are in accordance with the words, song, prayer, and supplication, which are repeated 24 times in the prayer of Solomon (1 Kings viii.). R. Zeira, on the authority of R. Jeremie, says: Every one on fasting days should insert in the Amida a few words relating to the fast, and which would be the best place? Between the 7th and 8th blessing. These are the words which he should add: "Hear us, O Lord, in these times and in these days, for we are in great

[5] The 4 letters which spell Jehovah, so sacred that they are generally replaced by the word *Adonai*.

[6] Cf. *Bereshith Rabba*, ch. lxix.; *Wayyiqra rabba*, ch. i.

[7] Probably because only the names of two patriarchs are found in it.

[8] The 3 patriarchs are mentioned: He (Jacob) and his ancestors, Abraham and Isaac.

[9] The connection established by the Rabbis between the prayers and the temple is easily understood.

[1] It is well known that the prayer of the 18 is not the same on Saturdays and festivals as that of ordinary days; the three first and three last blessings alone remain unchanged.

[2] According to the Rabbis, the new year is a day of judgment for all creatures.

[3] See the Mishna, tr. *Taanith*, ii. 2. It refers to public and general times of fasting, not the same as the great fast or *Yom Kippur*.

affliction; turn not Thy face away, and hear our supplications; for Thou, Eternal God, assisteth in times of trouble, Thou deliverest and savest in times of sorrow and oppression. *They called unto the Eternal God in their trouble, and He brought them out of their humiliation* (Ps. cvii. 28). Be Thou praised, O Eternal God, Who hearest in the time of trouble." R. Janai, on the authority of R. Ismael, who repeated it in the name of R. Janai's school, is of opinion that these words should be inserted in the 16th blessing, and that a separate paragraph should not be made of them, as the before-mentioned Rabbi advises.

R. Yona, on Rab's authority, says: A private individual who has vowed to observe a fast should insert the words which refer to this fast in his prayer, and it is the same thing for this as for the Sabbath, says R. Zeira, on the authority of R. Ḥoona: It should be mentioned at each of the three services (evening, morning, and afternoon). R. Mana says: I did not know which opinion was admitted—if it was R. Jeremie's or that of R. Janai on R. Ismael's authority; but when I went to the place where the rules were established,[4] I heard R. Hoona, on the authority of Rab, saying that a private individual who has made a vow that he will observe a day of fasting, should insert the prayer concerning the fast in the eighteen blessings. But R. Yosse objects, saying: Does not the Mishnâ formally observe that an individual should recite the 'Amida every day, even on Saturday evenings, on the evenings of Kippur, and of public fasting? (If in this prayer words relating to the solemnity were inserted, there would be one blessing more.) What does R. Yose mean by these words: "which the Mishnâ questions"? It is an argument against the opinion which maintains that the prayer relating to the solemnity is inserted between the seventh and eighth (and the opinion of R. Janai is admitted, which inserts it in the sixteenth without making a separate paragraph). R. Aḥa b. Isaac, in the name of R. Ḥiya of Sephoris, says:[5] On the day of Ab (the anniversary of the destruction of the two temples) he should insert in the 'Amida words relating to these events; this is what he should say: "Eternal God, spread Thy infinite mercy and Thy ever-faithful goodness upon us, upon Thy people Israel, over Jerusalem Thy town, over Sion, where Thy glory resides, on this town of mourning, destroyed, shaken, rendered desolate, given up into the hands of the proud, devastated by the wicked, which the armies conquered and the idolaters polluted; Thou hadst given it to Thy people Israel, as an inheritance for the posterity of Yeshurum; it has been destroyed by fire, and by fire Thou wilt rebuild it in future, as it is said, *I shall be to her* (said the Eternal) *as a wall of fire all around, and I will reside in her for her glory*" (Zacharie ii. 9). R. Abdima of Sephoris asked of R. Mana: At which place (in the Prayer) are these words inserted? Didst thou not know that

[4] The Beth-Hamidrash, or Sanhedrin.
[5] See J., *Taanith*, ii. 5.

yet? All that concerns the future is inserted in the *'aboda* (the 17th), and whatever concerns the past in the *hodaah* (the 18th); the Mishnâ says so: the *hodaah* is said (gratitude) for the past, and prayers are made for the future (by the *'aboda* we beseech God for His blessings). How is the prayer which resumes the eighteen composed? According to Rab, the end of each of the eighteen is said (always composed of these words: "Mayest Thou be praised, Eternal God, &c."). According to Samuel, the initial sentence of the eighteen blessings. Some say the prayer should be composed of seven blessings resuming the eighteen [6]; others that it is a prayer of eighteen which recapitulates the eighteen. The former agrees with Samuel, the latter with Rab. R. Zeira sent R. Nissim to R. Janai from R. Ismael, to learn how the prayer of the seven blessings recapitulates the eighteen was composed according to Samuel. He answered that this was the formula: "Give us intelligence, accept our repentance, forgive us, deliver us, cure our sick, bless our years." In the time of rainy weather, R. Ḥagai recommends the following words to be said: "Bless unto us the rain;" and at the fall of the dew, "Bless unto us the dew, for Thou bringest together those that are scattered and whose hope is in Thy justice. Thou wilt hold out Thy hand over the wicked, and all those who trust in Thee shall rejoice, when Thy town shall be rebuilt, and at the reopening of the Tabernacle and the return of the children of David, Thy servant; for before we pray to Thee, Thou hearest us, as it is said: *Before they call unto Me will I hear them; whilst they are speaking their prayer shall be heard* (Is. lxv. 24); be Thou praised, O God Eternal, Who hearest our prayer." To this formula are added the three first and the three last blessings, and the end is, "Praised be God Who has heard the voice of our prayer." [7]

4. R. Eleazar says: If prayers are said only to fulfil a duty (as a charge), they will not be heard (by God).[8]

R. Abahoo, on the authority of R. Eleazar says (to explain the meaning of the Mishnâ): Prayers should not be recited as if they were simply the reading of an act or lawsuit. R. Aḥa, on the authority of R. Yose, says: Every day a difference should be made;[9] Ahitophel (David's counsellor) made three different prayers every day. As long as I acted thus, says R. Zeira, I was in error. The only interpretation is that of R. Abahoo, from R. Eleazar's authority (on ineffectual prayer): prayers should not be recited as if one were reading an act (or a lawsuit). R. Eleazar said every day a different prayer. R. Abahoo added every day a new

[6] The 3 first, 3 last, and those of the middle resumed together, according to the formula given hereafter by R. Janai.

[7] In the *'Amida*.

[8] Cf. *Aboth*, ii. 18.

[9] Independent of the prayers prescribed in the ritual.

blessing. According to R. Yose Tseidania (or from Sidon) on R. Yoḥanan's authority, before the prayer of the eighteen these words should be said: *Eternal God, open my lips, that my mouth may sing Thy praise* (Ps. li. 16). After the prayer, these words are added: "May the words of my mouth and the thoughts of my heart be agreeable to Thee, Eternal God, my rock and my Saviour" (Ps. xx. 15). According to R. Judan, both these verses should be said before the prayer.

Whoever says his prayers over again and remembers he is doing so, should stop according to Rab; and continue according to Samuel.[1] Simon bar-Aba repeated these words of R. Yoḥanan:[2] Why does not one pray all day (and why should one)? Because no prayer is ever lost.

R. Zeira objected to R. Yose: Has not R. Yoḥanan expressed an opinion regarding the person who remembers during his prayer that he has already said it? Has it not been repeated that R. Abahoo, when he came from Palestine to Babylon, said on R. Yoḥanan's authority, that whoever doubts whether he has said his prayers or not, should not begin again? R. Ḥanina answers that it is only through reasoning that such a conclusion should have been made (that R. Yoḥanan was of Rab's opinion), or when R. Yoḥanan was asked what one should do in a case of doubt, he answered: Why does not one pray all day? for no prayer is lost. Supposing one has said by mistake the prayer for a weekday on a Saturday;[3] there is a discussion on this subject between R. Yoḥanan bar-Yaacob and R. Shesheth; one says: Stop; the other says, Go on. Both agree that if the fourth blessing has been begun, it should be continued. And Rabbi used to say on this subject: I am astonished to see that the fourth blessing has been omitted, for without intelligence how could one pray?[4] R. Isaac used to say: Intelligence is a great thing, for it is placed (in Scripture) between the Divine name twice repeated: *God is of intelligence* (1 Samuel ii. 3). Others quote the following verse: *Then thou shalt understand the fear of the Lord, and thou shalt find the knowledge of God* (Prov. ii. 5).

5. R. Yoshua says: He who is in a dangerous place says a short prayer resuming the 18; he says, "Save Thy people Israel, even when it transgresses Thy Law; let its wants be before Thee; praised be Thy Name, eternal God, Who hearest prayers and supplications."

[1] R. Yoḥanan and Samuel are both of the opinion, contrary to Rab, that the 'Amida must be continued, even if during the recital of it one remembers having already said it.

[2] See above, i. 1.

[3] The prayer of eighteen is reduced to seven on Saturdays: the three first and last of the daily ritual, and in the middle a special blessing for the Saturday.

[4] See the fourth blessing of 'Amida.

R. Shimon b. Aba, on the authority of R. Ḥiya, says: All travelling is considered dangerous. When R. Jona intended passing a night at an inn (ξενία), he used to make his will. R. Mana did the same before entering into a warm bath. R. Ḥanina, son of R. Abahoo, and R. Shimon b. Aba, in the name of R. Yoshua b. Levi, say: All maladies are considered dangerous. R. Aḥa, in the name of R. Assa, says: He who recites the résumé of the prayer of the eighteen must say all that the officiating priest at the desk says: "The wants of Thy people," &c. R. Pinhas, R. Levi, and R. Yoḥanan, say, in the name of Menahem, the Galilean: To him who goes up into the desk (to say the prayers aloud) one does not say: "Go to say the prayers," but, "Come, draw near, present our offering, implore for our wants, sustain our combats, implore for our life." Others maintain (that the following is the formula of the résumé of the prayer of the eighteen): "The wants of Thy people of Israel are numerous, but their will is weak; let it please Thee, O Lord God, God of our fathers, to accord what is necessary for each one, and to each person that which he wants for; be praised, O Lord, Who hearest the voice of my supplications; be praised, O Lord, Who answerest prayer." According to R. Ḥisda, the rule is conformable with this latter opinion.

According to R. Hisda, one says first the three first, and the three last (of the eighteen blessings). There is an opinion which maintains that one must first recite the obligatory prayer, and then pray for one's personal wants; another opinion maintains the contrary. The first opinion rests on the verse of the Psalms: *A prayer of the afflicted when he is overwhelmed, and poureth out his complaint before the Lord* (Psalm cii. 1); the second rests on the verse: To hearken unto the cry and to the prayer (1 Kings viii. 28). This is in accordance with the wise men, according to R. Zeira, in the name of R. Ḥanna. A person wishing to say a special prayer must always insert it in the fifteenth of the eighteen benedictions. R. Aba and R. Ḥiya, in the name of R. Yoḥanan, say: One must say one's prayers in a place reserved for that purpose; he relies on this verse: *Wheresoever I shall have proclaimed My name, I will come to thee to bless thee* (Exodus xx. 24). Now, it is not said, wheresoever *one shall proclaim*, but wheresoever *I shall proclaim.*

R. Tanḥoma bar-Ḥanina, said: One should have a fixed place in the synagogue to say one's prayers, for it is not written (2 Samuel xv. 32): "When David was come to the top of the mount to worship;" but *where he worshipped* habitually. R. Yassa and R. Ḥelbo add, in the name of R. Abdooma of Man-Ḥipa, that one must, in praying, turn one's face to the wall, according to the verse: *Then he turned his face to the wall* (2 Kings xx. 2). What wall[5] is here alluded to? R. Josué b. Levi replies: It is Rahab's wall, of which it is said: For her house was

[5] See J. tr. *Synhedrin*, x. 2.

upon the town wall (Joshua ii. 15). R. Hiskiah expressed himself thus: "Master of the Universe, Rahab the harlot, for having saved two persons (the two spies) has obtained, from Thee, the lives of many people, as it is written: *And the young men that were spies went in,"* &c. (Joshua vi. 23)."

When referring to this subject, R. Simon-ben-Yoḥai used to say that even if a branch of Rahab's family, composed of 200 persons, had united itself to 200 other families (by each of these persons), all had a right to salvation through Rahab's merits. Ought not then, my ancestors, who brought all these strangers to Thee, have more right to save my life? R. Ḥanina-b.-Pafa says that he turned his eyes towards the walls of the sanctuary, as it is written: *Setting their threshold near My threshold, and their post by My posts, and the wall between Me and them* (Ezechiel xliii. 8). Those men (whom the prophet reproaches thus) were, however, pious men, and not being able to go every time to the temple, prayed in their houses, and this prayer was accepted as if they had prayed in the sanctuary: "As my ancestors have made all this splendour and dedicated it to Thine honour, with so much more reason they may save my life." In R. Samuel-b.-Naḥmeni's opinion, his looks were directed towards the wall of the Sunamite, as it is written: *Let us make a little chamber in the wall* (2 Kings iv. 10). Ḥiskia expressed himself thus: "Master of the Universe, this Sunamite built a wall for Elijah, and as a reward, Thou didst bring back her child to life; as my ancestors built all this splendour (the temple) in honour of Thy glory, with much more reason they ought to save my life." According to the Rabbi, he directed his attention to his heart: *My bowels, my bowels, I am pained, my heart maketh a noise in me* (Jeremiah iv. 19). He expressed himself in these words: "Master of the Universe, I have examined the two hundred and forty-eight limbs Thou hast put in me,* and I have not found one of them guilty of irritating Thy brain; therefore Thou oughtest to save my life."

6. (5). If one ride on an ass, he must dismount (to say the prayer); if he cannot dismount, he must turn his face (upon Jerusalem); and if he cannot turn his face, he must direct his heart towards the Holy of Holies.

It has been taught that if any one who is riding an ass has some one to hold it, he should dismount to pray; if not, he may remain in his place; according to R. Meir, however, he can remain, for he is quieter (and consequently prays with more fervour). R. Yuda b. Paze, on R. Josué b. Levi's authority, says: The rule agrees with R. Meir's opinion. R. Jakob b. Aḥa says: We have learned it

* According to the Talmud, the human body is divided into 248 limbs, in reference to the same number of affirmative precepts contained in the Tôra.

elsewhere; never mind towards which way he is turned, it is not necessary to turn it again, except when it (the mule) is turned towards the east. R. Yose b. Abin gives the reason: It is because they formerly turned their backs to the sanctuary of the Eternal; their face was turned towards the east, *and they prostrated themselves towards the East in the sun* (Ezechiel viii. 16). This has been taught: A blind man, and he who does not know the cardinal points (or on which side Jerusalem is situated) should, when they pray, direct their thoughts to God, as it is written, *They shall pray unto the Lord* (1 Kings viii. 44). Those who are in the countries (out of Palestine) should turn their face towards the Holy Land, as it is written: *They shall pray unto Thee towards their land, which Thou gavest to their fathers* (ibid. 48). Those who live in Palestine turn their face towards Jerusalem, because it is written, *They shall pray to Thee towards the city which Thou hast chosen* (ibid. 44). Those who pray in Jerusalem should turn their faces towards the mount of the Temple, as it is written, *Towards the house that I have built for Thy name* (ibid.) Those who are on the mount of the Temple should turn their face towards the Holy of Holies, as it is written, *And they shall pray towards this place, and hear Thou in heaven, Thy dwelling-place, and when Thou hearest forgive* (ibid. 30); so that those who are towards the north should turn their faces towards the south, those who are at the south towards the north, those of the east towards the west, and those of the west towards the east, so that Israel when in prayer, should all turn towards the same place, as it is written, *For Mine house shall be called an house of prayer for all people* (Isaiah lvi. 7). R. Yoshua ben-Levi says: The *hekhal* (Temple) (Ezechiel xli. 1) means the inside of the sanctuary, the place towards which all the faces are turned.[7] This is right as long as the Temple existed; but since it has been destroyed, how should we know that it is the place towards which we should turn for our prayers? Because it is written: *It is built to be an arsenal* (*talpioth*), that is to say a mountain towards which all should direct their looks. R. Aboon interprets the word *talpioth*,[8] thus (Canticles iv. 4): A mountain for which every mouth prays; it is thus in the Shema and in the prayer (of 'Amida). In one verse it is said: *I will go and return to my place* (Hosea v. 15); and in an another verse: *Mine heart and mine eyes shall always be there* (1 Kings v. 3). How can that be?[9] By keeping one's face turned towards heaven, the eyes and heart towards the earth.[10]

In the Mishnâ it is said: That he who cannot turn himself should address his

[7] The coincidence between these words is difficult to explain: the word *interior* is in Hebrew: *penim*, and the word "face" is *panim*.

[8] If the word *talpioth* is decomposed, one finds *tal* which means "hill," and *pioth* means "mouths."

[9] These two verses contradict each other.

[10] Some versions of the Talmud say the contrary.

thoughts towards the Holy of Holies. Of which Holy of Holies does it speak? According to R. Ḥiya Raba's opinion, it means the heavenly Holy of Holies; according to that of R. Shimon, son of Ḥalaphta, it refers to the earthly Holy of Holies; and R. Pinḥas remarks: These two Rabbis do not dispute; the earthly Holy of holies (in Jerusalem) is just under the heavenly Holy of holies. He interprets in the following manner these words: *The place which Thou hast made* (Exodus xv. 17), that is to say, placed before Thy dwelling.[1] With reference to Moria, R. Ḥiya and R. Yanaï debated whether this name does not mean that the learning of the world was derived therefrom (in Hebrew *horáah*). According to Caḥana, fear came from thence for those who transgress God's word.[2] R. Ḥiya Raba (the great) and R. Yanaï explain this word thus: From thence came light (in Hebrew *orah*); in Cahana's opinion it expresses malediction (in Hebrew *arirah*, for those who transgress the law).[3]

Debir (the sanctuary) is, according to R. Ḥiya and R. Yanaï, a name which means that from thence came the plague (for those who violate God's law, in Hebrew *Deber*). According to Cahana, it means that from thence came the words (the commandments, in Hebrew *dibroth*).

6. (7). If one be seated in a ship, or in a carriage, or on a raft,[4] he must direct his mind towards the Holy of Holies.

The words *assade*, *raphsodoth*, and *σχεδία*, all mean the same thing (a raft), as it is written: *We will conduct them towards thee on a raft* (2 Chronicles ii. 15).

8. R. Eleazar b. Azaria said: The additional prayers, *Mussaph*, are only to be said in a public congregation. But the sages said: If there be a public congregation or no public congregation. R. Judah said, in R. Eleazar's name: in every place where there is a public congregation, individuals are exempted from additional prayers.

R. Bivi, on R. Ḥana's authority, says: It agrees with R. Juda's opinion, who speaks in R. Eleazar ben-Azariah's name, and a fact relating to Samuel agrees with him, for Samuel relates that he had only said the additional prayer (in private) on the day of the funeral of the son of the chief of the captivity;[5]

[1] Reading, instead of *makhôn*, "makhonan."

[2] In Hebrew *Yerah*, from whence *Arôn*, the Ark of the Lord.

[3] It is well known that the Book of the Law was placed in the Ark of the Lord.

[4] Maimoni translates it by מעדיה, a word that the Arabs of our days still use for Raft, Bark.

[5] They had lingered at the funeral, and it had been impossible to say in public the additional prayer.

"the congregation not having said it, I said it myself." As to the opinion of the Rabanan, who discuss (against R. Juda), it is explained by R. Yaakob b. Idi, in the name of R. Shimon the pious. The Mishnâ speaks of the shepherds and workmen whose work it is to dry the figs (as they are obliged to be always out of the town, they are exempted from the additional prayer by the public recitation); but any other man is not exempted (and although it has been said in the synagogue, he who prays in private is obliged to say it). The fact which R. Yoḥanan relates, agrees with this opinion. He said he had seen R. Yanai, when saying his prayers in a public place at Sephoris, walk four steps and then say the additional prayer. It is well known there was not any place of meeting for worship at Sephoris. We may draw therefrom a treble conclusion: 1. that the places of Sephoris are considered in the same light as the town[6] itself; 2. that the Rabanan were holding a discussion with R. Eleazar b. Azaria;[7] 3. that prayers being said (in private) one should walk a distance of about four steps, and then say the additional prayer. R. Aba says: It is not necessary to walk; it is sufficient if one pauses as long as it would take to walk the four steps. According to Rab, some words should be added to this prayer; and Samuel says: It is not necessary. R. Zeira asked R. Yossé's opinion on this subject; he answered it was sufficient to say: "And we will fulfil our duty towards Thee, by offering daily sacrifice and the additional sacrifice."

R. Shila, on the authority of Rab, says: He who, after having said his prayers, finds himself in the company of ten persons who are praying, should pray with them.[8] R. Zeira and R. Naḥman b. Yakob had already said their prayers, when ten persons arrived; R. Naḥman repeated the prayers with them. But, said R. Zeira, have we not already prayed? It is true, answered he, but has not R. Shila said that, whoever after having said his prayers finds himself in an assembly of ten persons who are praying, should pray with them? R. Aḥa and R. Yona, on the authority of R. Zeira, say: He who having said the morning prayer finds himself in the midst of an assembly of persons who are repeating the additional prayer, should repeat it with them; but if he has not yet said the morning prayer, he should see if he can repeat it,[9] and finish it before the person who officiates says (the prayer of the 18), so as to say *Amen* (with the Assembly), and he must do it; in the contrary case, no. What *Amen* is it that

[6] It means very probably a place outside the town.

[7] And consequently it is admitted that the private person is obliged to say the additional prayer.

[8] When ten persons are together, they make an assembly, and one of them says the prayers aloud.

[9] See above, iii. 2.

is mentioned here? Two *Amoraïms* discuss this subject. One says it is the *Amen* after the third benediction; the other says it is the *Amen* after the fifteenth benediction. Elsewhere[1] we learn that according to R. Gamaliel, the person who officiates exempts the people from repeating the prayers (by saying them himself aloud). R. Hoona Rabba says on this subject, on R. Yoḥanan's authority, that the rule only agrees with the opinion of R. Gamaliel for the *tekioth*.[2] R. Zeira and Bar-Ḥisda had repeated the prayers of the Shophar with the assembly (they had assisted whilst the officiating person repeated them), when some other persons came in. Ḥisda began the prayer again with them. Have we not prayed already, said R. Zeira? It is true, answered he, I have prayed a second time; for the Rabbis who came from Palestine (in Babylonia) said on R. Yoḥanan's authority, that the rule agrees with the opinion of R. Gamaliel for the *tekioth;* and during the first recitation my idea was not to fulfil my duty (by following the prayers which were said by the person who officiated); for if such had been my idea, I should have fulfilled my duty (and should not have begun a second time). That is true, R. Zeira answered, for if all the *tanaïmes* have expressed this opinion in the name of R. Gamaliel, R. Oshia has said it with regard to the wise men (so it makes the law). R. Ada, of Cyprus, adds (that in order to make the recitation of the officiating person sufficient), one must be present from the beginning (of the additional prayer). R. Tanḥuma, son of R. Jeremiah, remarks that the Mishnâ itself says so. The order of the *tekioth* is as follows: 1. the 3 first of the 18 benedictions are said[3] (therefore one must assist at the beginning of the prayer in order to make the recitation by the person who officiates suffice, and the Mishnâ says that so).

CHAPTER V.

1. Men should not stand up to pray except with reverential head. The pious of ancient days used to pause one hour before they began to pray, that they might direct their hearts to God. Though the king salute, one must not respond, and though a serpent were wound round one's heel, one must not pause.

[1] Mishnâ, ii. tr. *Rosh ha-shana*, iv. 9; J. ibid.

[2] Prayers which are said before the *Shofar* is blown during the additional prayer.

[3] Tr. *Rosh ha-shana*, ibid.

R. Jeremiah b. Aba says: On arriving from a journey, it is forbidden to pray before taking a little rest (because of the anxiety one feels). And which is the verse which proves it? The following (Isaiah li. 21): *Therefore, hear now thou this, thou afflicted and drunken, but not with wine.* (This verse proves that one is considered as being drunk if one is absorbed; and as it is forbidden that a drunken man should pray, it is the same for the man who is absorbed.) R. Zerikan and R. Yoḥanan, on the authority of R. Eliezer b. R. Yose the Galilean, says that he who is in grief (has not his mind at rest) should not for this reason say the prayers.[4] This opinion is doubtless founded on the same verse.

It has been taught that one should not begin to pray after having spoken of frivolous subjects,[5] nor after having jested, nor after behaving in a giddy manner, nor after heedless conversation, but only after Bible-reading. Therefore, it is noticed that the first prophets[6] finished their address by the praise of God and consolations of Israel. R. Eliezer says, however, that Jeremiah alone finished with remonstrances. R. Yoḥanan answers that even this prophet finishes with consolations: *Thus,* says he, *will Babel fall* (Jeremiah xxi., end). As Jeremiah was prophesying again on subjects which bore reference to the sanctuary, must it be concluded that he prophesied the ruin of the temple at the end? Therefore, it is said: *Thus far are the words of Jeremiah* (ibid.); this proves that this prophet finished by announcing the fall of his destroyers, and not by remonstrances and threatenings. On the contrary, is it not written: *There shall be misery for all creatures?* This malediction is addressed to pagans. But is it not also said: *Thou hast utterly rejected us* (Lament. v. 22)? Yes, but these words are accompanied with the hope of forgiveness; *Turn Thou us unto Thee,* it is said, *because Thou didst forsake us* (ibid.).

In the same manner the prophet Elijah did not leave Elisha, before having conversed with him on religious subjects: *They walked on, and talked* (2 Kings ii. 11). On what subject? R. Aḥa b. R. Zeira says: They were talking of the reading of the Shema; it is in the same spirit of exegesis that the verse says: *Thou shalt teach them* (Deut. vi. 7). R. Juda b. Pazi says: They were speaking of the creation of the world, according to this verse (Ps. xxxiii. 6): *By the word of the Lord were the heavens made.* R. Judan, son of R. Aibo, says: They spoke on subjects of consolation for Jerusalem, according to this verse (Isaiah xl. 2): *Speak ye comfortably to Jerusalem.* The Rabbis say: They spoke of the heavenly chariot; it can be proved by this verse: *And behold there appeared a chariot of*

[4] See B., tr. *Erubin,* fol. 65 *a,* and parallel passages of the Midrash cited by R. Schuhl, *Sentences,* p. 303.

[5] One would be distracted during prayer, and could not be sufficiently recollected to address God. See Schuhl, ibid. p. 52.

[6] See *Shohar tob,* ch. 4.

fire, and horses of fire (2 Kings ii. 11). R. Jeremiah says: Before praying one should learn a rule of religion. R. Yossé says that he who is occupied with the interests of the country is as deserving as he who is busy with the study of the Law. And R. Hana taught this: It is wise that if a woman should see a drop of blood of the size of a grain of saffron[7] (sign of impurity), she should remain during seven days to purify herself. Then this Rabbi arose and began to pray.

R. Zeira b. Ḥanina says: He who draws blood from the sacrifices commits sacrilege upon them. That is a fixed rule. B. Kapara has taught: It is a traditional law, given by Moses from the revelations on Mount Sinai, that eleven days elapse between one state of impurity[8] and another (*mulieris menstruatæ*). R. Oschia has taught: The produce of the earth and of wheat may be accumulated with the refuse grain, so as to be exempted from taking off the tithe (if they are gathered in, mixed up in this way, after having sorted them, one is exempted from taking off the tithe). Abba Judan asked Rabbi: How many degrees are there in holy things? He answered: there are four. And how many degrees are there for the oblations? Three. Then he began to pray. R. Ezekia, R. Jacob b. Aḥa, and R. Yassa say, on the authority of R. Yoḥanan, that the following verse should never be forgotten (Ps. xlvi. 12): *The Lord of hosts is with us, the God of Jacob is our refuge.* R. Yosse b. R. Aboon and R. Abooha said: "May it please Thee, O Lord our God, and God of our ancestors, to save us from hours of rebellion, hard and bad, which escape and arrive stealthily on the earth."

"One should not begin to pray," &c.

R. Joshua b. Levi interpreted the verse (Ps. xxix. 2) thus: *Give unto the Lord the glory due to His name, worship the Lord in the beauty of Holiness.*[9] R. Yosse b. Ḥanina asked: How is this verse explained, *Adore the Lord with fear and rejoice with trembling* (Ps. ii. 11)? (Is there not a contradiction between fear and joy?) R. Aḥa answers: That means that when the day of terror shall come, you will rejoice, for you have served God with fear, and then you will not be afraid.

[7] Cf. Matthew xiii. 31. Mark iv. 31. Luke xiii. 19; xvii. 6.

[8] As soon as a married woman sees any impure blood (menstruæ), she is *nidda*, that is to say during 7 days she may not accomplish the conjugal converse. After those days, often begin the days of gonorrhea (in case of serious flux), which number 11; after which come the days of *nidda*, followed again by those of gonorrhea. The consequence of this teaching is this: if during the 11 days there has only been a loss once or twice, the woman is pure, after taking the usual bath; but if she loses 3 following days, she should count after that time 7 more days of purity before returning to her husband. Thus the difference about the number of days is explained.

[9] There is therein more than a play on words, it is nearly a confusion of the letters ה and ח between those of two words (1° to the *threshold*, and 2° with fear, respect).

R. Joshua b. Levi says: On beginning to pray one should sit down twice, once before and once after; before doing so one should repeat Psalm cxlv., first saying the verse (Ps. cxlv. 14): *The just praise Thy name, the righteous shall inhabit in Thy sight.* The first pious men retired within themselves during one hour before prayer, then they prayed one hour and remained serious again. In that case, when did they study the Law and attend to their work? R. Isaac b. R. Eliezer answers: As they were pious people, God's blessing was on their study and their work. R. Hoona says: The man who prays behind the Synagogue deserves the name of impious, for it is said (Ps. xii. 9): *The impious walk around* (or behind). R. Hoona says again, according to this same verse, that he who does not enter the temple in this world will not enter it in heaven either.

R. Yoḥanan says that the man who prays in his house surrounds it and strengthens it, as it were, with a wall of iron. Is not this opinion contradicted by another of the same Rabbi? Is it not said above (iv. 4) by R. Aba or R. Ḥiya that man should pray in a place specially reserved for prayer? And here he tells us to pray at home? Yes, when one is alone, but when there is a society, one should go to the synagogue.

R. Pinḥas says, on the authority of R. Oshia: He who prays in a synagogue offers as it were a pure oblation. What proof is there that it is so? This verse (Isaiah lxvi. 20): *As the children of Israel bring an offering in a clean vessel unto the house of the Lord.* R. Abahoo, or another on his authority, interprets in this manner the following verse (Isaiah lv. 6): *Seek ye the Lord while He may be found.* Where is He to be found? In the temples and the school-houses; and, *Call ye unto Him while He is near,* there where He is near. R. Isaac b. R. Eliezer adds that then God is near them. And why? It is the conclusion that is drawn from this verse (Ps. lxxxii. 2): *God standeth in the congregation of the mighty, He judgeth among the gods.* R. Ḥisda says:[1] When one enters a synagogue, one should walk on as far as the width of two doors,[2] for it is said (Proverbs viii. 34): *Blessed is the man that heareth me, watching daily at my doors;* it says, *At my doors* (at least two), and not at my *door.* If any one acts up to this advice, what reward may he expect? What the verse promises (ibid.): *For whoso findeth me findeth life.* R. Hoona says: On going to the temple, one should walk faster, because of this verse (Hoseah vi. 3): *Then shall we know, we follow on to know the Lord.* On coming away, one should walk slowly, according to these words (Job xiv. 16): *Now Thou numberest my steps.* R. Yoḥanan says: It is a positive fact that the man who studies the Talmud in the temple does not forget it easily. R. Yoḥanan of Anatoth added as an answer: It is not less positive that he who in private studies zealously does not forget it quickly, as it is said (Prov. xi. 2): *With the lowly is wisdom.* R. Yoḥanan said also, that it was a good thing to learn the exegesis from the books

[1] B., same treatise, fol. 8 *a.* [2] See Debarim Rabba, chap. vii.

(and not by heart), in order not to forget it; and R. Tanḥoom says that the man who knows how to understand what he has read does not forget it either, according to these words (Deut. iv. 9): *Lest thou forget the things which thine eyes have seen.*

R. Yona says, on the authority of R. Tanḥoom b. R. Ḥiya: When any one has had a painful dream, they should say, "May it please Thee, Lord my God, and God of my ancestors, to dispose of all the dreams I have had this night or any other night, whether I dreamt them, or whether others dreamed about me. If they are good, may they be accomplished for joy, happiness, blessing, and life. If they are otherwise, modify them in the same manner as Thou didst change the salt waters into sweet ones,[3] and didst make the waters of Jericho agreeable, through the interference of Elijah, as also the curse of Peor's son (Balaam) into a blessing; change in a like manner all bad dreams. Let the dreams of others about me be changed to good, blessings, health, life, and happiness, joy and peace, according to this verse (Ps. xxx. 12): *Thou hast turned for me my mourning into dancing; Thou hast put off my sackcloth and girded me with gladness, to the end that my glory may sing praise to Thee. O Lord my God, I will give thanks to Thee for ever.* And (Deut. xxiii. 5): *Nevertheless, the Lord thy God would not hearken unto Balaam, but the Lord thy God turned the curse into a blessing to thee, because the Lord thy God loveth thee.* And (Jeremiah xxxi. 13): *Then shall the virgin rejoice in the dance, both young men and old together, for I will turn their mourning into joy, and I will comfort them in their sorrow.*"

"Even if the king asks after thy health," &c.

R. Aḥa says: What has just been said is applicable to the Kings of Israel, but to strange kings the salute must be answered. It has been taught that if any one is writing the name of God, one should not pause, not even for a king.[4] If one is writing two or three of the different names of God, for instance, *El*, *Elohim*, or *Jehovah*, on finishing one of these the salute may be returned. R. Yoḥanan was sitting down reading the Shema at the door of the Babylonian synagogue of Sippori; he did not arise before a magistrate (ἄρχων) who was passing. Seeing that, some people approached the Rabbi to strike him. Let him alone, said the judge, he is studying the laws of his Creator. R. Ḥanina and R. Joshua b. Levi went one day to the proconsul (ἀνθύπατος) of Cesarea. As soon as he saw them, he arose. What! said those around him, you arise before these Jews? I see in them, answered he, the faces of angels. R. Yona and R. Yosse went to Ursicinus (governor of the town) of Antioch,[6] who arose when they approached. Why, was it also asked of him, do you arise for these

[3] Exodus xv. 25.
[4] Tr. *Sophrim*, v. 6.
[5] See J., tr. *Meghilla*, iii. (fol. 74 *a*).
[6] Legate of Gallus. Cf. J., tr. *Beça*, i. 7.

Jews? I have seen, said he, the faces of these people in the battle, and I was victorious. R. Abin, returning from an audience with the king, turned his back upon him. The courtiers wished to kill him; but as they saw that two bands of fire accompanied him,[7] they let him go, according to the verse (Deut. xxviii. 2): *And all the people of the earth shall see that thou art called by the name of the Lord, and they shall be afraid of thee.* R. Simon ben-Yoḥai said this verse also referred to spirits and demons. R. Yanai and R. Jonathan were walking in the streets (strata). Some one saw them and saluted them, saying: "I bow to you, masters" (as if they had been high personages). They answered (modestly): "We do not even look like students to deserve such a salutation." Resh Lakish studied the law with so much zeal that one day by mistake he exceeded the limits of the Sabbath. He did not perceive it directly, and thus he accomplished the words of Scripture: *Because of his love for her* (the law) *he erreth* (Prov. v. 19). That is to say, through thy love for the *Tôra*, thou shalt be mistaken in other things.

R. Judan b. R. Ismaël was so taken up with the study of the law that he neither saw his mantle fall, nor a serpent coming towards him. "Master," said his disciples, "thou art losing thy mantle." "Does not this serpent," said he, "preserve it from thieves?"

"Even if one had a serpent rolled round one's ankle, one's prayers should not be interrupted." R. Hoona, on R. Yossé's authority, says: This has been taught only with reference to the serpent; but were it a scorpion, one should stop. Why? Because it bites several times (which is much more serious). R. Ila says: They only spoke of the serpent being already round one's heel; but if it be seen approaching, it can be avoided by getting out of the way, without interrupting the prayer. It has also been taught that if one is standing saying the prayers in the street (strata) or public roads (palatium), one ought to get out of the way to let the asses or chariots pass, without however interrupting the prayer. It is related of R. Ḥanina b. Dossa, that being one day bitten, while praying, by a venomous reptile, he did not interrupt himself. When the people went to examine what reptile it was, they found it lying dead (it had died for its audacity in having bitten such a pious man). It was then said: Misfortune will befall any who had been bitten by the many coloured serpent; and may misfortune befall this serpent which has bitten R. Ḥanina b. Dossa. What is the gravity of these bites? If a man be bit, and if he get into the water soon enough, the serpent dies; if not, the man dies. "Master," said his disciples, "did you not feel anything whilst the serpent was biting you?" "I swear," answered he, "that I only thought of the subject of my prayer." Referring to this subject, R. Isaac b. R. Ḛliezer says: God has

[7] Allusion is here made to the lateral bands of the phylacteries.

created a sort of spring to the soles of his feet, according to this verse (Ps. cxlv 19): *He will fulfil the desire of them that fear Him, He will also hear their cry and save them* (even of the danger which is unknown to them).

2. Men should mention the heavy rain when praying for the resurrection of the dead, and entreat for rain in the blessing for the year, and the Habdalla[8] is to be said in the prayer. "Who graciously bestows knowledge."[9] R. Akibah said, the Habdalah is to be said in a 4th prayer by itself. R. Eleazar said, in the thanksgiving (17th).

In the same manner as the resurrection of the dead is to bring everlasting life,[1] it is hoped that the fall of the rain produces everlasting life also (so these two subjects are comprised in one prayer). R. Ḥiya b. Abba proves it by these verses (Hoseas vi. 2): *In two days will He make us to live again; in three days He will forgive, and we shall live before Him; let us go to find the knowledge of God*: (1 Kings xvii. 1)[2] *And Elijah the Tishbite, who was of the inhabitants of Gilead, said unto Ahab, there shall be dew nor rain these years, but according to my word.*

R. Berakia relates an interview which took place between R. Yossa and the Rabbis: The first said that he had been heard in his prayers for the dew and for the rain; the others said that his prayers for rain only were granted, and not for the dew. This last opinion is founded on this verse (ibid. viii. 1): *Go, show thyself unto Rahab, and I will send rain* (not dew) *upon the earth.* But, according to what was said about the two prayers having been granted, how is the reference to the dew to be explained? Has he been released from his vow in this case? R. Tanḥooma of Edrea answers: It may be admitted that a vow from which one has been released in part is made entirely free. Or else it is supposed that he was speaking of the son of the woman Sarphith:[3] *He cried unto the Lord and said, O Lord my God* (1 Kings xvii. 21).

R. Juda b. Pazi says: It can be compared to one who stole a doctor's case of instruments (*Narthecium*): at the moment of his going out, his son wounds himself. He goes back to the doctor and says: My master, doctor, cure my son. I am willing to do so, answers he, but first give me back my case, which

[8] Distinction prayer called *Habdalah*, between the Sabbath and week days.

[9] The 4th section of *'Amida*.

[1] See J., tr. *Taanith*, i. 1; *Debarim Rabba*, chap. vii.

[2] Here is also seen the connection between the verses relating to the resurrection and the rains or dew.

[3] When the dew was spoken of, it was only used as a metaphor representing the resurrection.

contains my medicines, and I will cure thy son. In the same manner the Most Holy said to Elias: Go, and release thyself from the vow concerning the dew, for the dead live only on the dew, and I will make the son of Sarphith arise from the dead. And how is it known that the dead only live on dew? Because it is written (Isaiah xxvi. 19): *Thy dead men shall live, together with my dead body shall they arise. Sing, ye that dwell in dust, for thy dew is like the dew of herbs, and the earth shall cast out the dead.*

R. Tanḥooma of Edrea interprets the end of the verse thus: The earth will give back its trust. R. Jacob, from the village of Ḥanan, gave this reason,[4] on the authority of Resh Lakish: At the moment when the patriarch Abraham was accomplishing My wishes, I swore to him I would never deprive My children of the dew (in summer). What proves it? This verse: *Thou hast the dew of Thy youth,* and the following: *The Lord hath sworn and will not repent* (Ps. cx. 3, 4).

It is an everlasting gift I have made to Abraham: I have made him this present, according to this verse: *Therefore God will give thee the dew of heaven* (Genesis xxvii. 28).[5] R. Samuel b. Naḥmeni says: When the Israelites do bad actions and transgress the Law, the rain does not fall. In this case, an old man, for instance R. Yosse the Galilean, intercedes for them before God, and the rain falls. However the dew does not fall from heaven because of the merits of a creature. Why? Because it is written: *And the remnant of Jacob shall be as a dew from the Lord, that tarrieth not for man, nor waiteth for the sons of men* (Micah v. 7).

R. Zeira says, on the authority of R. Ḥanina: If one is about to recite the prayer for rain (which is said in winter), and that instead of that one the prayer for the dew is said, it is needless to begin again; if, on the contrary, the prayer for the rain is said instead of the one for the dew, it is necessary to begin again. But has it not been taught that in the prayer for the dew and the one which relates to the winds, the wise men have not obliged the faithful to make a special mention, as it is only voluntary? That is different; he who curses himself by asking for rain in summer instead of dew, is not to be compared to another who neither prays nor curses (therefore there is no obligation in this case). It has just been said that if instead of mentioning the rain, the dew is spoken of, it is useless to begin again. Why? Has it not been taught that if one has forgotten to ask God for the rain (*Shaalah*) in the blessing for the seasons (9th), or to mention the rain in the prayer for the resurrection of the dead (2nd), it is necessary to begin again? It is true, and one must begin again if one has

[4] He explained thus God's word.

[5] This verse is followed by the words: *He will give thee the blessing of Abraham.* It is therefore to the patriarch that it has been given.

forgotten to mention anything, neither dew nor rain (but this latter would be enough).

R. Zeira, on the authority of R. Ḥoona, says: If one has forgotten to ask for the rain in the 9th blessing, it should be done in the 16th which is a general prayer; and also, if one has forgotten to ask for the rain in the 2nd blessing, it can be remembered in the 16th. And indeed, if the prayer, which is generally the expression of a wish in the section of the seasons, can be said in the general invocation, with more reason it is so with regard to the simple mention of such and such a divine attribute "who causeth the rain to fall." But has it not been taught that, if the rain has not been asked for in the ninth blessing for the seasons, or if the rain has not been mentioned in the second blessing, it is necessary to begin again? (It seems, then, that it is not sufficient to mention these things at the end?) R. Abdime, brother to R. Yosse, answers: If it is said that one must begin again, it is in the case where it would not have been mentioned even in the 16th blessing. At what place should it be resumed? In the same manner as R. Simon says, on R. Yoḥanan's authority, speaking of the Neomenia: If after forgetting to mention the solemnity, one has already begun to retreat, one should begin it all again, and if one has not finished, it is sufficient to begin again at the section which is devoted to worship (to intercalate the paragraph of the Neomenia); in the same manner, as to our subject of the rain, if one has already retired, everything must be begun again; if not, it is sufficient to resume at the 16th section, where the prayer for rain may be introduced. At Nineveh,[6] it was necessary to appoint a special day of fasting after Easter (because of the want of rain which was near producing a famine). Rabbi was consulted in order to ascertain in what part (of the 'Amida) this prayer was to be introduced (it was in summer). He answered: Do as you like, as long as you do not change the order of the prayer. In what place, however, must this prayer be introduced? R. Jeremiah says: it should be said in the 16th blessing, or general invocation. R. Yosse told them: it was not the opinion of R. Zeira, when speaking on the authority of R. Hoona: If one has not, said he, asked for the rain in the blessings of the seasons, or if it has not been mentioned in the second, it should be remembered in the 16th blessing. And in reference to this Rabbi says: Go and pray as long as you change nothing of the form of the prayer (that is to say: as we are in summer, after Easter, you ought not to ask for rain in the blessing for the seasons; and as it should not be mentioned in this blessing, it should not be mentioned either, if it has been forgotten, in the 16th). Where then should it be mentioned, if it cannot be introduced, according to the interpretation of R. Yosse? In the 6 supplementary blessings that are added, on the day of fasting, to the prayer 'Amida. This information is enough for those

[6] B., tr. *Taanith*, fol. 14 *a*.

who pray in a public assembly, where the 6 supplementary prayers are said; but what would a man (who does not say these additions) do? R. Ḥanina answers that R. Zeira has said, on the authority of R. Hoona: The man expresses his wishes in the general prayer, and the prayer for rain is a wish.

"And the formula of separation (Habdala) is said in the 4th section." R. Simon b. Aba asked R. Yoḥanan:[7] How is it that when a custom is established, the wise men discuss it? (that is to say: why introduce into the 4th section what forms the subject of a special ceremony, at the end of divine worship, with a glass of wine?) Because, answered he, the essential ceremony contained in the blessing of the wine having been forgotten in the prayer 'Amida (it was necessary to recall it); that shows that the ceremony of the wine is performed after the recital of the formula in the prayer, only in order to allow of the children participating in this religious practice (by making them taste the wine); that would demonstrate that the essential formula is found in the prayer. R. Zeira and R. Juda say, in the name of Samuel: If one has said the formula with the glass in the hand, one says it also in the prayer; if one has said it in the prayer, one repeats it with the wine; that proves that both the formulas are essential.

"R. Eliezer said that it is intercalated in the thanksgiving." R. Yoḥanan said in the name of Rabbi:[8] One conforms to R. Eliezer's opinion when it happens that a holiday commences on a Saturday evening. R. Isaac Rabba said, in the name of Rabbi: the opinion of R. Eliezer must serve as a rule in this latter case. R. Isaac b. Naḥman says, in the name of R. Ḥanina b. Gamaliel: R. Eliezer's opinion must always serve as a rule. This is also what R. Abahoo says, in the name of R. Eleazar (a Rabbi who lived a long time after R. Eliezer). R. Jacob bar Aḥa said that this is not the case, although you have both advocated this opinion, but because R. Isaac bar Naḥman and R. Eleazar both repeated it in the name of R. Gamaliel.

According to the wise men, the formula of separation (Habdalah) must be intercalated in the 4th section: R. Akiba says that a fourth special blessing must be made of it. This is also the opinion of R. Jacob b. Aḥa, on the authority of Samuel. R. Judan says that it is added to the usual benediction formula. This is conformable to the opinion of Rabbi, who says: I am astonished that one should have shortened, on a Saturday, the fourth section, in which we solicit from God the gift of knowledge, for without knowledge one could not pray, and in the

[7] The Talmud is surprised that there should be dissension between the Rabbis on a subject which is a familiar custom of the people; and it replies that, since it is not an essential part of a religious ceremony, the custom may have been varied, and thus give rise to a feeling of uncertainty with regard to it.

[8] B., tr. *Pesahim*, f. 103 *b*.

same manner, without knowledge one could not effect the distinction or separation. R. Isaac b. Eleazar says: One recites firstly the formula of separation, and then that of the prayer. R. Eleazar b. R. Oshia adds that one must not effect less than three distinctions. R. Yoḥanan says that one must not effect less than three, or add more than seven. And R. Levy says: These distinctions must be such as are established by the Law. Naḥum arrives, and says, in his father's name, that one distinction suffices. R. Abahoo says that the formula must be terminated by a distinction. But then, asked R. Mena, if one has commenced with the words, "who separates the holy day from the unholy," should one end with the same? Certainly, says R. Yosse bar R. Aboon, for it is one of the formulas of blessings which commence and end with the words "praised be God." R. Eliezer b. Antigonos says, in the name of R. Eleazar b. R. Yanai: That proves that it is forbidden to work without having said the formula of separation (on Saturday evenings), and in the same manner it is forbidden, before saying this formula, to petition for one's necessities (by means of the requests expressed in the 'Amida; for which reason it is said in the first of the sections relating to the necessities of life).

R. Zeira and R. Eleazar b. Antigonos say, in the name of R. Yanai and of R. Juda: If one has not recited the said formula on Saturday night, it must be said, no matter when, until Thursday evening; this rule, however, only applies to the formula of separation, but not to the blessing of the light, which must be said at once. R. Zeira, in the name of R. Juda, and R. Abba, in the name of Abba b. Jeremiah, say that, even after a festival falling in the middle of the week, one says the words: "Who distinguishes between the seventh day and the days of labour." But, objected R. Zeira to R. Juda, are there 6 anterior days of labour? That does not matter, was the answer; one does not observe the order in this any more than in the distinction established between "uncleanness and cleanness" (for, if the order of the words had a rigorous signification, the uncleanness would seem to be attributed to the festival: an inadmissible hypothesis). R. Jeremiah and R. Zeira, in the name of R. Ḥiya b. Ashe, say that these words must be recited (they are still in use in the additional songs of Saturday evening): "Make us to commence favourably the six days of labour which come to us in peace." R. Aba adds the words: "Make us to hear of joy and gladness." R. Ezechia, in the name of R. Jeremiah, says these words: "Make us to understand and teach us Thy Law." R. Ezechia, in the name of R. Jeremiah, says: When one answers *Amen* after the formula of blessing, one must raise one's eyes to the cup of wine and then to the light. R. Ezechia, in the name of R. Jeremiah, says yet (as being *à propos*): One must hold the four kinds of the bunch of *loolab*[9] in the manner that they grow (the roots downwards).

[9] On the Feast of Tabernacles, one holds in the hand, while in the Temple, a branch

3. He who says, Thy mercies extend to a bird's nest,[1] or for goodness be Thy Name remembered, or he who says, We give thanks, we give thanks,[2] is to be silenced.

R. Isaac in the name of R. Simon, explains these interdictions: One might be led to suppose that in saying these words, one criticizes God's attributes;[3] it is as if one said: "Thou hast had pity on birds' nests, but not on me." R. Yossé says, in the name of R. Simon: One would seem to impose a limit on God's qualities and to say: "Thy mercy has extended to the birds' nests" (but not beyond). According to some, it has been taught: that one may not say, "ON the nests;" according to others, "*unto* them." The former rely upon R. Isaac's version, the latter upon R. Yossé's. R. Yossé bar R. Aboon says: One does not do well in classing mercy among the qualities of the Almighty (for these are not effects of His goodness, but of the laws ordained by Him), nor to develop the passage of *Leviticus* (end of chapter xxii.), commencing with the words: *My people, the children of Israel*, and to say: "As I am merciful in heaven, be so on earth, and therefore you will not eat on the same day the cow or the sheep with its young." This interpretation is wrong, since it presents one of the laws of Divine justice as a simple effect of His mercy.

"He who says, 'We give thanks, we give thanks,' is to be silenced." It is, says R. Samuel b. R. Isaac, in virtue of the verse (Ps. lxiii. 11): *But the mouth of them that speak lies shall be closed.*[4] These additions, however, are only forbidden to be said in public, but in private they pass as supplications (and in that case there can be no possible heresy).

4. (3.) If a man pass up to the Ark (where the rolls of the Law are kept) and make a mistake, another must pass up in his stead; nor may he in such a moment refuse.[5] Where does he begin? At the beginning of the prayer in which the other made the mistake.

R. Yossé b. Ḥanina says, in the name of R. Ḥanina b. Gamaliel, that, if one

each of palm, cedar, myrtle, and willow, tied together, according as prescribed in Leviticus (xxiii. 40).

[1] In taking the young ones out, the mother must first be sent away, so that she may not suffer by seeing it done (Deut. xxii. 6, 7).

[2] *Bis*: as if there were two gods.

[3] See J., tr. *Meghilla*, iv. 10.

[4] This is said against the adherents of dualism, or doctrine of two Divine powers.

[5] During divine service the faithful are not allowed to withdraw themselves, through modesty.

has made a mistake at the three first blessings, the whole must be recommenced. Ada bar bar-Ḥana Gueniba says, in the name of Rab, that, if the mistake has been made at the 3 last benedictions, one recommences at the one relating to worship (the 16th). R. Ḥelbo and R. Hanna say, in Rab's name: If the mistake has been made at the 3 first blessings, the whole must be recommenced, if at the 3 last, the 16th (Retseḥ) must be repeated. If a man has made a mistake and is not certain where, he must recommence at the part which he is certain not to have said. R. Aḥa and R. Juda b. Pazi were seated together in the Synagogue. At the moment of prayer, one of them placed himself in front of the pulpit of the officiating priest (to pray), and he forgot one of the blessings. R. Simon was then asked what was to be done. He replied, in R. Yoshua b. Levi's name: The officiating priest who has forgotten 2 or 3 blessings is not obliged to begin again. He was subsequently found teaching and discussing the following rule: It is not necessary to recommence, no matter which section has been omitted, excepting if the section of the resurrection of the dead (2nd) has been omitted, or that of the proud being humbled (12th), or that of the reconstruction of the Temple of Jerusalem (14th), under pain of being considered a heretic. When Samuel the younger was one day performing the service,[6] he happened to omit, at the end of the section, the words: "he humbleth the proud" (or wicked). He turned round towards the congregation, thinking that they were going to take him to task; but he was told: Our wise men did not think of thee (in qualifying this omission as heresy).

R. Jacob bar Aḥa and R. Simon b. Aba say, in R. Eliezer's name: In case of doubt of the mention of the Neomenia (in this day, in the 'Amida), it is necessary to recommence. At what part? Simon b. Aba says, in R. Yoḥanan's name: If he has already drawn back (thus indicating having finished), the whole must be recommenced; if not, it suffices to recommence at the section of worship (16th). R. Juda b. Pazi says: If a man considered the prayer ended (without taking the 3 steps), it is the same as if he had stepped back; and as regards those who recite the supplications (after the 'Amida), there is a doubt[7] whether they are to begin again.

R. Aba b. R. Ḥiya bar-Aba, and R. Ḥiya, in R. Yoḥanan's name, say:[8] If a man be reading the Law, and stop, he who is assisting the public reader takes it up at the part where the former commenced. Verily, if it were admitted to be sufficient to recommence only at the part where the other interrupted himself, it would happen that with regard to the first verses read, the assistants would certainly have heard the blessing which precedes them, but not the one at the

[6] B., same treatise, fol. 29 *a*.
[7] The word *Zerikhâh*, in this Talmud, expresses doubt and uncertainty.
[8] See J., tr. *Meghilla*, iv. 1, 5.

end;[9] for the last verses, the final blessing will have been heard, but not the blessing at the commencement. Now, it is written (Ps. xix. 8): *The law of the Lord is perfect* (*complete*), *converting the soul;* therefore it must be read in a complete manner (with an even number of blessings).

The following has been taught:[1] In the official reading (of the section of the Pentateuch, on Saturday in the Synagogue), two persons must not read the text simultaneously whilst another translates it aloud. Why? R. Zeira replies: So that there be no difficulty with regard to the blessing (as to which of the 2 should say it). But has it not been taught: 2 persons must not translate and a third read the text? Now, if only one person read (and as the translator does not say the blessing), how can it be supposed that there may be an irregularity? Therefore another cause must be alleged: it is that the ear cannot distinguish 2 voices at the same time. It has also been taught that 2 persons may read the Law together (the second one following reading to himself), but 2 persons may not read together the additional chapter of the prophets.[2] R. Oolla says: Several calls are made (and divisions of sections) for the Pentateuch, but not for the chapters of the Prophets.

R. Josuah Droma[3] said: There are three things which are bad when either in too small or too large a quantity: leaven, salt and abstention. At the 1st request (to officiate), one refuses; at the 2nd, one should hesitate to accept; and at the 3rd, one accedes.

R. Hoona was seated in a Synagogue. The attendants entered and tried very much to get a certain new comer to go up to the tribune, but the latter did not accept the invitation. At the conclusion of the service he presented himself before R. Eliezer[4] and said: "Master, be not provoked at my abstention; I had no intention to wound your feelings, but I did not go up because I was not in the frame of mind" (so disposed). It is not against thee, replied R. Eliezer, that I am angry, but against this servant who importuned you to mount up (to the tribune). The officiant Batityi interrupted himself one day (during the morning office, before the *Kedusha*, blessing of God), on arriving at the prayer which mentions the *Ophannim* (celestial beings). R. Aboon was consulted on the subject, and he said, in the name of R. Yoshuah b. Levi: That he who replaces him take

[9] Every official reading of a section of the Pentateuch, made in the Temple, is preceded and followed by a blessing, repeated at every interruption, and it must be noticed that the person named must read his section himself.

[1] See ibid. § 5.

[2] It is no doubt on this account that the custom has been preserved to have it read by a person called to the Law, and not by the officiating priest.

[3] See above, p. 3, n. 2.

[4] According to him, one should not refuse to officiate.

up the prayer at the point where he stopped. But, was it answered, has it not been taught that one should recommence at the commencement of the blessing in which the error happened? However, answered R. Aboon, as you have made the response to the blessing of God (which precedes the passage relating to the *ophannim*), that corresponds to the entirety of the blessing (and thus it suffices to take up the service at this passage).

5. (4.) He who passes up to the Ark is not to answer "Amen"[5] after the priest, lest his attention be distracted. If no other priest than himself be present, he is not to lift up his hands[6] (to bless the congregation). But if he be confident that he can lift up his hands, and then resume, he is at liberty to do so.

The following has been taught: Neither he who (arriving late at the Synagogue) recites the abridged formula (of Kaddish) which precedes the Shema, nor he who passes up to the tribune to officiate, nor he who lifts up his hands to bless the assembly, nor he who performs officially the public reading of a section of the Pentateuch, nor he who finishes the service with the recital of a chapter of the Prophets, nor he who pronounces the blessing, thus accomplishing one of the precepts established by the Law, should answer *amen* to his words; if he were to do so, it would have no meaning. According to other opinions, it is an act of wisdom, which R. Ḥisda explains thus:[7] Those who say "it is wise to say *amen*" speak of him who says it at the conclusion (because it is then a sort of confirmation of everything he has said previously); but it is senseless to say *amen* for every blessing.

R. Ḥanina says: If there are in the Synagogue 2 ordinary Israelites and a Cohen, the latter is placed between the other 2 (to do him honour). Under what circumstances are they thus placed? When they are all three of equal rank; but if one be a learned man, he is placed in the middle (he takes precedence). R. Yoshuah b. Levi says:[8] I have never recited the formula of thanksgiving after meals, in presence of a high priest (so as to leave the honour to him), neither have I ever allowed an ordinary Israelite to do so in my place (so as to maintain, with dignity, my position as a Levite).

[5] The officiating priests pronounce, word by word, the blessing before the *cohanim*; it is therefore to be feared that he would become confused in pronouncing these words, were he to reply *Amen*.

[6] It is also for fear that he would not be sufficiently self-possessed to terminate the prayer.

[7] He explains that there is no contradiction between the 2 *Boraïthoth*, the same action being sometimes that of an ignorant man, and at other times that of an educated one.

[8] J., tr. *Guittin*, v. 9.

R. Juda b. Pazi says, in the name of R. Eleazar: Any Cohen who, being in the Synagogue, does not raise his hand to bless the assembly, transgresses a positive precept of the Pentateuch (which orders it: Numbers vi. 23). R. Juda b. Pazi, being ill one day, wound a turban tightly round his head,[9] and placed himself behind one of the pillars of the temple (to keep at a distance from the part of the temple which the priests blessed, and to excuse himself on account of his illness from taking part, as *Cohen*, in the solemn blessings). As for R. Eleazar, he left the temple when similarly situated.

R. Aḥa and R. Tanḥooma b. R. Ḥiya say in the name of R. Samlai: In the event of the entire community consisting of Cohanim, they must all nevertheless raise their hands to bless the faithful. But whom do they bless then? Their brothers of the north, south, east, and west. And who answers the *Amen?* The women and children. Abaye taught, on behalf of R. Benjamin: Those who stand behind the Cohanim are not included in the blessing, but those standing in front of them always profit of it; even were they separated by an iron wall, says R. Ḥiya b. Aba, the blessing would go through it. But what of those who stand aside? That is a case to be resolved by the following point:[1] If (in sprinkling the altar with the blood of the sacrifice) the one who officiates intends to sprinkle it in front of him and it falls behind him, or *vice versâ,* the aspersion is considered defectuous and insufficient (through want of care); if, however, the intention be to sprinkle it in front, and it fall at the sides, the aspersion is valid. That shows, for our subject, that the people standing at the sides during the function of the Cohanim are included in the blessing.

R. Ḥisda says that the officiating minister should be an ordinary Israelite (the request to give the blessing, which is made by him to the Cohanim, should not be made by one of the latter). R. Naḥman b. Jacob says: When the officiating minister makes this call, he words it in the singular number, in case there should be only one priest present, in the same manner as the plural is used if there are several priests present. R. Ḥisda, on the contrary, says that the request is always made in the plural, for the idea is that the whole tribe is called to bless the people.

6. (5.) If a man pray and make a mistake, it is a bad sign for him. If he be a representative of a congregation, it is a bad sign for his constituents, for a man's representative is like himself. They say of R. Hanina b. Dosa, that when he prayed for the sick, he used to say, "This one will die," or, "This one will live." The (Sages)

[9] To counteract the pain which he endured.

[1] Mishnâ, tr. *Para*, xii. 2.

said to him, "How do you know?" He said to them, "If my prayer be fluent in my mouth, I know that it is accepted; but if not, I know that it is lost."

R. Aḥa b. Jacob says: These presages can only apply to the 3 first sections (which are recited with ease, because they are more frequent, and form the commencement). When R. Gamaliel saw his son ill, he sent two clever men to R. Ḥanina b. Dossa to his town, to consult him. He said to them: Wait here for me, I am going up to my room (to pray), and then I will answer you. When he came down, he said to them: I have now the conviction (by the prayer I have said) that R. Gamaliel's son has recovered from his illness. They noted the precise moment, and at the same moment the convalescent asked for food.

R. Samuel b. Naḥmeni says: If a person applies his whole attention during prayer, he may be assured that his prayer has been granted.[2] Why? Because it is written (Ps. x. 17):[3] *Thou wilt prepare their heart, Thou wilt cause Thine ear to hear.* R. Joshuah b. Levi says: If a man's lips move alone (i.e. if the words come from him spontaneously), he may be sure his prayer is heard. Why? Because it is written (Isaiah lvii. 19): *I create the fruit of the lips; peace, peace to him that is far off, and to him that is near, saith the Lord; and I will heal him.*

CHAPTER VI.

1. How do we bless for fruit?[4] For fruit of a tree say, "Who createst the fruit of the wood," excepting the wine. For wine say, "Who createst the fruit of the vine." For fruits of the earth say, "Who createst the fruit of the ground," excepting the bread. For the bread say, "Who bringest forth bread from the earth." For vegetables say, "Who createst the fruit of the ground." R. Judah says, "Who createst various kinds of herbs."

[2] See *Debarim Rabba*, chap. i., *Wayyiqra Rabba*, ch. xvi.

[3] The fervour of the heart is a sign of the attention of the ears, and proves that the prayer is heard.

[4] The Mishnâ supposes that it is already known that a blessing must be made for each different article consumed; it is only therefore necessary to appoint the different formulas.

It is written (Ps. xxiv. 1): *The earth is the Lord's, and the fulness thereof;*[5] *the world and they that dwell therein.* And therefore he who enjoys anything whatsoever in this world before having said a prayer commits an offence (Levit. xxvii.); by accomplishing this precept he acquires it. R. Abahoo says: It is written (Deuteronomy xxii. 9): *Lest the fruit of thy seed which thou hast sown, and the fruit of thy vineyard be defiled,* that is to say that the universe with all it contains is considered as a vine; and how do we become entitled to these holy gifts? By blessing. R. Ezechia or R. Jeremiah and R. Abon, in the name of Resh Lakish, remind us of the words (Ps. xvi. 2), *Thou hast said unto the Lord, Thou art my Lord; my goodness, cometh it not from Thee?*[6] that is to say: If thou hast given thanksgiving after a meal, it is as if thou hadst eaten of thy own substance. In other terms, the words, *My goodness is not for thee,* signify, I destroy my goodness in thy body. And in still other terms these words mean, All goodness shall combine to come to thee. R. Aḥa says: What signify the words "*not on thee*"? They indicate that without the Divine assistance nothing has come into the world, as it is said (Genesis xli. 44): *And without Thee shall no man lift up his hand.*

R. Ḥiya taught that it is said (Leviticus xix. 24): *It shall be holy to praise the Lord withal,* in order to indicate that a blessing must be made both before and after the meal; R. Akiba deduces from this: Nothing may be eaten before pronouncing the blessing. When R. Ḥaggai and R. Jeremiah proceeded to render justice, R. Ḥaggai commenced by pronouncing the benediction. Thou hast done well, said R. Jeremiah, for all the precepts say that this must be done. How do we know this? R. Tanḥooma or R. Aba b. Cahana says, in the name of R. Elazar, that it is in conformity with the verse (Exodus xxiv. 12), *And I will give thee tables of stone, and a law and commandments;* the Law is likened to His commandments, and in the same manner as the necessary formula must be said before reading a section of the Law, we must act (in the same manner) before accomplishing any precept.

R. Yoḥanan, in taking an olive, recited a blessing before eating it, and another after. R. Ḥiya b. Aba looked at him in astonishment. "Babylonian," said R. Yohanan to him, "why lookest thou at me so? Is it not admitted that a blessing must be said both before and after eating any fruit belonging to the seven superior kinds?"[7] "I recognize that, and am only surprised at your blessing such a small quantity, diminished yet more by the seed being extracted." But does R. Yoḥanan contest that the taking out of the seed diminishes the value of the olive? No, but he blesses it because it is an entire fruit. He even went beyond

[5] See *Shoḥar tob.* chap. xvi. [6] Literally: *extendeth not unto Thee.*

[7] The 7 superior products of Palestine are: grapes (wine), olives, dates, pomegranates, figs, wheat and barley.

this, for in eating even one grain of a grape or pomegranate, he thought himself obliged to recite the two formulas, one before and one after.

As long as the wine is in its natural state, this blessing is said: "Blessed be the Creator of the fruits of the tree," and it may not be used for the ablution of the hands. When mixed with water, we say, "Creator of the fruits of the vine," and it may be used to wash the hands. This is the opinion of R. Eliezer. But the wise men say that for wine pure or mixed with water, is said, "Blessed be the Creator of the fruits of the vine," and it may be used for ablutions. R. Aba says that it is not a destruction of food (to wash with it). R. Jacob b. Zabdi says, in the name of R. Abahoo: For olive oil say: "Blessed be the Creator of the produce of the trees." R. Ḥiya b. Papa remarked to R. Zeira that the Mishnâ expresses itself in the same manner: excepting, it says, for wine, for which is said, "the Creator of the fruits of the vine" (*therefore for oil we say, Creator of fruits*). But is not wine an extract of grapes? (why not the same for oil?) Exception has only been made for wine; therefore all other produce, although extracts, are natural.

R. Aba says: Rab and Samuel both agree that for cooked herbs is said: "All has been created by His word." R. Zeira says, in the name of Samuel: For the cooked heads of radishes (roots), if they are entire, we say, "Blessed be the Creator of the fruits of the earth." If they are crushed, we say, "All is created by His word." R. Yosse says it is conformable to the Mishnâ, which says: "Excepting for bread, in which case is said, 'Blessed be He who produces the bread from the earth.'" But is not bread made of crushed wheat? Exception is only made in the case of bread; therefore, all other produce, even crushed, are considered as whole.[8]

R. Ḥipa b. Abba says, in the name of R. Yoḥanan:[9] For a preserved olive is said, "Creator of the fruits of the tree." R. Benjamin b. Japheth says, in the name of R. Yoḥanan: For cooked herbs is said, "All has been created by His word." R. Samuel b. Isaac says that the Mishnâ is in accordance with R. Benjamin b. Japheth's opinion, for we read there: The bitter things which we eat on Easter night must not be (so that they lose not their taste) either preserved, cooked, or boiled, and if they are in their natural state may serve to accomplish one of the Easter duties. R. Zeira asks: Which is he who remembers best having heard R. Yoḥanan's sentences? Is it R. Ḥiya b. Aba or R. Benjamin b. Japheth? It is certainly R. Ḥiya b. Aba; it may be proved by this: We see some of the illustrious Rabbis, when they sit down at table,[1] take some lupines and pronounce the formula: "Creator of the fruits of the earth."[2] Now, are not these lupines

[8] And we do not say: "All has been created," &c.

[9] See J., tr. *Pesaḥim*, ii. 5; B., tr. *Berakhoth*, fol. 38 *b*.

[1] Literally: if they go to take ברייה *eat* (2 Samuel xiii. 5).

[2] They do not use the formula, "all was created by His word," which is R. Ḥiya's opinion.

cooked? (How, then, does it happen that this formula is recited? It proves that, although boiled, they are still considered natural.) As regards the Mishnâ (just quoted), it says that "the bitter herbs must not be cooked," so that they may not lose their paschal bitterness required by the Law, for cooking deprives them of their bitterness (but, for the purposes of the blessing to be recited, they are considered natural, and we can understand that the Rabbis used this formula). R. Yosse b. Aboon says: There is no question about the olive, because it is customary to eat it raw; and, although preserved, it is considered to be in its natural state; but herbs, as soon as they are cooked, they change their form. R. Jacob b. Aḥa says that R. Naḥman and the Rabbis held a discussion on the following subject: The former said, "*Who* produced the bread from the earth" (in the past tense), and the others said, "*He* produces the bread from the earth" (in the present tense). This question is settled in the same manner as was the following one, referring to vegetables (cereals), discussed by R. Ḥinena b. Isaac and Samuel b. Imi; the former said that it is a vegetable, and not bread;[1] the other said that if it is not yet bread, it will never be bread, as it is said (Ps. lxxii. 16): *There shall be an handful of corn in the earth upon the top of the mountains* (the seed is, therefore, already considered as bread).

R. Jeremiah pronounced, in the presence of R. Zeira, the formula, "Who has produced the bread from the earth;" and the latter complimented him on his having adopted it. What is R. Nehemiah's motive for admitting the article (ה) in the formula? It is in order not to confound the sound of the words, the one commencing and the other ending with the same letter. This objection, however, might be repeated at the end in the case of the word *Lehem min* (it has not, therefore, much foundation). According to R. Naḥman, the same is to be said (for wine): "*Who* has created the fruits of the vine;" and according to the Rabbis, "*He* creates the fruits of the vine."

R. Zerikan or R. Zeira put the following question: If any one have taken a lupine and said the blessing (before eating it), but let it drop, must he repeat the blessing? How can you ask that? was the reply. Is there any difference between this case and that of a person wishing to drink from a running stream? (For the water which was before the person at the moment of saying the blessing would have flowed away during its recital, and yet he does not repeat the blessing. Would he not be in the same predicament as the person before mentioned?) No, was the reply; in the case of the water, one knows what to expect from the commencement; but in the case of the dropping of the olive, it was an unforeseen accident. (The problem has not yet been resolved.)

R. Ḥiya taught that the blessing of the bread was not said until at the moment of breaking it. R. Ḥiya b. Aba says: This proves that he who, having a radish

[1] The word לפת, *vegetable*, is composed of לא פת, and means either: "it was never bread," or: "it will never be bread."

in his hand, lets fall a piece, should recite the blessing for the pieces; but he who had not at the time a piece in his hand, must say a blessing apart. R. Tanḥum b. Judan says that these words should then be added: *Blessed for ever be His name and glorious reign,* so as not to repeat with disrespect the Divine name. What quantity must there be to require the blessings? R. Ḥanina and R. Mena do not agree on this subject. According to the one, the piece cut must be of the size of an olive; according to the latter, a smaller piece suffices. He who says that it requires a piece the size of an olive conforms to the opinion hereafter given, in which it is said: All the pieces[4] were of the size of an olive. He who says that it requires a smaller piece is of R. Ismael's opinion, who says: Were there even but so little that it might be assimilated with flour, the blessings must be said.

The following general rule has been taught:[5] Every time that the consumption of a certain dish is followed by the triple blessing of thanksgiving, it is preceded by the formula: "Who has produced the bread from the earth;" should the contrary be the case, the anterior formula is not said. An objection has been offered to this general rule: If, it is said, there is less bread than of the size of an olive, the 3 complete blessings are not said afterwards. Would the anterior formula, however, be said? Verily, said R. Jacob b. Aḥa, this rule has been formulated for superior products, other than bread. R. Aba says, in the name of Rab: It is forbidden for any of the guests to taste of anything before the person charged with the giving of the blessing has done so. R. Joshuah b. Levi says: But they may partake of drink. The subject of their difference is relative to certain circumstances. Rab speaks of the case in which a loaf of bread is divided among all (and for which it is necessary to go the round of the company); and R. Josuah says that they may drink at once, because each person has their goblet to hand.

He who recites the blessing is the first to reach out his hand for bread, unless he wish to accord this honour to his master, or to his superior in science. When Rab cut bread for the guests, he tasted it with his left hand whilst distributing it with the right. R. Hoona says: It is not an interruption between the recital of the blessing and the tasting to say: "Go and bless;" but it is an interruption to say: "Give some fodder to the cattle." R. Hoona also says: For a dish composed of wheat flour roasted, or pulverized horseradish, the following formula is said: "All has been created by His word." R. Hoona also says: If anybody has taken something into his mouth, and remember that he has forgotten to say the blessing, he must reject it if it be a liquid; and if it be a solid, he must put it to one side of his mouth, and recite the formula. R. Isaac b. Mare said, in the presence of R. Yosse b. R. Aboou, in the name of R. Yoḥanan: Even if it be a solid, it must be rejected, because it is written (Ps. lxxi. 8): *Let my mouth be filled*

[4] Of oblations, Leviticus ii. 6.

[5] See J., tr. *Succa*, ii. 7.

with Thy praise and with Thy honour all the day. If a person chews[6] some wheat he must say: "*Blessed be the Creator of all sorts of grain.*" If it be roasted or cooked, and the pieces be whole, the following formula is said: "Who has produced the bread from the earth," and afterwards the three complete blessings after meals. If the pieces are no longer entire, say: "Blessed be the Creator of the different kinds of food," and afterwards an abbreviation of the three thanksgivings after meals is said. Of what size should the fragments be? R. Yosse, whilst with R. Aboon Cahana b. Malkia, said, in the name of Rab, about the size of an olive. He who chews rice says the formula: "Blessed be the Creator of all kinds of grain." If the rice is baked or cooked, although the grain be entire, he says: "Blessed be the Creator of all kinds of food," without any other blessing after it. According to R. Jeremiah, he says: "The Creator of the fruits of the earth." Bar-Merina recited, in the presence of R. Zeira and R. Ḥiya b. Aba, the formula: "All has been created by His word."

R. Simon the pious said: "Blessed be the Creator of all kinds of delicate food." R. Yosse, whilst with R. Abin, says that these 2 opinions are not contradictory: he who says: "Creator of all kinds of food," speaks of the case in which a mixture has been made (by crushing them in a mortar); he who maintains that we must say: "Creator of the fruits of the earth," speaks of the case in which the grains are still entire; he who maintains that we must say: "All was created by His word," speaks of the case in which it has been boiled; and finally, he who says: "Creator of all kinds of delicate food," speaks of the case in which the different grains have been shaken up and mixed together. Up to the present we have learnt the anterior formula. What is the posterior one? R. Yona, in the name of R. Simon the pious, says as follows: "Who has created different kinds of agreeable foods to rejoice the soul of every living being; be praised, O Lord, for the earth and its pleasures." R. Aba b. Jacob says, in the name of R. Isaac Raba (the great), that when Rabbi ate meat or an egg, he recited the formula: "Who has created numerous animals to nourish the soul of every living being; be praised, O Lord, living spirit of the world." We know now what is to be said in this latter case, after the meal. What is to be said before? According to R. Ḥaggai: "Blessed be the Creator of diverse souls." But, objected R. Yosse, does not the Mishnâ (§ 3) contest this? It says: For vinegar, for certain kinds of locusts, and for windfall (of fruit) is said: "All has been created by His word;" now, these locusts, are they not in a certain sense beings?[7] The opinion of R. Simon (whose formula we have just mentioned) was the reply, is conformable to Rabbi's opinion, and both are in accordance with R. Gamaliel's. The following is the general rule, taught by R. Juda in the

[6] *Crush, chew,* from which is derived the name of an Arab dish, *cuss-cussu,* which is no doubt meant here.

[7] It would therefore be necessary to say: "Creator of beings."

name of R. Gamaliel: With regard to one or other of the seven superior products[8] (excepting wheat), and for wheat not made into bread, the consumption must be followed, according to R. Gamaliel, by the recitation of the 3 blessings, and according to the wise men by only one blessing; as for the other fruits which belong neither to the seven superior fruits or which are not of the wheat tribe, we must, according to R. Gamaliel, say the blessings both before and after, and according to the wise men only before. R. Jacob b. Ida, in the name of R. Ḥanina, says: For everything farinaceous, in the shape of a paste, and which is composed of one of the five kinds of grain, the anterior formula: "Creator of all kinds of food," is said, and is followed by the three blessings for meals, in an abbreviated form. But what is to be said of an article which, whilst fulfilling the two first conditions, does not belong to either of the five species? R. Yona says that R. Zeira caused information to be asked for on this subject at R. Janai's house, and the answer was, that nothing was known about it. And yet what is to be done in this case? It seems, says R. Yossé, that we must say the formula: "All has been created by His word" (general formula).

R. Jeremiah asked: What should he do after the meal, who has eaten of baked flour? As a fact, says R. Yosse, R. Jeremiah never ate flour.[9] That is not the question, replied he; what we require to know is, why is the formula terminated by the final mention of the Holy Land? It is because this is considered to be the blessing of the workpeople; for it has been taught[1] as follows: The workmen working on their master's estate say the 1st blessing, summarize the 2nd and 3rd, and finish by reciting the final of the 2nd; but if, as pay for their work, they receive their repasts, or if the master eats with them, they must say the 4 complete blessings. R. Janai appointed a fixed formula for the ceremony to be said by the workmen.

Is the solemnity of the day also to be mentioned therein? R. Aba b. Zimna replied that sometimes it was done; R. Jeremiah adds: As R. Zeira paid attention to this, we must do the same.

It has been taught that, when the blessing of the bread is made, the best should be chosen:[2] of a loaf of fine bread, and the ordinary household loaf, the former should be chosen; of a piece of fine bread, and an entire household loaf, the latter should be preferred (because it is more presentable). Of a wheaten loaf, and one made of barley meal, the former is taken; of a piece of wheaten bread, and an entire loaf made of barley meal, the former is chosen; of a loaf made of barley, and one of maize, the former is selected. And yet, is not this

[8] See page 119, note 5.

[9] On account of the doubt existing with regard to the terminable blessing; we know what to commence with in a doubtful case; but what is to be said after?

[1] See above, ii. 5.

[2] Tosseftâ on *Berakhoth*, section 4.

second kind the superior one? It has the disadvantage of not being one of the 7 superior kinds. This latter opinion, says R. Jacob bar Aḥa, in the name of R. Zeira, is that of R. Judah, who says: If amongst the different sorts of bread, there is a single loaf made of one of the 7 superior fruits of Palestine, to it is given the preference. Of an impure loaf and a pure one, says R. Ḥiya b. Abba, the pure one is naturally chosen. R. Ḥiya b. Ada, in the name of R. Aḥa, says, that if one has before one a nicely-made loaf of impure bread, and one less nicely made, but pure, the blessing is made over the one which one prefers. According to R. Jacob b. Aḥa, in the name of Samuel, the formula to be said for the young shoots of the first year of the palm-tree is the following: "Creator of the fruits of the tree." According to R. Joshuah: "Creator of all kinds of verdure." A Mishnâ[3] of R. Oshia contests this opinion by enumerating the different verdure (not including the shoots of the palm-tree); they are: the artichoke, *κινάρα*, the orach (goose-foot), ἅλιμος, a pickly herbaceous plant, and the thistle.

2. He who blessed the fruits of the tree (thus), "Who createst the fruits of the ground," is free from his duty. And for the fruits of the ground, if said, "Who createst the fruits of the wood," he is not free. But, in general, if one say, "(who createst) everything,"[4] he is free.

R. Ezechia says, in the name of R. Jacob b. Aḥa,[5] that R. Juda considered the tree as a stalk (that is to say, that the tree is to the fruit what the stalk is to the ear of corn). R. Yosse replies that it is an idea, generally admitted, that the fruit of trees may be classed among those of the ground, but the reverse is not permissible. R. Hoona says that bread and wine must be excepted; the Mishnâ expresses this: Excepting wine, says the Mishnâ, for which is said this formula: "Creator of the fruits of the vine," and excepting bread, for which is said: "Who bringest forth bread from the earth." R. Yosse says: From the moment that one changes the formula adopted by the wise men, the duty is not accomplished. R. Juda says: The obligation is not fulfilled if, in the event of an article changing form, the formula is not modified. R. Meir says that it suffices even to say: "Blessed be the Creator of this object which is so beautiful." And R. Jacob b. Aḥa says, in the name of Samuel, that this opinion is adopted as a rule. It is proved by the following incident which occurred to Rab: A Persian came to his house and said: When I eat bread, not knowing the proper formula of blessing to be used, I say: "Be blessed, Creator of this piece of bread." Have I in this manner accomplished my duty? Yes, replied Rab.

[3] See tr. *Kilaïm*, v. 7, and at the end.

[4] The text only gives the first word of the formula (*shehakôl*).

[5] See J., tr. *Bikkurim*, chap. i. § 8 (6).

R. Juda narrated,[6] in the name of Aba b. bar Ḥana, that when Bar-Kapara and two of his pupils stopped to pass the night at an inn in Berakhta,[7] some small cakes (tarts), plums, and some leeks (capitatus) were placed before them. Is it necessary to recite the blessing for these latter? asked one of the pupils. No, replied the master; it would answer for the plums, but not for the cakes; and if you said a blessing for the plums it would not answer for the two other things. Thereupon the other pupil rose up hastily and said the blessing for the cakes with this formula: "All has been created by His word." His comrade railed at him for his mistake. Bar-Kapara said: I have not so much to complain of in him, as in thee: he has just committed an act of gluttony; but then, why doest thou mock him? And he said to the mocker: It is a case in which the following may be applied: If they respect not my knowledge, should they not respect my old age? (i.e. you had no regard for my old experience, and you did not ask counsel of me in this case). It is said that they died before the close of the year (for their want of respect). However, says R. Yosse, these 2 men died, and we have learnt nothing of them. What is the real solution? It appears that firstly the blessing should be said for the leeks: "Fruits of the earth," for the formula: "All has been created by His word," is only a secondary one, and is insufficient.

3. For the thing which groweth not from the earth, say, "(who createst) everything." For vinegar, unripe fruit, and locusts, say, "everything." For milk, cheese, and eggs, say, "everything." R. Judah says: "Whatever it be, which had its origin in a curse, is not to be blessed."

If wine has become soured, say: "Be blessed, Judge of the truth" (the formula for misfortunes); if use has just been made of it, say: "Everything was created by His word." On seeing locusts, say: "Be blessed, Judge of the truth." If one has just eaten of them, say: "Everything was created by His word." On seeing unripe fruit fall to the ground, say: "Be blessed, Judge of the truth." If one has just eaten some, say: "Everything was created by His word.

4. If a man have before him many kinds of fruits, R. Juda says: "If there be among them of the 7 kinds,[8] he is to bless them." But the sages say: He may bless whichever of them he pleases.

R. Joshuah b. Levi says: On what point does the discussion, between R. Juda and the Rabbi, bear? In case there was an intention to eat bread with these

[6] See B., tr. *Berakhoth*, fol. 39 *a*.

[7] A locality to be included in the Talmudic geography (perhaps Anath ?).

[8] They are: Wheat, grapes, figs, pomegranates, olives, and honey (or dates). See Deuteronomy viii. 8.

fruits, that of the bread suffices; but in case there is no intention to eat bread, everybody recognizes the necessity to give the preference to one of the 7 superior sorts, if there is one, and to pronounce the benediction over it. R. Aba says that the final blessing must also be said (according to the wise men, when the blessing has been pronounced over one of the chosen kinds, the blessing at meals does not suffice; a special one must be made). Therefore, says R. Yosse, it is R. Aba's opinion which is in dispute (since according to him a posterior blessing is necessary), whilst R. Joshuah b. Levi's opinion is, that there is only a difference of opinion when bread is eaten with any of these products (and according to his opinion, the blessing of the bread alone suffices); for R. Aba says that a final blessing is necessary. The fact is, that if no blessing is recited for this special fruit, it would be considered an accessory, and it has been taught that, where there is an accessory to the diet, the blessing is said for the principal object (and it would be impossible to apply this to any of the superior produce of Palestine). If a man has a mixture of several sorts (or dessert), *γαρίσματα*, before him, R. Jeremiah says, in the name of R. Ame, that the blessing is said for the lupines. R. Levi says that it is in virtue of this verse (Prov. xxii. 22): *Rob not the poor, because he is poor* (i.e. he must not give the preference to the superior sorts, but say also the blessing for the lupines). We know now what is to be said when a man intends to eat bread afterwards. But what is to be said if he does not intend to eat any? It is not decided. R. Gamaliel Zooga went one day to R. Janai's house, and he saw that the latter said the opening blessing and the final one on partaking of some olives (although the intention to eat bread afterwards would have exempted him). R. Gamaliel said to him, is that the proper thing to do? (Have we not been taught that, on the contrary, the blessing for bread suffices?) R. Zeira sent to R. Samuel b. Naḥman, to ask for a solution of this question, and the latter replied, that according to Rab, in the name of R. Mena, every one recognizes the necessity to give the preference to one of the seven superior kinds, if there is one (and when one is not eating bread). The decision is good, says R. Zeira, since we see the Rabbis, when they are travelling to proclaim the Neomenia,[9] eat grapes without reciting the blessing afterwards. Why do they not recite it? Because they intend to eat bread, and exempt themselves by a comprehensive blessing (in conformity with the decision above quoted). When a man has before him several sorts, all belonging to the 7 superior classes, which one should he choose to recite the blessing over? Over the one standing first in biblical order,[1] as has been said elsewhere, and the one coming nearest to the word *land* in the verse indicated (therefore wheat takes precedence of all).

[9] It was announced at the time of the first phases of the moon.

[1] See p. 119, note 5. The verse begins with the word *land*.

5. If one blessed the wine before food, the blessing frees the wine after food. If he blessed the adjuncts before the food, it frees the adjunct. But the blessing of the adjuncts does not free the bread. The school of Shammai say, neither does it free the cookery.

It has only been shown that the blessing of the wine before the meal exempts one from blessing it after the meal; but one has blessed the wine drunk during the repast, that does not exempt the wine after. At other places (Babylon), it has even been taught that the blessing before the meal does not exempt the wine drunk after it (on account of the long interval). How reconcile this with the Mishnâ (which teaches that the blessing of the wine before exempts that drunk after)? R. Hoona, and R. Josuah b. Levi both answered this objection: the former says that the anonymous author of this passage of the Mishnâ had in view the case of a man drinking conditum (spiced wine) (which is not pure) after the meal; the latter says that it alludes to a man drinking wine after the bath (Βαλανείον); otherwise another blessing is necessary.

R. Helbo and R. Hoona or Rab say, in the name of R. Ḥiya Rooba, that for the cakes eaten after the meal, a blessing both before and after eating them is necessary (the blessing of the meal not being sufficient to cover them). R. Ama says that R. Yoḥanan contests this and does not admit it. He only contests it, says R. Mena to R. Ezekiah, in the case of a person eating them during the repast. No, answered the latter, he contests it even if one has not eaten of them during the meal. And R. Haggai, in the name of R. Zeira, confirms this. The people of the house of the *naci* (prince) sent some fruits[1] to R. Ḥanina b. Kissi, and he put them aside to eat them after the meal, reciting two special blessings. R. Ḥana ate bread with dates (so that the blessing of the bread availed). R. Ḥiya b. Ashe said to him: Thou contesteth the decision of thy master (which was contrary)? Leave what thou art eating there, until the end of the meal; and then thou canst recite the necessary special blessings. R. Ḥana replied: The bread is the principal for me (and therefore I recite not the blessing for the fruit).

R. Yona and R. Yosse went to a feast given by R. Ḥanina Antonieh (? of 'Anath), and at the dessert some cakes with roasted ears of corn were brought to them. In the present case, said they, let us lay aside our studies and personal opinions, and let us conform to the rules of the Mishnâ: now, R. Mena taught, in the name of R. Judah, who had it from R. Yosse the Galilean, that special blessings are needed for these cakes, served at dessert. Therefore, said they, as the opinion of this particular Rabbi is contested by the Rabbis, the opinion of the latter must be adopted (and no new blessing be recited).

[1] The produce of a certain palm-tree, or hard dates, called *Nicolai* (Plinius, xiii. 4).

R. Marinos, whilst at R. Josuah's house, said that he who eats a sort of caviar[3] and a dish made of fine flour, besides the blessing said after this mixture, must say a second one for the flour. Who says so? R. Shammai, who says that the principal blessing does not cover these cooked dishes. R. Yosse says: It is an unanimously admitted opinion that the blessing of the bread covers the adjuncts; as regards cooked food, Hillel says one is exempted, but Shammai says not so. If, however, one has recited *ab initio* the blessing for the accessories, every one (including even Hillel) admits that this does not cover either the bread or the cooked food. R. Aba b. R. Papa asked: If a man eat some flour food, intending to eat bread afterwards, must he recite a special final blessing for the flour? Yes, answered the Cesarean Rabbis (because the one does not carry with it, nor does it cover the other).

6. If several persons sit down to eat, each blesses for himself; but if they recline together, one blesses for all. If wine come to them during food, each blesses for himself; but if after food, one blesses for all. He also blesses for the incense,[4] even though they have not brought it till after the repast.

The Mishnâ alludes to the repast which follows the ceremony of circumcision, and not of a repast given by the master of a house to his guests (for in this case they are not obliged to sit in a circle, for one to pray). According to R. Ḥiya, it means also at an ordinary repast. The order of the meal has been defined: the visitors enter and sit down on the forms and chairs (cathedra) until all the company are assembled. Wine is brought, for which each one recites a blessing; when water is brought every one washes his hand (the right one, which holds the cup); each one says his blessing for the accessories; then the company recline on sofas, and when wine is brought, a second blessing must be said, in addition to the first one, by one of the assistants, and then the guests wash both hands. When any adjuncts are served, one of the guests recites the blessing, and it is not proper that a stranger should enter after the third service.

We have learnt elsewhere:[5] If a man is to remain in the *Succa* for just[6] 7 days only, what is done for the last day? After the repast of the seventh day, the Succa must not be abruptly taken down, but the different fixtures must be gradually taken down, commencing at midday, so as to honour, without incon-

[3] J. Levy translates: *Garonbrei.*

[4] According to Oriental custom, incense and spices are burnt after meals.

[5] See J., tr. *Succa*, iv. 5. In the following explanation it is shown at what time the blessings are to be repeated.

[6] It is said: "You shall remain in your tents 7 days;" but the festival lasts for 8 days.

venience, the last day. R. Aba b. Cahana, or R. Ḥiya b. Ashe, says, in the name of Rab: The Succa must be rendered unfit for use before night (so as to show that it will not be used again). R. Joshuah b. Levi says that it suffices to sanctify the last day at home. R. Jacob b. Aḥa says, in the name of Samuel, that if a man has sanctified the festival in a house,[7] and that, on reflection, he decides to take his meal elsewhere, the formula must be recommenced (on account of the change of place). R. Aḥa and R. Ḥanina say, in the name of R. Joshuah, that, if a man be at his ease in the Succa, he shall sanctify the festival in the evening at home, and then he may go to take his meal in the Succa (and in spite of the change of place, the blessing need not be recommenced). In any case, says R. Abin, Samuel and R. Joshuah are not at variance. R. Joshuah (who does not exact the recommencement) does not refer to the case in which a man has decided to take his meal elsewhere, and Samuel speaks explicitly of this latter contingency. R. Mena, on the other hand (who admits of no distinction on account of premeditation), says that Samuel conforms to R. Ḥiya's opinion as given above, whilst R. Joshuah conforms to R. Joshuah b. Levi's opinion. In fine, says R. Ame, this proves (with regard to this subject) that there is a difference of opinion on the first question (and each of the guests must bless them himself before eating).

Ben-Zoma was asked the following question: Why must each guest pronounce his own blessing when wine is brought in during the repast? It is, replied he, because the throat is full (and he could not answer *amen*). This is a proof, says R. Mena, that if a man sneezes during meals, it is forbidden to wish him good health (ἴησις or ἴασις), on account of the danger (because, in speaking, a piece of food might get into the trachea).

"For the spices and incense, one person only pronounces the blessing."

What difference is there between the spices and the spiced wine, for which it sometimes happens that each person pronounces separately the blessing? It is because every one can inhale the good odours, even while eating, but it is not so with the wine, which each one tastes separately. R. Zeira, in the name of R. Jeremiah, says that the blessing for the spices must be said as soon as their fragrance ascends. R. Jeremiah, wishing to question R. Zeira, asked him: What blessing is said for perfumed oil? He replied that one must say: "Blessed be He who has given an agreeable odour to perfumed oil," or, according to others, "to scented woods." Isaac b. Aba b. Meḥasia and R. Ḥananel, being together, the one said the formula: "Blessed be He who has given an agreeable odour to scented woods," and the other said: "Blessed be He who gives an

[7] See J., *Succa*, iv. 5 (3), and B., tr., *Pesahim*, fol. 101 *a*.

agreeable odour to the verdure of the fields." The latter objected to the former: Are they woods? How, then, can you call them so? They are so called in the same manner as it is said (Joshua ii. 6): *She hid them with the stalks of flax* ('EZ), which are also called *wood.* They went to Rab and Simon (to ask for a solution of the question). R. Ḥanna replied, in the name of R. Ashe, that one must say: "Blessed be He who gives an agreeable odour to scented woods." Gueniba says that a man is exempted from saying a blessing for the oil which is used to wipe away the perspiration (to clean the hands), and even also, according to R. Judan, if they are condensed on the hands (in the shape of perfume). R. Ḥelbo and R. Ḥanna say, in the name of Rab, that the blessing is unnecessary if a man prepares in his own house some liniment (*linteum,* for perfume), composed of wine, oil, and water. R. Ḥisda says that for all these articles one must say the formula: "Blessed be He who gives the good odour to scented woods,"[8] excepting for musk (*muscus*), for which say: "Blessed be He who gives a good odour to the spices."

7. If they first set salt food before a man and bread with it, he blesses the salt food which frees the bread, and the bread is only an appendage. The rule is, whenever there is principal and with it appendage, the blessing on the principal frees the appendage.

R. Simon b. Naḥman says, in the name of R. Yonathan: The decision of the Mishnâ only holds good as long as a man is not familiar with royal feasts, and when the salt foods form the principal diet;[9] but in the contrary case there is no fixed rule. R. Jeremiah says, in the name of Rab, that if a man eat bread and vegetables together, he only says the blessing for the vegetables, if they form the principal. R. Simon says, in the name of R. Simon b. Lakish, that if a man eat bread and sweet things, he says the benediction for the latter, if they form the principal; but if the contrary, there is no fixed rule.

8. If one has eaten figs, grapes, and pomegranates, he must say after them 3 blessings, a summary of the 3. R. Akibah says, If one has eaten boiled (pulse), and it is his meal, he must say after it 3 blessings. Whoever drinks water for his thirst says, "By whose word everything is," &c. R. Tarphon says, "Who createst many souls," &c.

R. Simon and R. Judai say, in the name of R. Joshuah: If a man eat on the east side of a fig-tree, and go to finish his meal on the west side of it, he must say the blessing. Aba b. R. Hanna says: Be the wine old or new, it must be

[8] B., tr. *Berakhoth,* fol. 43 *b.*

[9] Gastronomical observation.

blessed; if a man change his wine he need not bless, but must do so if he change his place. If a man have his attention turned away, it is as if he had changed his place (and he must recommence). Rabbi said the blessing on every cask he opened. What did he say? R. Isaac Rooba replied, in Rab's name, that he said this formula: "Blessed is He who is good, and who does good." R. Akiba gave a feast to his son Samson; he blessed every cask that was opened, and said: "The good wine! To the health of the Rabbis and their pupils."

"Whoever drinks water for his thirst," &c.

R. Yona says that an exception must be made in the case of medicinal waters which are drunk for reasons of health. But, says R. Yosse, a man says the formula for any liquid he drinks with pleasure. Even also for medicinal waters, says R. Abahu, in drinking them say this formula: "Blessed be He who has created medicines." According to others, it means palm waters.[1] According to the former, it means waters used to pierce or drive away the bile; others say it means a water which has its source between two palm-trees.[2]

CHAPTER VII.

1. Three men who have eaten together are bound to bless[3] after food. If a person have eaten of that which is doubtful, whether it has paid tithe or not, or of 1st tithe from which the bread offering has been taken, or of 2nd tithe or consecrated things, which have been redeemed; also if the waiter have eaten the size of an olive; or a Samaritan[4] be of the party, the blessing must be said. But if one have eaten the untithed, or 1st tithes from which the bread-offering has not been taken, or consecrated things which are unredeemed, or if the waiter has eaten less than the size of an olive, or a tranger be of the party, the blessing is not to be said.

[1] There is a word's-play between *Deqarim*, medicinal waters, and *Deqalim*, palm-waters.

[2] See B., tr. *Shabbath*, fol. 110 *a*.

[3] It is what the German Jews call *benschen*, from the Latin *benedicere* (with Italian pronunciation).

[4] The slight illegalities affecting all these cases do not affect the common prayer; they are shown in the first treatises following the *Berakhoth*.

How is it that it has at one time been taught, that when 3 men are together they must not separate without saying the grace, and again, that they must remain together for it? (Is it not a useless repetition of words?) Samuel replies, that on the one occasion it refers to a principle and on the other to an accomplished fact. In what does this difference consist? It is explained by two *amoraim*: according to the one, it is called a principle when one has the intention of eating with others, and an accomplished fact when one has eaten together with others, be it but the equivalent of an olive; according to the other, no account is taken until the size of an olive has been eaten, and they call *end* the termination of the whole of the repast.[5] R. Aba says, in R. Hoona's name, and R. Zeira says, in the name of R. Aba b. R. Jeremiah: 3 persons being together are bound to pray together, but for 2 it is optional. R. Zeira repeated this before R. Yosse, who said that we have only to follow the text directions of the Mishnâ, which says: 3 persons having eaten together are bound to pray together;[6] each Rabbi acts in a manner consistent with his own opinion.

With regard to these numbers, Samuel says that the judgment of 2 men is valid;[7] but it is a presumptuous action for 2 to judge (instead of there being at least 3). R. Yoḥanan and Resh Lakish both say that the judgment of 2 people is not valid. R. Hoona says that 3 persons who have eaten separately, and afterwards come together, pray in common.. That takes place, adds R. Ḥisda, if they come from 3 companies who have already arranged to pray together. According to the opinion of R. Zeira and his companions (R. Yosse, R. Yoḥanan, and Resh Lakish), they must all 3 have eaten together (it does not suffice to come together after the meal).

R. Yona says (*à propos* of R. Hoona's opinion) that if 3 hyssops have been dipped into the water of the ashes from the sin offering,[8] and these 3 hyssops subsequently become mixed, the priest may nevertheless make the aspersion with them. According to R. Zeira and his companions, the 3 must have been dipped in together; and, according to R. Ḥisda, they may have been taken from 3 separate bundles. One cannot object to the comparison of the rules of the hysops with that of the prayers, as mentioned above, for we see that the Rabbis, when they are occupied with the Succa (tent of the tabernacles), deduce, from another

[5] The new teaching, which was deemed superfluous, has therefore a reason, viz. to teach us that after having eaten together (the equivalent of an olive, or after having simply sat down together), they should not separate without reciting the blessing in common.

[6] The discussion about the propriety of praying together is a pendant to the other discussion: is a judgment pronounced by two judges valid or not?

[7] See J., tr. *Synhédrin*, i. 1.

[8] Numbers, the whole of chapter xix.

subject, a rule concerning the use of clay. For indeed it has been taught at Babylon[a] that, if the roof of the Succa be raised so as to leave a breadth of 3 hands, the Succa is unfit for service; but if the interval is less, it is good. May one also sleep there? R. Isaac b. Elishah replies to this question by a comparison: The clay serves to stop up the cracks in a bath; but one may not thereupon take a bath of legal purification therein (it is still considered defective); the same with the Succa, the lessening of the space suffices to make it of use, but not to allow of sleeping therein.

If after a repast partaken of by 3 men, one of them wish to go, he must, according to Rab's school, say the first blessing. What is meant by that? Rab's school say that it is a call to say the thanksgiving; R. Zeira says, in the name of R. Jeremiah, that it is the first section, and this is also what R. Ḥelbo, and R. Ḥanan say, in Rab's name. R. Shesheth made an observation and said: Does not the Mishna contradict that? for if one person cannot recite the thanksgiving from memory (and only says the 1st section), another says the 2nd section, and another the 3rd, so as to fulfil the obligation to recite them, without there being any question of a 4th; now, if the call forms the 1st special section, one would have to speak of 4. And indeed it sometimes happens that there is question of a 4th one.

Thus we have learnt that there are 4. But if the 1st blessing includes the call and the 1st section, how can we find this number? We cannot suppose that it alludes to the 4th one of the final section, for it differs from the others in that, instead of having been established by the Law, it has been subsequently appointed by the Rabbis; since R. Hoona says[1] that when the Israelites killed at the siege of Bethar were buried, the said section was appointed, and it is said of God *that He is good*, because the corpses did not decompose; and *He does the good thing*, because it was possible to inter them (how then explain this number four?). That may be explained, says R. Ḥana, by R. Ismael's opinion, who tells us that, the said section is indicated to us by the allusion in the Pentateuch; for it is written (Deut. viii. 10): ***When thou hast eaten and art full, then thou shalt bless;*** this part corresponds to the summons to say the grace; the words following: *the Lord thy God,* correspond to the first blessing; the fragment of the verse: *for the (good) land,* corresponds to the second, and the word *good* to the third, as it is further said (Deut. iii. 25): *that goodly mountain;* and finally the words: *which He hath given thee,* represent the final blessing.

For the reading of the Law, it is said[2] that an opening blessing is said, but

[a] *B.*, tr. *Succa*, fol. 16 *b*; see ibid. i. 7 (10).

[1] See above, i. 8, p. 24; tr. *Taanith*, iv. 8 (fol. 69 *a*).

[2] See J., tr. *Meghilla*, iv. 1; *Mekhilta*, section *Bô*, chap. xv.; *Debarim Rabba*, chap. viii.; Medrash *Rabba* on Samuel, chap. xiii.

nothing is said about a 2nd one to be uttered afterwards. Where is it said that one must be recited before? In this verse (Deut. xxxii. 3): *Because I will publish the name of the Lord: ascribe ye greatness unto our God.* At the repast it is said that it should be recited after it, but nothing is said about the prayer before it; and what proves that it must be recited after it, is this: *Thou shalt eat, thou shalt be full, then thou shalt bless.* How do we know that the precept relative to the repast is to be attributed to the *Tôra*, and *vice versâ*? R. Samuel b. Naḥmeni replies, in the name of R. Jonathan, that this attribution is made by confronting the passages, identical on both sides (and the secondary prayers are also deduced from it); in the same manner as the mention of the Lord's *name* for the Law indicates a prayer to be said before it, as also the analogous mention for the repast indicates the same thing; and as the legal precept indicates a blessing to be made after the repast, so also one must be recited for the reading of the Law.

Thus up to the present R. Akiba's opinion seems to be admitted, contrarily to R. Ismael, who says, through R. Yoḥanan, that the necessity for these blessings may be proved by reasoning *à fortiori*: if, for the repast, which does not (legally) exact an opening blessing, one must be recited afterwards, much more so is one required after the reading of the Law, for which one is already prescribed to be recited before it. This now determines the principle to be followed for the Law. After this it is analogically reasoned that a blessing must be recited before meals. R. Juda and R. Nehemias each cite verses in support of this deduction. The former recalls to us the verse (1 Samuel ix. 13): *Because He doth bless the sacrifice, and afterwards they eat that be bidden* (here the blessing is before). The latter says that it is written (Exodus xxiii. 25): *And ye shall serve the Lord your God, and He shall bless thy bread and thy water*, this signifies that: although it be *thy bread*, ye must recognize, before eating it to whom thou dost owe it. Rabbi adds this: If after having eaten and been filled, we must bless God, with much greater reason must we do so when we are hungry and can sit down. Behold now the rules of meals explained. In order to give a motive for the prescriptions of the Law, the following reasoning is put forth: If we must recite a blessing before and after our food which provides for our ephemeral existence, with more reason must it be so for the reading of the Law, which concerns our eternal life.

R. Zeira asked (*à propos* of these diverse parallels of the Law and repasts): To what can we compare 3 successive readings? Is it to 3 individuals who have eaten together (and of whom one prays for all), or to 3 persons having eaten separately (and praying in the same manner)? Must we compare it to the 1st case, so that the 1st reader would say the anterior blessing, the 3rd reader the final formula, and the 2nd nothing? Or is it like the 2nd example, in which case the 2nd reader would, like the others, recite a blessing before and after? R. Samuel b. Abdoma replied that the rules for the reading of the Law, are only

deduced from those ruling the meals in so far as concerns the plural number, and indeed, one person recites, for several others, the blessing for the reading of the Law. R. Aba-Mare, brother of R. Yosse, says: It is considered the equal of the other prescriptions of the Law, and in fulfilling it, a blessing is required as for all the others.

"If one has eaten *Demai*, &c." Can we deduce from this that if a man has eaten of fruit of which he is doubtful whether the tithes have been taken off for the Levites and the oblations for the priests,[3] &c.? R. Simon, brother of R. Berakhia, says: When an order was promulgated regarding these doubtful fruits, which forbade that they should be carried to the market before the legal tithes had been taken off, the greater part of the peasants took their produce back home (which led one to suppose that they followed the precepts of the Law).

How is it that the Mishna says that the Samaritan may be included so as to make up the legal number necessary to say the prayer for meals in common? Is not his Jewish faith doubtful? It is admitted, replies R. Abahoo, that he is considered as an Israelite in everything; for we have learnt, through Rabbi, that he is a stranger. But, according to R. Gamaliel, he is considered in everything an Israelite.[4]

2. There is no blessing at food for women, slaves, and children. What quantity is required for the blessing at food?[5] The size of an olive. R. Judah says, the size of an egg.

R. Simon, in the name of R. Josuah b. Levi and R. Yosse b. Saul, says: A child (under 13 years of age) may be taken to make up the 10, if there are already 9 men. But have we not been taught the child is accepted without examination? (Would he not count without any conditions?) A distinction must be made, say R. Yosse, R. Simon, and R. Ḥanina, in the name of R. Josuah b. Levi: If the child is quite young he is only admitted as an auxiliary, if he is adolescent he is considered as a man. R. Juda bar-Pazi says, in the name of R. Yosse: If nine men represent ten, they say the formula prescribed for an assembly of ten. How is that? Can 9 men, of whatever importance, ever numerically represent ten? We must therefore conclude that this number may be completed by the addition of a child. R. Berakhia says that R. Jacob bar-

[3] The question is the elucidation of a *Halakha*, a particular case which has been compared firstly to *Demai* and then to the *Cuthean*. Neither the one nor the other comparison were found right, and the question is not decided.

[4] See J., tr. *Demai*, ch. vi., § 11; tr. *Sheqalim*, i. 5.

[5] Ten men are necessary for *minian* (religious number).

Zabdi asked R. Yosse b. R. Eliezer: Since we have learnt that a child may be added to make up ten, can the same method of proceeding be adopted to make up the number? Yes, as he is added so as to join in the utterance of the name of the Lord, which is part of the formula for ten, with more reason may he be taken for the third one, in which formula the Lord's name does not appear. This reasoning, was the reply, is not good, for in order to utter the Lord's name one may go so far as to admit a child, whilst it may not be so for the formula prescribed for 3. We are taught that, in admitting the child he is provided with a roll of the Law (a symbol of knowledge and aptitude for religion). R. Judan adds that a child may in case of need be added to the number of those called to the Law. What age must he have? R. Abina says that R. Hoona and R. Juda transmit us, in Samuel's name, different opinions on this subject: according to the one, the child must know well the blessings and their meaning;[6] according to the other, the child must know to whom this prayer is addressed. R. Nassa says: I have often eaten with my father, R. Taḥelipha, and Anania[7] b. Sisi, my uncle, and I was never added to the number of those reciting the formula of the blessing in common until I had arrived at the age of puberty (about 12 years). Samuel b. Shilath asked Rab (others say the question was addressed to Samuel) the following question: If 9 persons have eaten bread and one green food, may they recite the thanksgiving together? Yes, was the reply. If only 8 have eaten bread, is it the same? Yes. If there are only 7 to 3? Again, yes. But, asked R. Abina, if only half of them have eaten bread and the other half not, may they also pray together? R. Zeira replied: Until I was there the question was a doubtful one for me; but I did not dare to raise it. Then, asked R. Jeremiah, even he who has not eaten bread at all, may he recite the blessing for all? Has R. Jeremiah changed his opinion? replied they.

300 Nazarenes[8] came forward, during the time of the Doctor Simon b. Shetach (brother-in-law of King Alexander-Jannus); for 150 of them motives were found to render their sacrifices unnecessary,[9] but not for the other 150. Simon went to King Jannus and said to him: There are here 300 Nazarenes who have to offer 900 sacrifices, give them from thy treasury wherewith to pay

[6] Cf. B., the same treatise, fol. 48 *a*.

[7] For Ḥannania (by softening the first letter).

[8] See Numbers, chap. vi. Those who had made vows of abstinence, *nasireat*, had, after the accomplishment of the vow, to offer three sacrifices in the Temple. This fact is also spoken of in *Bereshith-Rabba* (fol. 101 *b*) and *Koheleth-Rabba* (fol. 103 *a*). See also J., tr. *Nazir*, v. 3 (fol. 54 *b*); Derenbourg's *Essai*, &c., pp. 96 and 98.

[9] The Rabbis did not approve of the *nazireat*, and were very ingenuous in rendering null those engagements, which were often inconsiderately and imprudently made. On this occasion our Rabbi remained faithful to the doctrines of the prophets.

the half, and I. will provide for the other half. The king therefore sent the 450 sacrifices; but meanwhile a slanderer went to the king, and told him that Simon had given nothing at all (this was a perfidious action, Simon had contributed nothing because of the 300 Nazarenes he had been able to annul the vows of 150). On learning this, Jannus was irritated. R. Simon b. Shetach was terrified and fled. Some time afterwards, certain great personages of the kingdom of Persia (or some Parthians) came to Jannus. Whilst at table, they said to him: We remember that on the occasion of our first visit here, there was a venerable man (a sage) who expounded to us things full of wisdom. In reply, the king told them what had passed. They asked the king to have him brought back. The king therefore sent after him and promised him (that he would be safe). Simon returned and seated himself between the king and the queen (the highest place of honour). The king said to him: Why didst thou mock me by saying that 900 sacrifices were required, when the half would have sufficed? I did not mock thee, replied Simon; thou hast paid thy share, and I mine (by my knowledge in examining the aspirants). Verily it is written (Eccles. vii. 12): *For wisdom is a defence, and money is a defence.*[10] Then why didst thou fly? I heard that my master was angry with me, and I put into practice the advice of the prophet (Isaiah xxvi. 20): *Hide thyself as it were for a little moment, until the indignation be overpast;* and it is further said (Eccles. vii. 12): *But the excellency of knowledge is that wisdom giveth life to them that have it.* Why, said the king, hast thou seated thyself between me and the queen? It is written, replied Simon, in the book of Ben-Sirah (xi. 1): *Exalt her* (the Law) *and she shall promote thee* (Prov. iv. 8), *and thy seat shall be among the princes.*[1] Let a cup be brought to him, said the king, so that he may recite the blessing for the meal. It was brought, and the Rabbi said: Let us bless God for the repast that Jannus and his companions have had. Thus, thou art bent on railing me? said the king. No, said the Rabbi, but what shall I say for a meal of which I have not partaken? Let food be given to him. The Rabbi ate,[2] and included in the formula the words, "for the repast which we have eaten."

R. Yoḥanan says that R. Simon b. Shetach's opinion is questioned. R. Jeremiah contests it for the first part of the history, when Shetach wished to give the blessing for a meal in which he had not taken part. R. Aba contests even the resolution he took at the end to bless it, since Shetach had not taken

10 A flattery and compliment in the mouth of the king.

1 M. Derenbourg says (*Essai*, &c., p. 50): Sometimes the Rabbis confounded the sentences of Ben-Sirah with those of the Book of Proverbs.

2 Apparently without taking bread, for it is not said that he washed his hands; this must be noted on account of the conclusions to be drawn from this fact.

bread. But, as R. Jeremiah does not share this opinion (and if, according to him, it suffices, e.g. to have eaten vegetables), does he not contradict himself in putting the above question, viz. to know whether in this case he is allowed to bless the repast? The answer is that indeed, for the above case, it is evident that it is a decided question. In asking this question, he was guided by the Rabbis, who had not decided it; but it is, according to R. Simon b. Gamaliel, an established point, as results from the following teaching: If a person go up to a dining-room, and sit down with other guests and eat near to them, he prays with them in common, even if he has eaten less wheat than the size of an olive. This is the opinion of the wise men. R. Jacob b. Aḥa says in the name of R. Yoḥanan: A man may never take part in the prayer if he has eaten less wheat than the size of an olive. As to the teaching, according to which two persons may take another to them, who has only eaten green food, to say the prayer in common, it is a decision of R. Simon b. Gamaliel.

3. How do we bless at food? If there be 3, one says, "Let us bless," &c.; if 3 and himself, he says, "Bless ye," &c. If ten, he says, "Let us bless our God," &c.; if ten and himself, he says "Bless ye," &c.; and so if there be ten or ten myriads.[3] If there be 100 he says, "Let us bless the Lord our God," &c. If there be 100 and himself, he says, "Bless ye," &c.; if there be 1000, he says, "Let us bless the Lord our God, the God of Israel;" if there be 1000 and himself, he says, "Bless ye," &c.; if there be a myriad, he says, "Let us bless the Lord our God, the God of Israel, the God of Hosts, who sitteth between the cherubims," &c.; if there be a myriad and himself, he says, "Bless ye," &c. As he pronounces the blessing, so they respond after him, "Blessed be the Lord our God, the God of Israel, the God of Hosts, who sitteth between the cherubim, for the food we have eaten." R. José the Galilean says they should bless according to the number of the assembly; for it is written, *Bless ye God in the congregation;* (even) *the Lord from the fountain of Israel.* (Ps. lxviii. 26.)

One day, R. Zeira, R. Jacob b. Aḥa, R. Ḥiya b. Aba, and R. Ḥanina, all companions of the Rabbis, were eating together. R. Jacob b. Aḥa took the

[3] Up to this point it is R. Akiba's opinion; hereafter it is R. Yosse the Galilean, who speaks, as is shown by the following *Mishnâ*.

cup, in order to pray, and said, "Let us bless," instead of saying, "Bless ye." Why, asked R. Ḥiya b. Aba, hast thou not said the formula, "Bless ye?" Have we not learnt, replied he, that the terms are of little importance? Whether one says, "Let us bless," or "Bless ye," no notice is taken. It is only the exacting people that look so closely into it.[4] R. Zeira was displeased that R. Jacob b. Aḥa should call R. Ḥiya b. Aba an exacting person. Samuel replied: One must not exclude oneself from the assembly.[5] But, was the objection, do we not say "Bless ye" at the blessing given for the reading of the Law? Would not that also be an exclusion? No, replied R. Aboon; since the term "who is blessed" is added, this is not a case of exclusion. R. Aba b. Zemina served R. Zeira and poured him out some drink; the latter asked him to pronounce the blessing. Be it so, said he, but bear at once in mind that thou wilt drink again, because we have been taught that he who serves must pronounce a blessing for each glass of wine, if not for every morsel of food. R. Zeira replied: In the same manner as I, if I pronounced the blessing, would exempt you from it, by thinking of you; so also am I released when I answer *Amen* to your blessing in my place. R. Tanhum b. Jeremiah says that a *baraitha* teaches as follows: Neither he who recites a blessing while working, nor he who listens to this person, has sufficiently fulfilled their duty (therefore he is not exempted).

"When there are a hundred persons he says, &c." R. Yoḥanan says that it is the opinion of R. Yosse the Galilean; but, according to the wise men, it matters little whether there be ten or a hundred thousand. This last enunciation, says Rabba, serves for a rule. From where do we learn that an assembly is composed of at least ten persons? R. Aba and R. Yassa explain it, in the name of R. Yoḥanan, from the moment that the same word ('Eda) is used twice to designate the assembly,[6] and that once the number *ten* is indicated, this term also represents it here. R. Simon says that the word among (*Tŏkh*) is comparable to that of the verse (Genesis xlii. 5): *And the sons of Israel came to buy corn among those who came;* each time this word represents *ten*. R. Yosse b. R. Aboon says that the comparison of these terms might suffice; but, in addition, the expression *sons of Israel*[7] used in each term proves that it always is *ten*. To what do the Rabbis, who do not admit a higher formula than that for ten, apply the term on which R. Yosse the Galilean, who differs in his opinion, bases himself, and according to whom the term *among the assemblies* signifies that a special formula is necessary for each assembly (according to the number of those

[4] Because it is making an exception to the general rule.

[5] In speaking in the 2nd person, instead of the 1st, it seems that one does not take part in it.

[6] Numbers xvi. 21; xvii. 10. J., tr. *Meghilla*, iv. 4 (7); *Synhedrin*, iv. 4.

[7] The sons of Jacob, leaving out Benjamin and Joseph, were *ten*.

composing it)? R. Ḥanina b. R. Abahoo says that this term is written in such a manner that it may mean *community* in the singular number, and may not be applied to what R. Yosse says.

4. R. Akivah says: What do we find in the synagogue? Whether many or few, the minister says, "Bless ye the Lord,"[8] &c. R. Ismael says, "Bless ye the Lord, who is ever blessed."

When R. Ḥiya b. Ashe got up to read the Law, he said: "Bless ye the Lord," without adding the term, "who is ever blessed." On hearing him the others tried to reduce him to silence, on account of his irregularity. Rab interposed and said: Let him alone, he is guided by R. Akiba's opinion (as above). R. Zeira stood up and read for the priest, in place of the Levite (who is in the second row), and he said the 2 blessings—the anterior one and the final one. They tried to silence him. Leave him alone, said R. Ḥiya b. Ashe, for such is the custom in their country.

It is written (Nehemiah viii. 6): *And Ezra blessed the Lord, the great God.* By what did he exalt Him? By saying the holy tetragram. R. Matna says that he exalted him by blessing.[9] R. Simon asks, in the name of R. Josuah b. Levi: Why are the Doctors, contemporary with the restoration of the Temple, called the men of the Grand Synagogue? Because they had re-established on their ancient footing the splendours of religion.[1] R. Pinhas says that Moses established the following formula, to be found in the *'Amida:* "God the great, the strong, the terrible." R. Jeremiah did not include the last attribute. He said *the strong,* because it is right, according to him, to style thus, He who assists in silence at the ruin of his house. Why did he not call Him *the terrible?* Because, said he, there is nothing terrible but the sanctuary, as it is written (Ps. lxviii. 35): *O God, thou art terrible out of Thy holy places.* Daniel (ix. 4) said: "God, the great and the terrible," but he did not say the *strong;* when His sons are in chains, where then is His strength? Why then did he call Him *the terrible?* In remembrance of His miracle of the fiery furnace. It was when the men of the Grand Synagogue returned that the religious splendours were re-established in their primitive glory, and that the following formula came into use again: "God the great, the strong, the terrible." But how can a mortal have the power, and how dare he impose a limit to the attributions of the Divinity? The prophets, replied R. Isaac b.

[8] In other words: he does not think, like R. Yossè, that the formula is modified according to the number of guests present.

[9] See J., tr. *Meghilla*, iv. 7, at the end; B, tr. *Yoma*, fol. 69 *b.*

[1] In citing this passage, M. Derenbourg, *Essai,* &c. p. 34,, translates it: "they had restored the ancient grandeur."

Eleazar, know that the Lord is a God of truth, and they do not flatter Him by thus qualifying him.

5. (4) When 3 have eaten together, they are not permitted to separate without blessing; not 4 or 5, but 6 may divide into 2 parties, and so may any number up to ten. But ten may not separate without blessing, nor any number less than 20.[2]

We have learnt that, if after the Saturday's meal, one has forgotten, while reciting the blessing, to refer to the solemnity of the day, the blessing must, according to Rab, be recommenced; Samuel holds a contrary opinion. Simon b. Aba, in the name of R. Yoḥanan, says that in case of doubt of having mentioned the Neomenia, there is necessity to recommence. It has been found, however, that this subject had been discussed and taught in the following manner: every day on which the additional sacrifice is offered, as for instance on the day of Neomenia, and on semi-festivals, the solemnity must be referred to, and in case of omission the blessing must be recommenced; but if the additional sacrifice be not offered, as for instance on the day of 'Hanooca (feast of the Machabees), or of Purim (Esther), the solemnity should be referred to; but, if forgotten, it need not be recommenced. Hanan b. Abu was eating once with his companions on Saturday; after the repast, followed by the blessing, he left; he returned after a while and found them repeating the blessing. Have we not already said it? asked he. Truly, replied they; but we recommence because we had forgotten to mention the Sabbath. This is not, however, what R. Aba says in the name of R. Hoona, or R. Jeremiah in the name of Rab: according to their opinion, if the mention of the Sabbath has been forgotten, the following formula is said: "Blessed be He who has given rest to his people Israel." This may only be said if one's attention has not been turned from the grace after meals (otherwise one must recommence).

When ten persons travel together, each one pronounces his blessing on the meal himself, even if they eat of the same loaf; but if they sit down to table together, one says the prayer for the others, even if they eat different dishes. When R. Jeremiah ate with his companions in an inn, he said the prayer for all.

6. (5) If 2 companies have eaten in one house, and some of each company be able to see some of the other company, they may join in the blessing; but if not, each company blesses for itself. They should not bless the wine till it has been mixed with water. These the words of R. Eleazar; but the Sages say they may bless it unmixed.

[2] Divisible in two parts, on account of the formula: "*Let us bless our God*" (see the preceding Mishna for the distinction).

R. Jona and R. Aba b. Zimna say, in the name of R. Zeira, they must mention it, even if they are in different houses.[3] R. Yoḥanan, however, imposes the condition that they must from the commencement have entered the house with that intention. How is one to act with regard to the scattered meals in the houses of the prince (Naci)? Is it like one house (as belonging to the same owner), or like two houses? It may be answered that if the guests are accustomed to serve themselves, or to pass the dishes from one to the other, they pray together. In the same manner R. Brakhia placed his interpreter in the middle doorway of the study-chamber, and as a result of this junction he could say the blessing for one and the other party.

"They should not bless the wine till it has been mixed with water, &c." R. Zerika says, in the name of R. Yosse b. Hanina: The Sages are of R. Eleazar's opinion as regards the addition of a little water to the benediction cup, and indeed the Sages adopted this custom for the glass of sanctification. R. Yosse's opinion is in opposition to that of R. Yona, for the latter tasted the wine first, and then added water. How admit this mixture? Have we not learnt that it is dangerous to drink a mixture on which a night has passed? That only applies, says R. Yoḥanan, in case the mixture has been kept in metal vessel. R. Jeremiah says, in the name of R. Yoḥanan, that the ancients asked whether the left hand may help the right in holding the cup at the blessing. 3 points may be deduced from this question: 1st, that it must be held in the right hand; 2nd, that the hand must be raised a palm's height from the table; and 3rd, that the eyes must be fixed on the cup. R. Aḥa reminds us that the cup must fulfil 3 conditions:[4] It must be full, ornamental, and agreeable. All three conditions are indicated in the same verse (Deut. xxxiii. 23): *O Naphtali, satisfied with favour, and full with the blessing of the Lord*; the *satisfaction* is equivalent to ornaments, *favour* represents agreeableness, and the term *full* naturally explains itself. If we act in this manner, says R. Ḥanina, we shall see the accomplishment of the remainder of the prediction (ibid.): *possess thou the west and the south*, that is to say that we shall enjoy this life here below and the life to come.

R. Eleazar says that the blessing must not be pronounced over an imperfect glass, and the moment it has been tasted it is rendered unfit for service. We learn three points from this Rabbi: 1st, that the blessing is forbidden if one has tasted; 2nd, that the glass must contain the measure; 3rd, that by tasting it it is rendered unfit. R. Tanḥoom b. Judan says that the honour to be accorded to the solemnity of the day takes precedence of that of the night, although the

[3] In this case, if the two parties see each other, they must unite; on the other hand, if they do not see each other, they do not join together, be they even in the same house.

[4] B., tr. of the *Yôma*, fol. 51.

sanctification of the night takes precedence of that of the day. How do we honour the day? R. Yosse, in the name of R. Jacob b. Aḥa, and R. Eleazar b. Joseph, in the name of Rab, say by the formula: "Blessed be the Creator of the fruit of the vine." R. Zerikan, son-in-law of R. Zerikan, mentioned the day of Ḥanooca in the second section of the thanksgiving, and he was complimented on it. R. Aba, son of Ḥiya b. Aba, mentioned the words "judge of truth" in the 4th section (the last), and he was praised for it. If R. Aba b. R. Ḥiya happened to eat while walking, he stopped to pray; if he ate while standing up, he sat down to pray; if he was sitting down, he leant on his elbows to pray; if he ate leaning on his elbows, he wrapped himself up to pray. In doing so, he did as the angels do, of whom it is said (Isaiah vi. 2): *With twain he covered his face, and with twain he covered his feet.*

CHAPTER VIII.

1. These are the controversies relating to meals, between the schools of Shammaï and Hillel. The Shammaites say, one must say the blessing of the day and then bless the wine; but the Hillelites say, one must say the blessing on the wine, and then bless the day.

(2) The Shammaites say, men must pour water on the hands, and then mix the goblet; but the Hillelites say, the goblet must be mixed, and then water poured on the hands.

(3) The Shammaites say, one is to wipe his hands on the napkin,[1] and lay it on the table; but the Hillelites say, on the cushions.

(4) Shammaï says (after the repast), one must first sweep the chamber, then perform the ablution (a fresh one); Hillel prescribes the reverse.

What is Shammaï's reason? It is, says he, because the sanctification of the day is the cause of the wine being brought, therefore one is obliged to do it before the wine comes.[2] What is Hillel's motive? It is that the wine is the cause of this sanctification; and also the wine is a more frequent thing than the blessing (and the most frequent is said first). R. Yosse says that it results from the words of these two doctors that for the wine of separation (*Habdala*) it is blessed before anything (and this is why): Shammaï gives for a reason that the sanctification of

[1] The use of the table-fork was unknown.

[2] J., tr. *Pesaḥim*, x. 2.

the day is the cause of the arrival of the wine; now, as the separation does not here precede the coming of the wine, priority is given to the wine. In the same manner Hillel alleges as a motive for his opinion, that the wine is the more frequent; now, as it is also more frequent than the ceremony of separation, it is given the preference. R. Mena says, on the contrary, the result of their assertions is, for both of them, that the blessing of separation is said before that of the wine. Shammaï maintains, in support of his opinion, that the sanctifying of the day is obligatory before that of the wine; now, as the obligation of the separation precedes that of the blessing of the wine, the former should be done first. And Hillel maintains that the wine is the cause of the recital of the sanctification of the Saturday; now, as it is not the wine which is the motive for the separation, the wine should be blessed first. R. Zeira says: Above all, the result of their words is that the ceremony of separation may be performed without wine, but not so the sanctification of Saturdays and festivals. This opinion is conformable to what the same doctor has said elsewhere, viz. that the separation may be performed with a strong drink; the wine, however, is sought after on account of the holiness of the ceremony. R. Yosse b. Rabbi says: In Babylonia it is the custom in localities where there is no wine for the minister officiating to pass up to the tribune and recite a summary of the seven blessings forming the *'Amida* prayer, and terminating with the words: "He sanctifies Israel and the Sabbath."

We ask ourselves, in view of Shammaï's opinion, what is to be done on Friday evenings? If on that evening being seated at table, the night surprise one, and there only be left one glass of wine, what is to be done? May it be put aside until after the meal, and then be used to fulfil several duties? Would there not be anyhow a something wanting? If it be used to perform the blessing of the solemnity of the day, it would be wrong, for the repast which preceded it should have taken precedence; were the blessing after the meal recited, the wine would receive the preference; and finally, were the wine to be blessed, the Sabbath should take precedence. How extricate oneself from this position? The following indicates the solution: We know that if wine be presented after the repast, and there be only one glass, it must be blessed, for it is to be feared, says R. Aba, that being a little blessing it might be forgotten, and the wine be drunk without saying it. Therefore, for the case in point, as the glass of wine is to serve for several ceremonies, there is no danger of its being forgotten. Acting on Shammaï's opinion, what should be done? The grace is first said for the meal, then the day is blessed and then the wine. It remains to be seen how one would act, granted the same case and in accordance with Hillel's opinions. Is the cup to be reserved until after the meal, and use it for the fulfilment of several duties at the same time? And with which should one commence? Should the wine be blessed? The meal has taken place before it. Should the meal be blessed? The light must come first. Should the light be blessed? The separation has taken place

before it; what is to be done? The following shows: R. Juda says that Hillel and Shammaï do not disagree on the order of the blessings; they admit that the thanksgiving for the meal must come first, and the celebration of separation last. They differ only with regard to the order of prayers for the light and the spices. Shammaï says that the spices are blessed first, and then the light; Hillel says that the light is blessed before the spices. R. Aba and R. Juda say the first of these opinions serves as a rule. How then is Hillel's opinion to be acted upon? First bless the meal, then the wine, and finally the light.

When a festival commences on Saturday evening, the following order, says R. Yosse, is to be adopted: the wine, sanctification of the solemnity, the light, and finally separation. Ḥanina bar-Aba gives, in Rab's name, the following order: the wine, the sanctification, the light, separation, *Succa,* and the special solemnity. R. Ḥanina says: wine, light, separation, sanctification. Samuel says: R. Ḥanina's opinion is right; for R. Aḥa says, in the name of R. Josuah bar-Levi: When a king goes (it is Saturday), and a governor arrives (it is the festival which is of minor sacredness), the king is first conducted away, and then the governor is admitted (i.e. the Saturday is celebrated before the sanctification of the festival). Levi proposes this order: wine, separation, light, sanctification. It seems that this last opinion is mostly accepted, for it conciliates the other opinions. R. Zeira asked R. Yosse: How does one act when the case presents itself? As Rab did, he replied, because the accomplished facts are proofs in his favour. When R. Abahoo went to the south, he acted as did R. Ḥanina; and when he went to Tiberiade, he acted like R. Yoḥanan did (R. Yoḥanan resided there), so as not to vex the wise man there where he lived. One can understand that he adopted R. Ḥanina's opinions (for if the festival is only sanctified after having blessed the light, one may, in accordance with established custom, extinguish it before the festival commences); but how can one imagine that he followed the decisions of R. Yoḥanan? For, if during the whole year, one bless not the light without extinguishing it, what does R. Yoḥanan make of this light? As soon as he has wine, was the reply, he does not put out the light, so as to profit of it while drinking, and he only blesses the light at the end, so as not to neglect the custom of the other Saturdays.

"Shammaï says (§ 2) that one washes first the hands, &c." What is Shammaï's motive? This order was made so that the impurity of the hands (if not washed) attach not themselves to the glass, which would render the glass itself impure. What is Hillel's motive? The sides of the glass are always considered impure (if therefore one wash one's hands before mixing water with the wine, the hands might become impure by contact with the humidity of the glass). According to others, the reason is that one should not wash one's hands before the moment immediately preceding the opening blessing. R. Bivi says, in the name of R. Yoḥanan, that Shammaï's opinion is conformable with that of R.

Yosse, and that of Hillel's to that of R. Meir; for as we have learnt elsewhere,[3] R. Meir says that in taking a vessel up by the handle, it matters little whether the hands be pure or impure (one is not preoccupied with the thought that the impurity might be communicated to the vessel by contact); according to R. Yosse, a man does not take notice of this if the hands be pure (and the vessel be not so, which is conformable to Shammaï). R. Yosse says, in the name of R. Shabtaï, and R. Ḥiya says, in the name of R. Simon b. Lakish,[4] that one must, if necessary, make a journey of four miles to obtain, with purity, the lump of dough, or to get pure water to wash the hands (if there be none in the neighbourhood).

In any case, says R. Abahoo, in the name of R. Yosse b. Ḥanina, a man is not required to do this unless there remain to accomplish a like distance on the road which he is following; but not to retrace his steps. What is, in this case, the rule for the keepers of public gardens, and orchards? We can see that, by the following: A woman may, if she be seated, take off the paste[5] (dough), even if she be naked, for she can hide her nakedness (by bending herself), but not the man (whose nakedness is visible even if he be seated); now, in speaking of this woman, she is of course supposed to be at home, and yet she is not obliged to disturb herself; it should therefore be the same for the keeper.

We have learnt that to wash oneself before meals is optional; but to do so after meals is obligatory;[6] to wash oneself, however, before meals is an interruption, but not so after meals. What does this interruption mean? According to R. Jacob b. Aḥa, it means that one should wash twice. R. Samuel b. Isaac asked: Why do they insist so strongly upon the accomplishment of an action which has just been stated to be optional? It is of importance, says R. Jacob b. Idi, for it happened once that pork was given to a man to eat, as not seeing him wash himself before the meals (they did not know he was an Israelite);[7] for not having washed herself, a woman was once obliged to leave her house, as being repudiated (she was wrongly suspected); through her not washing herself, some traces of the meal remained on her fingers, and this was taken to be a sign or evidence of a convention with a gallant. Others say that three persons died, as a consequence of this negligence. Samuel went to R. Ḥama, and ate as if ashamed (with his hands enveloped). What does this mean, said R. Ḥama, art thou not washed? I am in delicate health (ἀσθενής), was the reply, and (for fear of the cold) have covered my hands (although they are washed). When R. Zeira went to Babylon, he saw the Cohanim eating in this manner; they followed, said he, the opinions

[3] Mishna, tr. *Kelim* (of vessels), xxv. 7.
[4] See J., tr. *Hallâ*, ii. 2; B., tr. *Pesaḥim*, fol. 46 *a*.
[5] See J., tr. *Hallâ*, ii. 2.
[6] It is a hygienic precaution, B., tr. *Ḥoollin*, fol. 105—107; tr., *Yoma*, fol. 83 *b*.
[7] See *Bamidbar Rabba*, chap. xx.

of Rab and Samuel. R. Yosse b. R. Cahana said, in the name of Samuel, that one washes the hands for profane dishes, but not for the oblations. R. Yosse exacts it also for these last. He says further, in the name of R. Ḥiya b. Ashe and of R. Yona, that, for the oblations, the hands are to be washed to the wrists, and for ordinary meals, up to the finger-joints.[8] Meisha, grandson of R. Josuah ben Levi, says: He that was invited to my grandfather's house, and did not wash himself to the wrists, was not admitted to table. R. Hoona says: A man only washes his hands to eat bread; according to R. Oshia, a man washes himself when he eats anything soaked or accompanied by a sauce. R. Zeira washed himself, even in cutting lupines (because in cutting them one squeezes out the juice). Rabbi says that if a man has washed himself for the morning meal, he is not obliged to recommence for the next meal. R. Abina recommended this to the donkey drivers when they travelled: When you find water, said he, wash your hands and make a mental condition that this act shall suffice for the day.

R. Zeira went to see R. Abaha at Cesarea.[9] As soon as the latter perceived him, he invited him to dinner and handed him a loaf of bread to cut, asking him at the same time, to say the blessing:[1] The master of the house, replied R. Zeira, knows better the quality (strength) of the bread and can cut it properly (it is therefore for him to cut it). He was also asked to say the blessing after the meal: Master, replied he, recognize in R. Hoona a great man, for he said that he who says the first blessing is also to say the last one. There is, however, replied the host, a *boraitha* which contests the opinions of R. Hoona: we learn there that, as regards the order of washing the hands, if five persons only are present, the one who is held in the highest consideration does so first; if there are more present, the youngest one commences. The ablution during the meal is commenced by the most important one present; the ablution after it is first made by the one who has recited the blessing, so as to give him time to prepare himself for the recital. Now, if he who says the first blessing, says them all, there would be no necessity for preparation, and it would be known beforehand; therefore, one changes sometimes. R. Isaac says that this dissertation applies to the meetings of small companies where each one says himself the initial blessing, and it is not known who will say the final formula (but this does not apply to a company, the members of which are present from the commencement).

"Shammaï says (§ 3) that one first sweeps, &c." Shammaï gives as his motive, that fragments of the food be not spoiled by the water; Hillel says that, if the

[8] It must not be forgotten how scarce water is in the east, and that these parsimonies are excusable.

[9] A town on the shores of Palestine. See Neubauer's *Geographie*, pp. 91—95.

[1] One prefers to recite the formula *Moci* on an entire basket, as being more presentable. B., tr. *Berakhoth*, fol. 46 *a*.

servant be an intelligent man, he withdraws beforehand the pieces of the size of an olive (for those which are smaller than this receive no attention), then the hands are washed, and finally the room is swept. As regards what the Mishna says and which forms the subject under discussion, it refers to a marble table or a table made of pieces of marble which are not susceptible of impurity.

"Shammaï says that one is to wipe his hands on the napkin, &c." What is Shammaï's motive? He fears that the humidity of the napkin, which has become impure by contact with the cushion (on which one reclines), may in their turn render the hands impure. What is Hillel's motive? It is that, on principle one always supposes any liquids which come in contact with the hands are pure; or also, it is admitted that the hands are not so susceptible of impurity from contact with profane things,[2] but Shammaï holds a contrary opinion. That is explained according to the opinions of R. Simon b. Eliezer, or of R. Eleazar b. R. Zadok; the one says, in the name of R. Meir, that, through contact with profane objects, the hands become susceptible of only the first degree of impurity (transmittable in the second degree to the food), whilst by contact with the (sacred) oblations, they become impure in the second degree (transmittable in the third). We learn elsewhere[3] that profane meats which have been raised to a state of sacredness, are considered profane; R. Eleazar b. Zadoc considers them equal to the oblations, to the extent of becoming impure to the second degree, and even to the third degree, and so become unfit for sacred purposes (without, however, the owner being obliged to destroy them). We have learnt also:[4] "If a man rub himself with pure oil and subsequently become impure, and take a bath of purification, Shammaï says he becomes pure, although the oil still drip off of his body; Hillel says he remains impure as long as there is sufficient oil on his body to spread over a small member. Should the oil be impure from the commencement, the man remains impure as long as there is enough left on his body to spread over a little member, and according to Hillel, he remains impure as long as the hand, when applied to the body, becomes humid; or according to R. Juda, in the name of Hillel, he is impure as long as the hand thus rendered humid is sufficiently so as to moisten anything else. These several opinions of R. Hillel do not vary one with the other. For it has been said just now that the person remains impure as long as there is sufficient humidity on his body to moisten another object through contact with the hand, and here Hillel says, in this *Mishnâ*, that the napkin is put on the cushion, for fear of its communicating impurity, through being wet, to the food, although it take up no more room on the table than the width of the hand?

[2] See tr. *Yadaim*, ii. 4.

[3] *Mishna*, tr. *Taharôth* (of purities), ii. 8; Tosephta, section 1; B., tr. *Hoollin*, fol. 33 *b*. Cf. *Biccurim*, ii. 1, and tr. *Ḥaghiga*, ii. 5 (79 *b*).

[4] Mishna, tr. *Eduyoth*, iv. 6.

In the case mentioned above, was the reply, Hillel mentions this quantity as the limit, because it is in its natural state, whilst here it is imbibed by the napkin.

5. (4) Accordingly the Shammaites, they bless[5] the light, the food, the spices, and the distinction of the day. The Shammaites say, "Who created the light of fire;" but the Hillelites say, "Creator of the light of fire."[6]

6. Men must not bless light and spices of idolatrous Gentiles, nor light and spices of corpses, nor light and spices before an idol. They must not bless the light until they have enjoyed the light.

7. If one have eaten, and forgotten, and not blessed, the Shammaites say he must return to his place and bless; but the Hillelites say he may bless in the place where he recollects. How long is one obliged to bless? Until the food in his stomach be digested.

8. If wine come to the company, and there is but one goblet, the Shammaites say that one must bless the wine and then bless the food; but the Hillelites say that one must bless the food and then bless the wine. Men must answer "amen" when an Israelite blesses; but they must not answer "amen" when a Samaritan blesses, until the whole blessing be heard.[7]

R. Juda says: The Shammaites and Hillelites agree on this point, viz. that the blessing of the meal comes first and then the ceremony of separation. They only differ with regard to the relative order of the light and the spices; according to Shammaï the spices are blessed before the light, and according to Hillel it is the contrary. R. Aba and R. Juda say, in Rab's name, that we should adopt for a rule the pre-eminence of spices over the light. Shammaï says that the goblet of wine is carried in the right hand and the perfumed oil in the left; the wine is blessed first, and then the oil; according to Hillel the contrary is the case. A little of the oil is poured on to the servant's head, or if he be a man of learning a little is rubbed on the wall, for it is not proper that a learned man should be perfumed when he goes out (it is the custom of the libertines).

When Aba b. Ḥana and R. Hoona were eating together, R. Zeira got up and served them, carrying the oil and the wine in the same hand. What have you got in the other hand, asked b. Ḥana (that you hold these two objects in one hand)?

[5] On being seated at table, at nightfall, on Saturday night.

[6] On the colours of the light.

[7] For it is to be feared that his prayer may be addressed to an idol.

This remark irritated his father: Thou art not satisfied, said he, to be seated at your ease whilst being waited upon by a member of the family of priests, although Samuel has said that it is a sacrilege[8] to use the services of a priest (destined to God), and yet thou mockest at his acts; I order therefore that he sit down, and that thou get up to serve him. Where do we learn that it is a sacrilege to avail oneself of the services of a Cohanim? R. Aḥa answers, in Samuel's name, because it is written (Ezra viii. 28): *And I said unto them, Ye are holy unto the Lord; the vessels are holy also;* now, as it would be a sacrilege to empty these vessels for a profane purpose, so also is it with the priests.

Shammaï says one must say the formula: "Who created the fruit of the vine;" and Hillel says: "Who createst (in the present tense) the fruit of the vine;" why is not the same formula employed for this as for the light said on Saturday evening? The wine is renewed every year (and every time there is an actual new creation), but the fire is not renewed every moment (it exists always in principle, and it is only its creation which is recalled); for if the fire and the mixture of heterogeneous products were not created from the six first days of the creation, they at least entered into the plan of the creation. With regard to the heterogeneous products,[9] we find it in this verse (Genesis xxxvi. 24): *These are the children of Zibeon, both Ajah and Anah; this was that Anah that found the mules in the wilderness.* What does the word *Yémim* (mule) signify? R. Juda b. Simon says[1] that it indicates wild animals; the Rabbis say that it is the produce of a horse and a female ass. According to R. Juda these are the distinctive signs; if the ears are short it is the offspring of a mare and an ass; if they are long, it is born from a female ass and a horse. R. Mena recommended the young men of the house of the Naci (prince) in buying mules to choose those having short ears, being the offspring of a mare and an ass. What did Zibeon and Ajah do? They put a female ass and a stallion together, which produced the mule. The Most High said to them: You have brought into the world a bad object, I will do the same. What did He do? He brought a serpent (ἔχιδνα) and a saurian together, which gave birth to the asp. Now, a man has never been known to recover from the bite of an asp or of a mad dog, or of the kick of a mule, especially if it be white. This determines the origin of heterogeneous mixtures; but why say that fire was not created at the time of the creation of the universe? R. Levi replies, in R. Nezira's name: The light which was created at the beginning served for thirty-six consecutive hours, twelve hours on Friday, twelve hours the next night, and twelve hours on Saturday; thanks to it the first man was able to examine the earth from end to end. When, during the night of Friday to Saturday the light

[8] See *Mekhilta*, section *Mishpatim*, ch. ii.; *Oraḥ Ḥayim*, § 98.

[9] *Bereshith Rabba*, section 82; B., tr. *Pesahim*, fol. 24 *a*.

[1] See J., tr. *Kilaim*, viii. 3.

did not cease to shine, the whole universe commenced to sing songs of joy, as it is written (Job xxxvii. 3): *He directed it under the whole heaven, and His lightning unto the ends of the earth.* As soon as Saturday's work was completed darkness began to predominate. Adam was afraid and said: Behold, perhaps the moment when will be fulfilled the biblical prediction, according to which I will tread upon the serpent's head, and it will bite my heel (Genesis iii. 15), and he cried out (Ps. cxxxix. 11): *Surely the darkness shall cover me.* At this moment, says R. Levi, God caused him to touch two bricks, which he knocked together, and light sprang out, as it is written (ibid.): *Even the night shall be light about me,* and he blessed God, saying: "Be praised He who createst the light of fire." This is why, says Samuel, light is still blessed on Saturday evening, in remembrance of this creation. R. Hoona says, in the name of R. Abahoo or of R. Johanan, that this blessing is also uttered after *Kippur,* for light has ceased to shine for the whole day.[2]

"Men must not bless light and spices of idolatrous Gentiles." R. Jacob taught, in the presence of R. Jeremiah, that the blessing may be said in this case. What! he contests the writings of the Mishna? The reply is, that it applies to the case in which a man burns spices in front of his shop as an advertisement. The blessing may be said on seeing a lantern left burning (from the night before). In the same manner, if one see light on anybody's knee, or in a lantern, or in a transparent glass, *speculare,* if one see a (flickering) flame without profiting of the light, or if the contrary be the case (through separation), the blessing may not be made for this until all the conditions are fulfilled. Five propositions have been made relative to coal,[3] and five concerning flame: 1st. If one make use of coal which has been used for burning the sacrifice, it is a sacrilege; but it is not a sacrilege to see the flame, of which, however, one must not profit; 2nd. Coals, having been used for idols, are forbidden, but a man may light himself by their flames; 3. If a man make a vow not to profit at all by his neighbour he may not profit by his fuel, but may profit of the light of it; 4. It is forbidden (on festivals) to carry fuel on the public roads, but it is not forbidden to direct the flame from them on to the public way; 5. The Saturday evening's blessing is to be made over a flame, but not over live coals. R. Ḥiya b. Asha says, in Rab's name, that the blessing may even be said over coals, if they are flaming. R. Yoḥanan, of Karcion, says, in the name of R. Naḥoom b. Simaï, that it applies to those which burn after the air has ejected them from the stove.[4] We have been taught that, whether an idolator has lit his light at that of a Hebrew, or *vice versâ,* the Saturday evening's[5] blessing may be said. Shall we conclude from this that if

[2] For it is forbidden to light anything on this day.

[3] See J., tr. *Beza,* v. 4; B., ibid. f. 39 *a*; Tossefta, ch. 4.

[4] In this case one may use the fuel of an idolator.

[5] On seeing it. B., the same treatise, fol. 53 *a*.

an idolator has lit his light at that of another idolator, one may also in this case bless this light? No, it is forbidden.

R. Abahoo says, in the name of R. Yoḥanan: If one sees a light in a narrow street entirely inhabited by idolators, and only one Israelite live there, the light may be blessed on the supposition that it belongs to the Israelite. The same author says that the blessing is not made on the spices of Friday evening at Tiberias, nor it is said on the spices of Saturday evening at Sephoris, nor on the spices which have been in the latter town since Thursday evening, because they have been prepared with another object in view (not to serve as perfumes, but for embalming), neither may it be said on the lighter spices which have been used in honour of the dead. R. Ezekia and R. Jacob b. Aḥa say, in the name of R. Yosse b. Ḥanina, that this last rule only applies to things placed above the bed on which the dead body is placed; but the things in front of it may be used to say the blessing over, for he says that they are put there for the living. It is also said that neither the light nor the spices of the idolators are blessed. Is not this a repetition of the injunction not to bless the objects of the idolators? It may be replied that, in this second case it refers to the idols set up by Israelites.[6]

"They must not bless the light until they have enjoyed the light." R. Zeira b. R. Abahoo interprets thus the verse (Genesis i. 4): It is written, *God saw that the light was good, and God divided*[7] *the light from the darkness.* R. Berakhia says that, according to the interpretation of two great personages, R. Yoḥanan and R. Simon b. Levi, a real distinction is signified. R. Juda b. R. Simon says that he separated (adopted) heaven for himself, and the Rabbis say that he destined it for the just in the future life. What does this resemble? It is like a king who has two generals (strategus), both of whom wish to be on day service, and so the king limits the services of one to the day and of the other to the night. And so it is written: *And God called the light Day, and the darkness He called Night* (ibid.). This is, says R. Yoḥanan, what God said to Job (xxxviii. 12): *Hast thou commanded the morning since thy days; and caused the dayspring to know his place?* That is to say: Knowest thou the origin of the light? the 6 days of the creation. This, says R. Tanḥooma, is the reason for the formula, "He forms the light, creates darkness, and makes peace" (Isaiah xlv. 7). God, in appearing, made peace between them.

It is said that a man does not say the blessing unless he enjoys the light. Rab says: The light must be suited to the man (יאותו), and Samuel says that it must be timely.[8] The former bases the sense which he adopts on the verse

[6] And who eventually repent themselves.

[7] This is an allusion to the *Habdalá* ceremony.

[8] This is a play upon words between the two terms, which read the same, but have a different meaning. See J., tr. *Erubin*, chap. v. § 1; tr. *'Aboda zara*, i. 2.

(Genesis xxxiv. 15): *But in this we will consent* (נאות) *unto you, if ye will, &c.* The latter bases himself on this (Isaiah L. 4): *that I should know how to speak a word in season* (לעות) *to him that is weary.* In the same manner, with regard to the question of enlarging the towns, Rab says that one must read *Meabdin*, and Samuel says to read *Me'abrin*. According to the first, it means that one adds as it were a member to the town, and according to the second, that one makes it fruitful, like a woman with child.[a] Again, in one of *'Aboda Zara's* Mishnas, according to Rab this expression is in reference to the testimony of strangers,[1] and, according to Samuel, to their festivals (unfortunate for us). The second bases himself on this verse (Deut. xxxii. 35): *for the day of their (festival or) calamity is at hand;* and the former takes his stand on this (Isaiah xliv. 9): *and they are their own witnesses; they see not, nor know, that they may be ashamed.* How does Samuel explain the verse on which Ṛab bases his opinion? He says that these idols will be a cause of shame in the future, i.e. on the day of judgment, to those who made them. One may not bless the light, says R. Juda in Samuel's name, unless women be able to weave by it; according to R. Yoḥanan, one must be able by its light to distinguish between the contents of a glass and the saucepan, or, according to R. Ḥanina, between one piece of money and another. R. Oshia teaches that one may say the blessing even in a room (triclinium) of ten cubits in length by ten cubits in breadth, and at a great distance from the light. R. Zeira used to go close to the light. Why, said his disciples unto him, dost thou improve upon the opinion of R. Oshia, who authorizes us to say the blessing at a distance? R. Yustes b. Shoonam replied, That depends on the 2 ways of interpreting this opinion, of which the one interpretation is conformable to Shammaï and the other to Hillel. The 1st, according to Shammaï, says that if a man had forgotten somewhere a bag of pearls and precious stones he would certainly return to fetch it; therefore a man must also return and draw near for divine service. The 2nd says, conformably to Hillel, that a man need not inconvenience himself any more for this, than for any other prayer, which he may, in case of need, say on the top of a tree or at the bottom of a pit (as we have seen above).

"How long is one obliged to bless? &c." R. Ḥiya replies, in Samuel's name: as long as one is thirsty after the meal (this is the digestion). R. Yoḥanan says: until one feels hungry again.

"If wine come to the company, &c. (§ 8) one must bless the wine after the thanksgiving, according to Hillel." That is, says R. Aba, because this short blessing might in the ordinary way be forgotten; but in this manner there is no fear of it being forgotten, the cup of wine having to serve several purposes at the same time.

[a] Again a play upon words; B., tr. *Erubin*, fol. 53 *a*; tr. *'Aboda Zara*, fol. 2 *a*.

[1] By this is meant the idolators, that the Talmud calls in abbreviation: 'Akoom.

"One must not answer *amen* (§ 9) when a Samaritan blesses until the whole blessing be heard." It seems, therefore, that they answer *amen* after the prayer of an Israelite, even if they have not heard him. Is not this contrary to what has been taught: that the hearing without the answer *amen* counts as an accomplished duty, but that the reverse is not sufficient? Ḥiya, son of Rab, replies that the Mishna refers to the case in which one has not eaten the equivalent of an olive (therefore it is not sufficient to answer *amen* without having heard all, because the blessing is not obligatory). We have just been taught that the hearing of it without the response *amen* is admitted to be an accomplishment of the duty, but that in the reverse case it is not so. Rab says, in Aba bar-Ḥana's name, or Aba bar-Ḥana says, in Rab's name, that one must at least have replied to the heads of the chapters of the prayers.[2] What are these commencements? asked R. Zeira. *Praise ye the Lord. Praise ye the name of the Lord; praise Him, O ye servants of the Lord* (Ps. cxxxv. 1). R. Ḥiya b. Aba was asked: How is it known that the hearing of a prayer, without answering *amen*, is considered to be a duty fulfilled? It is, was the reply, because we see important Rabbis act thus: when they are in public some of them commence the verse and the others continue it. All of them have accomplished their duty.

R. Oshia teaches that a man may answer *amen*, to the grace after meals, even if he has not eaten anything; but he must not say the formula, "Let us bless Him through whom we have eaten," if he has not taken part in the repast. We are taught that one must not answer *amen* too late (which would seem like an orphan *amen*, as it were), nor too quickly (before the end), nor brokenly, or in swallowing the letters. B. Azaï says that he who answers too late will have orphan children; if he answers too quickly, his life will be shortened; if he says a furtive *amen*, his soul will be cut off; if he says it opportunely, his years will be happy and prolonged. What is meant by an orphan *amen?* That which has been said after a blessing without knowing what one says, or unthinkingly. One answers *amen*,[3] even when one hears a non-Israelite bless the name of the Lord. R. Tanhooma says that if a pagan bless you, you must answer *amen*, in conformity with the verse (Deut. vii. 14): *Thou shalt be blessed above all people.* A pagan once met R. Ismael and blessed him. What thou sayest, replied R. Ismael, has already been written;[4] that is to say, it is useless that I reply to you. Another met him and cursed him. Ismael replied again that his words were already written (ibid.). What does that mean? asked his disciples. Thou makest the same reply to the one as to the other? Verily, replied he, it is what is written

[2] J., tr. *Succa*, iii. 12; tr. *Meghilla*, i. 11.
[3] See *Revue des Etudes juives*, vi. 73.
[4] At the preceding verse.

(Genesis xxvii. 29): *Cursed be every one that curseth thee, and blessed be he that blesseth thee.*

CHAPTER IX.

1. He who sees a place where signs were wrought for Israel, says, "Blessed be He who wrought signs for our fathers in this place;" for a place where idolatry has been rooted out, says, "Blessed be He who hath rooted idolatry out of our land."

The miracles referred to in the Mishna must be those affecting the whole of Israel; but if it be a case of a miracle affecting only one particular person, his descendants only may say the blessing. Ought we to say it on seeing the effects of the miracles which happened to our parents, or to our master, or to a distinguished man, like unto Joab, son of Serooya, and to his companions,[1] or to a man who has adored God at the risk of his life, as did Ḥanania, Michael, and Azaria,[2] or for the miracles which have happened to certain tribes? The solution of this question depends upon the possibility of knowing whether an isolated tribe constitutes a community or not: according to the first opinion, a man must bless for isolated miracles; and according to the second opinion, he is exempted. At the sight of Babylon a man must recite five blessings,[3] viz.: on seeing the Euphrates this formula, "Blessed be the author of creation;" on seeing the statue of Mercury, a man always says: "Blessed be He who is long-suffering" (who has the patience to let them exist); on seeing the ruins of Nebuchadnezzar's palace, say: "Blessed be He who has destroyed the palace of this impious man;" on seeing the site of the furnace in which Ḥanania, Michael, and Azaria were thrown, or the lions' den in which Daniel was put, say: "Blessed be He who has performed miracles in favour of our ancestors here." If a man see the place (now a desert) from whence earth was taken to sprinkle on animals (which forms a sort of baptism), he says: "Blessed be He who speaks and acts, who commands, and keeps His promises" (to destroy idolatry); according to others, on seeing Babylon this verse is said (Isaiah xiv. 23): *and I will sweep it with the besom of destruction.*

R. Zeira and R. Juda say, in Rab's name: No blessing is valid if it does not contain the recognition of the divine royalty. Behold the reason, according to R. Tanḥooma: it is written (Psalm cxlv. 1): *I will extol Thee, my God, O King.*

[1] See 1 Samuel xxvi. 6.
[2] Daniel i. 6 and the following.
[3] B., the same treatise, fol. 57 *b.*

Rab says: a man must address God as *Thou* (in the second person), and Samuel says that it is not necessary. When R. Yoḥanan and R. Jonathan went to re-establish peace in the centre of a community in the south,[4] they stopped in a certain town, where they heard the officiating minister say: "O Lord, great, strong, terrible, powerful, valiant." They silenced him, saying that one must not modify the formulas of blessings established by the wise men. R. Hoona explains, in the name of Rab, the following verse (Job xxxvii. 23): *we cannot find Him out: He is excellent in power;* that is to say, that we cannot explain what is the force and power of the Lord. R. Aba also explains, in R. Abahoo's and in R. Yoḥanan's name, these words (Job xxxvii. 20): *Shall it be told Him that I speak? If a man speak, surely he shall be swallowed up;* that is to say, if a man were to attempt to explain completely the qualities of the Lord, he would deserve to be swallowed up by the earth. R. Samuel bar-Nahman recalls the verse (Ps. cvi. 2), *Who can utter the mighty acts of the Lord?* neither I nor my companions. R. Aboon says: Who can praise the greatness of God? Jacob of the village of Nebooria, in Tyr, interpreted the words: *Praise waiteth for Thee* (in silence), *O God, in Zion* (ib. lxv. 2). The best of medicaments consist in being silent,[5] like a pearl, which is inestimable, τιμή, loses in value the more it is extolled.

We have learnt that it is wise to commence and end the blessings, when the formula admits of it, with the tetragramme (Lord); but it would be absurd (and contrary to established rules) to begin and end them by the word EL, *God;* it is an intermediary measure[6] to commence with the term God and finish with the term Lord; but the reverse might pass for heresy (and make it supposed that God is not the eternal Lord). And indeed, some bad men asked R. Samlaï:[7] "How many Gods[8] created the universe?" What are you asking me? replied he; you have only to consult the words of Adam, the first man: *Ask now of the days that are past,* it is written; *which were before thee, since the day that God created* (and not in the plural) *man upon the earth* (Deut. iv. 32). But, replied they, "Is it not written, following the textual order of the words (Genesis i. 1): *the beginning*[9] *created God?*" "The verb, replied he, is not in the plural,

[4] B., tr. *Meghilla*, fol. 25 *a*; Midrash on Psalm xix.

[5] See B., tr. *Meghilla*, fol. 18 *a*, and the parallels of the Midrash, as also the analogous modern proverbs, cited by M. Schuhl, *Sentences*, p. 403.

[6] That is to say, the medium expression to be chosen. Lattes, in *Giunte al Lessico Talmudico*, p. 41, n. 3, translates: "è un metodo alieno" (eretico).

[7] *Bereshith Rabba*, viii.; *Debarim Rabba*, ii. A trace of Christian apology may be seen here, says Mr. Graetz, *Septuaginta im Talmud*, in *Monatschrift*, 1845, ii. 434.

[8] It is a sort of argument against the word *Elohim*, "God," which has the plural form and is called by grammarians *plurale majestatis*.

[9] This is a repetition of the preceding observation. They say: the plural is used from the beginning of the Bible to designate God.

because the subject is in reality in the singular." In general, says R. Samlaï, every time that the unbelieving have sought to contest the biblical text, they have found immediately afterwards the refutation of their assertions. They also asked him this: "How is it, according to the doctrine of the unity of God, that the Bible says (Genesis i. 26): *Let us make man in our image,* after our likeness? It is written, replied he: *God* (in the singular number) *created man in His own image.*[1] This reply, answered his disciples, is but a subterfuge amongst ourselves; what answer would you make to us if we asked the same question? In the beginning, replied he, Adam was created from earth and Eve from Adam; from that moment, the propagation of the human race was continued according to many images and likenesses; for man cannot do without woman, or woman without man, and both require the aid of the Divinity." The unbelievers asked again: How is it that, according to your doctrines, it is written (Joshua xxii. 22): *The Lord God of gods, He knoweth* (does not this indicate that there are several divinities)? In spite of that, replied he, the verb is employed in the singular number (because it treats of a single God). Master, said his disciples, that reply is a forced one; what would you answer to us? These 3 expressions, replied he, are the attributes of a single name, as people say indifferently, Cæsar, Augustus, or Emperor, βασιλεύς.[2] He was again asked: How is it that it is written (Psalm l. 1): *The mighty God, even the Lord, hath spoken and called the earth?* The verbs, here also, are in the singular number, replied he; and to his disciples, who made the same observation to him, he added that they are also attributes of the same name, as people say: labourer, mason, or architect, ἀρχιτέκτων. He was further asked: How is it that it is written: *He is a holy God* (in the original text the substantive and adjective are in the plural number)? No matter, replied he, the verb is in the singular number, as it is said elsewhere (Exodus xx. 5): *For I the Lord thy God am a jealous God* (singular). To his disciples, who made the same observation, R. Isaac replied that in this verse the plural sign is used to show that several degrees of holiness are meant. Indeed, says R. Judan in R. Aḥa's name, everything regarding God is holy,[3] His footsteps, His word, His seat, the movement of His arms; the Lord is terrible and majestic by His holiness. A verse may be found in support of each of these degrees. For the footsteps (Ps. lxxvii. 14): *Thy way, O God, is in the sanctuary.* His ways are holy (ib. lxviii. 24): *The goings of my God, my King, in the sanctuary.* He sitteth in holiness (ib. xlvii. 9): *God sitteth upon the throne of His holiness.* He speaketh in holiness (ib. cviii. 8): *God hath spoken in His holiness.* He lifteth His arm in holiness (Isaiah lii. 10): *The Lord hath made bare His holy arm.* He is

[1] The plural is not used because only one God is in question.

[2] See *Bereshith Rabba,* chap. xciv.; *Wayyiqra Rabba,* section *Beḥuqothai,* on Leviticus xxvi.

[3] See *Shoḥar tob,* chap. ii.

strong and terrible by His holiness (Exodus xv. 11): ***Who is like Thee, glorious in holiness, fearful in praise, &c.?***

He was also asked: Why is it written (Deut. iv. 7): ***For what nation is there so great, who hath God so nigh unto them?*** (Why is the word ***nigh*** in the plural?) The pronouns, he replied, are in the singular number to show that only one God is meant; and to his disciples, who asked him the same question, he added that the plural adjective *near* refers to diverse objects and causes of nearness. And so says R. Pinehas, in R. Juda b. Simon's name, an idol even when it appears near[4] to us is far from us. It is to the false God that the prophet alludes when he says: *They bear him upon the shoulder, they carry him, and set him in his place, and he standeth; from his place shall he not remove; yea, one shall cry unto him, yet shall he not answer nor save him out of his trouble* (Isaiah xlvi. 7); in other terms: The idol in the house lets you cry and die without hearing you or succouring you; but although the Lord seems far, there is nothing nearer than He. R. Levi reminds us on this subject that from earth to heaven is a journey of 500 years,[5] and the like between one heaven and another, and also the same to traverse heaven itself. R. Berakhia and R. Ḥelbo say, in R. Aba Semooka's name, that even the soles of the feet of the celestial animals or angels have also a journey of 515 miles in size. How do we know this? Because it is written (Ezekiel i. 7), speaking of them: *And their feet were straight*, ישרה.[6] We see, in fine, the distance between the celestial home and the earth. And yet, let a man enter the synagogue, let him stand aside, and pray in a low voice, the Almighty immediately gives ear to his invocation, as it is written (1 Samuel i. 13): *Now Hannah, she spake in her heart, only her lips moved; but her voice was not heard,* and yet God answered her prayers. He does the same towards all creatures, as it is written (Psalm cii. 1): *Prayer of the afflicted, when he is overwhelmed and poureth out his complaint before the Lord,* as a man speaks in the ear of his neighbour who hears him.

Can one imagine a God nearer to us, and who for every one of His creatures is ready to approach his ear to their mouths?

R. Judan, in R. Isaac's name, has made hereon four similitudes: To a man, for example, who has a friend, one comes to tell him: Thy son is taken; I will be security for him, says the protector (patronus), to save him. But if he has already been judged, and is going to be hanged, no one can save him. With the Lord it was quite otherwise; He saved Moses from Pharaoh's sword, as it is written (Exodus xviii. 4): *And delivered me from the sword of Pharaoh.* R. Janaï asked himself: How can it be said (ibid. ii. 15): *But Moses fled from the face of Pharaoh?* Can a man escape from the power of a king? At the moment that the king, after having had Moses seized, gave the order to cut off his head, the

[4] *Debarim Rabba*, chap. ii. [5] See chapter i. 1, above.

[6] The numerical values of these 4 letters give 515.

blade rebounded from Moses' neck and broke; it is to this that the following verse alludes (Cant. vii. 5): *Thy neck is as a tower of ivory;* it is Moses' neck that is meant. R. Abiatar thinks that the sword killed the executioner in the rebound, *Quæstionarius.*[7] That is why it is written: *He saved me from the sword of Pharaoh;* I was saved, and the executioner perished. R. Berakhia reminds us hereon of the verse (Ps. xxxvii. 32): *The wicked watcheth the righteous and seeketh to slay him;* and R. Aboon of this one (Prov. xi. 8): *The righteous is delivered out of trouble, and the wicked cometh in his stead.* According to Bar-Kapara, Moses escaped in another way. An angel descended from heaven and took the form of Moses, who thus escaped whilst they seized the angel. According to R. Josuah b. Levi, at the moment that Moses fled before Pharaoh all Pharaoh's soldiers, ὄχλος, became deaf, dumb, or blind. The king, addressing himself to those who were dumb, asked them where Moses was, and they could not reply; he spoke to the deaf ones, and they did not hear him; and then to the blind, and they did not see him. So also God had said to Moses (Exodus iv. 11): *Who hath made man's mouth? or who maketh the dumb, or deaf, or the seeing, or the blind? have not I the Lord,* that is to say, that as I have succoured you when thou wast in danger, shall I not assist thee again to deliver Israel? That is why it is written (Deut. iv. 7): *As the Lord our God is in all things that we call upon Him for.* R. Judan, in the name of R. Isaac, makes the following comparison thereon: If a man have a friend, and one say to him: "Thy son is taken prisoner," this friend might well try to defend him; he can do nothing if the son has already been condemned to be thrown in the water; but the Lord saved Jonas even from the whale's belly; as it is written (Jonas ii. 11): *And the Lord spake unto the fish and it vomited out Jonah upon the dry land.* It would be the same were a mortal to wish to save his friend from the fire; but the Lord saved Ḥanania, Michael, and Azaria from the fiery furnace. So it is written (Daniel iii. 28): *Then Nebuchadnezzar spake and said, Blessed be the God of Shadrach, Meshach, and Abed-nego* (the Chaldean names of the three young Israelites). And again a man cannot save him who is thrown to wild beasts; but the Lord saved Daniel from the lions' den, as it is written (Daniel vi. 23): *My God hath sent His angel,* and hath shut the lions' mouths. R. Judan says that a man, if he have a friend, and trouble come upon him, his friend does not come to him suddenly; but the friend will stand at his door, will call his servant, or one of his family, and will send him word that he is waiting outside; for it is still doubtful whether they will let him in or leave him at the door. But as regards God, it is not so: if trouble come to a man, he must not invoke either Michael or Gabriel, but God, who will hear him, even as it is written (Joel iii. 5): *Whoever shall call on the name of the Lord shall be delivered.*

R. Pineḥas recounts that Rab coming out of the warm baths of Tiberiade,

[7] See tr. *'Aboda Zara*, iii. 1 (fol. 42 c); *Medr. Hazith*, chap. vii.; *Shoḥar tob*, chap. iv.; *Mekhilta*, section *Yithro*, chap. i.

happened to meet some Romans, who asked him who he was. I am of Vespasian's suite, replied he. After that reply they let him go. In the evening they came to the governor himself, and said to him: Wilt thou much longer sustain these Jews? Why? asked he. Because, said they, we met a Jew of whom we asked his name, and he tried to pass himself off as one of your people. And what gift did you make him? asked the governor. Should we have recompensed him? said they; was it not enough to have let him go? You have at least done well not to do him harm; for if, being dependent on man, he has been saved, the more so would he have been saved if (being arrested) he had depended on God alone, as it is written: *Whoever shall call on the name of the Lord shall be delivered.* R. Alexandre recounts that an Archontus named Alexandros was judging a brigand: Thy name? asked the judge. Alexandros, replied the accused. At this name the judge had him released. If this man was saved because he had the same name as his judge, much more so would he be saved in the name of the Lord,[8] in virtue of the verse quoted above.

R. Pinebas added 2 interpretations to this, 1st in R. Zeira's name, 2nd in R. Tanhoom b. Ḥanilaï's name. In the first place, he says, if the man have a defender and he fatigue him by his impórtunities, he would complain of it; but with God it is not so; however, a man beset Him with prayers, they are all heard, as it is written (Ps. lv. 23): *Cast thy burden upon the Lord, and He shall sustain thee.* The Rabbi then said in the name of the second: If a man, having a friend, be attacked by his enemies and taken at his friend's door, before he would have time to call for help or receive aid, the sword would have passed over his head and he would be killed; but the Lord saved Jehoshaphat from the sword of Aram, for it is written (2 Chronicles xviii. 31): *But Jehoshaphat cried out, and the Lord helped him;* these expressions show that he was very near having his head cut off.

R. Zeira b. R. Abahoo,[9] or the latter in the name of R. Eliezer, interprets the following verse (Ps. cxlvi. 5): *Happy is he that hath the God of Jacob for his help;* and what comes after? *Which made heaven and earth.* Now, what relation is there between the two ideas? This is it: A king may make a friend of the governor of one province (ἐπαρχία) and not of another; and, be he the universal monarch (κοσμοκράτωρ), his power is limited to the bounds of the earth, and he does not dominate the seas. But the Lord is the sovereign, as well of the sea as of the land; on the sea He saves men from death by water, and on land, from fire. Thus He saved Moses from the sword of Pharaoh; Jonah from the whale's belly; Ḥanania, Michael, and Azaria from the fiery furnace, and Daniel from the lions' claws. And so it is written (ibid. 6): *Which made heaven and earth, the sea, and all that therein is.* R. Tanhooma relates that a Jew boy was once on board of a

[8] This name (*el*) is found in the first syllable of Alexander.
[9] See J., tr. *'Aboda Zara,* iii. 1.

ship filled with foreigners, and which was making sail for the great sea (Mediterranean). A great tempest arose, and every one, seized with fear, took his idol in his hand and invoked it; but it was in vain. Seeing this, they said to the young lad: My son, get up, and invoke thy God; for we have learnt that He hears you when you pray to Him, and that He is all-powerful. The child immediately arose, and prayed with so much fervour that God heard him favourably. The sea became calm and they were able to disembark. When on land each one went to buy what he required, and the young man was asked whether he wanted anything. What can you find, said he, in those miserable inns? We can understand, they replied, that, for thee, this inn is little worthy, but not so for the other passengers; for among those who are here, some have their idols at Babylon, some at Rome, and the others have them even with them, but in vain; thou, wherever thou goest, thy God accompanies thee. That is why it is written (Deut. iv. 7): *For who hath God so nigh unto them, as the Lord our God is in all things that we call upon Him for.* R. Simon ben-Lakish says, that a man only recognizes his friends if they are rich, and that he denies them if they are poor; but the Lord acts not thus. The Israelites, be they of the lowest degree, God still calls them His friends and His brothers. R. Aboon, R. Aḥa, and R. Simon b. Lakish say, that a man only recognizes his relative if he is a learned man (philosophus); in which case he says that such a one is his relative; but God calls all the Israelites His relatives; as it is written (Ps. cxlviii. 14): *He also exalteth the horn of His people.*

"One blesses the place where idols have been rooted out." The Mishna speaks of the suppression of idols in all Palestine; but if it be a case of only partial rooting out, say the formula, "Be blessed He who has rooted out the idols from this place." If they have only been transported from one place to another, and one see their new position, say: "Blessed be the long-suffering;" on seeing the place where there are no more left, say: "Blessed be He who has rooted out idolatry from this place; let it please thee, O Lord God and God of our forefathers, as Thou hast rooted out idolatry from this place, to root it out from everywhere, to turn to Thee the hearts of those who adore the false gods."[1] Does not this formula of prayer prove that one must pray for their conversion? R. Ismael b. Gamaliel says that this formula is also to be recited outside of the Holy Land.

R. Yoḥanan interprets the following verse (Eccles. ix. 4): *For to him that is joined to all the living there is hope,* &c.; that is to say that man does not lose all hope until after death;[2] for when the wicked dies, all is over with him (because he does not believe in the immortality of the soul). R. Judah taught 3 things

[1] It is therefore proved that one must pray also for the conversion of all idolators, and not only for the renegade Jews. See *Sefer Hassidim*, No. 882.

[2] See Rabba on Ecclesiastes, chap. ii.; on Ruth, chap. ii.

that a man should say every day: "Blessed be God; 1, for not creating me a pagan; 2, nor foolish; 3, nor woman."[3] He should thank God for not having been created a pagan, for he would be little esteemed, according to this verse (Isaiah xl. 17): *All nations before him are as nothing;* for not being a fool, because the fool feels no fear of sin; and finally, for not being a woman, because they are not subject to all the precepts of religion. R. Aḥa interprets the preceding verse of Ecclesiastes in another manner: "Even those, said he, who have contributed to the destruction of Jerusalem, have still some hope of not being condemned to eternal damnation; now, they cannot approach paradise, for they have turned their hand against the Temple; and yet they are not completely lost, for they have repented of their work of destruction." It is to these that the following words apply (Jeremiah li. 39): *That they may rejoice, and sleep a perpetual sleep, and not wake,* &c. The Cesarean Rabbis also say,[4] that the emissaries of the oppressors of Judea, and the armies of Nebuchadnezzar, will neither live nor be judged (for their acts were ordered by their masters, who are alone responsible), still in virtue of the above verse.

When a man passes before a temple of idols, he says these words (Proverbs xv. 25): *The Lord will destroy the house of the proud,* &c. R. Yosse b. R. Aboon says, in the name of R. Levi, that if a man see them offering up incense, he recalls the law of the Pentateuch (Exodus xxii. 20): *He that sacrificeth unto any god, save unto the Lord only, he shall be utterly destroyed.* If one see a nigger, a red-skin, an individual startlingly white (*albino*), λευκός, a giant, or a dwarf (*nanus*), he says: "Blessed be He who changes creatures;" or seeing a cripple, a blind man, or a leper, say: "Blessed be the just judge." This rule, however, only applies to those who were born sound, and who have been crippled by an accident; but if they have been so since their birth, say: "Blessed be He who deforms creatures." On seeing fine trees, or even fine men, say: "Blessed be He who has made such beautiful creatures on the earth."

R. Gamaliel once pronounced[5] the formula of blessing on seeing a very pretty pagan woman. Is it possible? cried the doctors. Has not R. Zeira said in R. Yosse b. R. Ḥanina's name, and R. Aba, or R. Ḥiya, in R. Yoḥanan's name, that one must not attribute the gift of beauty to pagans? Is it not written (Deut. vii. 3): *Neither shalt thou make marriages*[6] *with them?* So he did not cry out, ἀβάσκαντα (in admiration of her beauty), but he said: "Blessed be the Lord for having created beautiful things on this earth!" which is what the Rabbi

[3] The Talmud does not reproach women with not fulfilling their duties so well as the men; it states that there are some duties which they are not obliged to observe.

[4] Cf. tr., *Shebiith*, iv. at the end.

[5] See J., tr. *'Aboda Zara*, i. 9.

[6] The Talmud takes, as it often does, the simple sense away from the word, in order to apply the word to a particular question.

would also have said for a fine camel, or a horse, or a donkey. But yet, returned the others, was it R. Gamaliel's custom to look at women? It is to be supposed that he met this one suddenly, face to face, in a narrow and winding path, *σπεῖρα*, and thus looked at her involuntarily. On hearing the cock crow, say: "Blessed be he who hath knowledge of mysteries." Thus the following verse expresses it (Job xxxviii. 36): *Who hath put wisdom*[7] *in the inward parts.*

R. Levi says that in Arabia the goat is called *yoobla;* so also is it used in this verse (Exodus xix. 13): *When the trumpet soundeth long,* &c. In Africa, they call a woman in her courses, *galmooda;*[8] it is the term used in the verse (Isaiah xlix. 21): *I have lost my children, and am desolate.* At Rome, the cock is called *sechwi;*[9] that is why it is used in this verse (Job xxxviii. 36): *Who hath given understanding to the heart* (cock). On seeing troops, *ὄχλοι*, say: "Blessed be He who is wise in mysteries" (without us understanding them); for, in the same manner as their faces do not resemble each others, so also their ideas are not similar. When Ben Zoma saw some troops at Jerusalem, he said: "Blessed be He who has created all these men to defend us." The same Rabbi also said: "How hard the first man must have worked before being able to eat a piece of bread! he had to till the ground, sow, pluck out the weeds, dig holes to receive the rains, reap the corn, bind it into sheaths, thresh it, winnow it, select it, grind it, dry it, knead it with water, bake it, and then only eat it; whilst I, as soon as I get up in the morning, I find it all ready for me. See what trouble Adam must have had to clothe himself! He had to shear the sheep, bleach the wool, stretch it, dye it, spin it, weave it, wash it, he sewed the pieces of cloth together, and at last clothed himself; whilst I, on getting up in the morning, find it all ready. How many workmen get up early and retire to rest late on account of their work; whilst I find everything to my hand in the morning." Ben Zoma also said: A bad guest arriving at a certain house, says to himself: I have hardly been any expense to the master of this house, neither for drink or food: I have eaten a morsel of bread and drunk a glass of wine, but all the trouble he took was only on account of his wife and children." A good guest, on the other hand, says: "Blessed be the master of this house, and may his name be held in good repute; what wines he has presented to me, what a number of dishes he has offered me, what trouble he has given himself! And all this he has done for me alone," as it is written (Job xxxvi. 24): *Remember that thou magnify His work, which men behold.*

2. On comets, earthquakes, lightnings, thunder, and tempests, say: "Blessed be He whose strength and might fill the world."

[7] That is to say, one does not expect to find it there.
[8] See *Bereshith Rabba*, chap. xxxi.; *Bamidbar Rabba*, chap. xxi.
[9] B., *Rosh-Hashana*, fol. 26 *a*. It is perhaps: "In Idumea."

On mountains, hills, seas, rivers, and deserts, say, "Blessed be He who made the creation." R. Judah says when a man sees the great sea he is to say, "Blessed be He who made the great sea." When he sees it at intervals of time, say: "Blessed be He who made the creation."

3. On rains and on good news, say, "Blessed be He who is good and beneficient." On bad news, say, 'Blessed be the true Judge."

Bar-Kapara says that for earthquakes they fast and sound the *Shofar* (horn). Samuel says[1] that if a comet appeared in the Zodiacal sign *Orion* the world would perish (by the shock). But we have seen this happen, was the objection made to Samuel. It is impossible, replied he;. the comet must have passed a little above or a little below the sign, without traversing it; for, said Samuel, I am as familiar with the vault of heaven as with the streets of Nehardea, my native town, only I do not know where the seat of the comet is. But did Samuel ascend to the heavens that he should know them so well? No, he only learnt the description of them, according to this verse (Job xxxviii. 37): *Who can number the clouds in wisdom?*

Elias (of happy memory) asked R. Nehoraï (Lucius): Why do earthquakes come unto this world? On account of the sin, replied he, which people sometimes commit in not taking from the fruits of the earth the oblations and tithes.[2] For it is written (Deut. xi. 12): *The eyes of the Lord thy God are always upon it;* and it is written elsewhere (Ps. civ. 32): *He looketh upon the earth and it trembleth; He toucheth the hills and they smoke*. How can these two verses agree? In the following manner: When Israel accomplishes God's will and takes off from the fruits of the earth the tithes due to the priests, to the Levites, and to the poor God looks favourably upon the earth, and it is not in danger; but in the contrary case the Divine look makes the earth to tremble. Certainly, my son, replied they; this explanation is very reasonable. But this is the real sense: When God looks upon the earth, and He sees the theatres and circuses (theatrum and circenses) seated in security, whilst the sanctuary is in ruins.[3] He threatens (ἀπειδῶν) the earth with destruction, as indicated by these words (Jeremiah xxv. 30): *He shall mightily roar upon His habitation.* R. Aḥa said that this misfortune comes upon the earth in punishment for the unnatural traffickings, for the Lord says: I will shake the earth also because of this criminal (sicut membrum in alienum ab illo intulit). According to the Rabbis the earthquakes are caused by discussion, as indicated by this verse, which recalls

[1] Cf. same treatise in the *Babli*, fol. 58 *b*.
[2] Midrash on Psalm civ.
[3] See *Shemoth Rabba*, chap. xxix.; *Wayyiqra Rabba*, chap. xxii.

the same cause (Zechariah xiv. 5): *And ye shall flee to the valley of the mountains; for the valley of the mountains shall reach unto Azal; yea, ye shall flee, like as ye fled from before the earthquake in the days of Uzziah, King of Judah.* According to Samuel, on the contrary, this verse does not refer to an earthquake, but to a political storm, to the interruption of the royal power, as it is said (Jeremiah li. 29): *And the land shall tremble and sorrow; for every purpose of the Lord shall be performed against Babylon, to make the land of Babylon a desolation, without an inhabitant.* Elias also asked R. Nehoraï: Why has God created worms and insects in the world? It was for our interest, replied he, that they have been created. When men behave themselves badly God considers these little animals, and says to Himself: If I let these little creatures, who have no end in view, live, with more reason should I let those live who have one. Besides, adds he, a certain benefit may be drawn from them: a dead fly is a counter poison against the bite of a wasp, the bug is useful as a leach, the serpent for a sort of leprosy, the snail is good for skin diseases, and the lizard for the scorpion's bite.

"One blesses at lightning, &c." R. Jeremiah and R. Zeira say, in the name of R. Ḥisda, that it is sufficient to recite the blessing once in the day. R. Yosse says: it is established that when it is continuous one blessing a day suffices, but if the lightning is repeated from time to time, one must bless each time. R. Yosse bases[4] his assertion on the following grounds: If a man be seated all day in his spice shop (grocer's shop) he only says one blessing for inhaling the good odours, but if he go in and out several times during the day he must repeat the blessing each time. R. Aḥa and R. Ḥanina said, in R. Yosse's name: Since it is so, if a man be present in the place of execution (speculatores) or in a place still more impure, and have time enough to go out and say the blessing immediately, he is considered to have fulfilled the prescription, but not in the contrary case. R. Jeremiah was doubtful on the question whether a man, being naked in his house, may consider the room as a garment and recite the blessing by putting his head out of the window; and whether he may do the same if he be on the top of a tower in the same state. (It is not decided.)

"What blessing is made for storm winds, &c." The rule of the Mishna only applies to winds in the shape of hurricanes; but when the wind is a gentle one, one only says: "Blessed be the author of the creation." R. Josuah b. Ḥanania says: When the wind comes upon the world[5] the Lord breaks it as it were against the mountains, puts it between the hills, and enjoins it not to harm man. What proves it? This verse (Isaiah lvii. 16): *For the spirit* (wind) *should fail before Me;* that is to say, it becomes weak, as it is written (Ps. cxlii. 4): *When My spirit* (breath) *was overwhelmed within Me.* And what good is all that? R. Hoona replies, in the name of R. Aḥa: *it is because of the souls I have created.*

[4] Literally: the strength of Yosse's opinion is based on.

[5] See *Bereshith Rabba*, chap. xxiv.; *Wayyiqra Rabba*, chap. xv.

Three times, says the same author, the wind appeared out of all bounds, and nearly destroyed the world; once under Jonah, once under Elias, and once under Job. Of Jonas the text says (Jonah i. 4): *But the Lord sent out a great wind into the sea;* of Job it is said (Job i. 19): *And behold there came a great wind from the wilderness;* and, finally, about Elias it is written (1 Kings xix. 11): *And behold the Lord passed by and a great and strong wind rent the mountain.* According to R. Judan bar-Salom, it is supposed that the storms of Job and Jonah took place on account of them; but that of Elias was universal, *κοσμικόν*, for after speaking of the passage of the divinity, the storm is mentioned, which in its turn is followed by fire from heaven.

R. Judah says a man blesses when he sees the sea at intervals. What should be their duration? Thirty days. Simon Kamatria asked R Ḥiya b. Aba: I who am a donkey driver, and who go several times during the year to Jerusalem, must I each time rend my garments? Thou art exempted, replied the Rabbi, if thou returned within the same month; but if a longer time has elapsed the rending must be renewed. R. Hoona and the same Simon Kamatria also asked, in the name of R. Samuel b. Naḥman: what is the signification of נ (n) appended to the name of Manasseh of this genealogy (Judges xviii. 30): *And Jonathan the son of Gershom, the son of Manasseh.* This is the meaning: If he proves himself worthy he will be considered as the son of Moses;[6] if not, he will be the son of Manasseh. His companions asked R. Samuel b. Naḥman: How is it that this same man, after having become an apostate to idolatry, should have lived so long? Because, replied the master, his conversion was caused by want and not by conviction. How is this proved? Because when a man came to offer sacrifice to the idol, a bull, a goat, or a ram, he dissuaded him from doing so, saying: that will not profit you, because the idol neither sees, hears, eats, drinks, nor does either good nor evil, and cannot speak. Is that true? said the giver. With what shall I then replace my sacrifice? Go, said he, and bring me a jar of the finest flour, on which thou wilt prepare ten eggs; thou wilt give it to me, and I will eat it, and render the god favourable to thee; when the man had departed, the converted man ate the offerings. One day, however, a great man presented himself with this intention, and the converted man addressed him in the same manner. But if the idol is no use, replied he, what doest thou here? It is to feed myself, replied he, that I am here. When King David was raised to the throne, he sent for this Jonathan, and said to him: How is it possible that thou, the son of a just man, can adore false gods? Behold, was the reply, the teaching which was transmitted to me by my ancestors: Rather than have recourse to charity a man may engage himself to a false religion. Does heaven spare you to explain things thus? said the king. Behold what we have learnt: Rather than have recourse to the charity of man,

[6] Because the word *Manasseh* without *n* reads: Moses.

sell thyself to the work to which thou art the least accustomed, the work the most unimportant and the most menial. And David seeing that he loved money, named him head of his finances, *comes*. And so it is written (Judges xviii. 30): *And Sabuel, the son of Gershom, the son of Manasseh, he and his sons were priests to the tribe of Dan.* The name of Sabuel shows that he returned to God with all his heart and with all his strength when he directed the treasures which he was charged to administer. The following objection was made to Samuel bar-Naḥman: Is it not written (ibid.), that his family remained relapsed until the captivity of Babylon? How then admit that this priest returned to Judaism under David? He replied that at the death of David, Solomon changed all the council, *συγκλητικός*, so that the treasurer returned to the adoration of the false gods; therefore it is written (1 Kings xiii. 11): *Now there dwelt an old prophet in Beth-el;* this applies to him.

When one sees the sun complete [8] (at the equinox of the month of Nissan, at the commencement of the solar cycle of 28 years), and the full moon (when, at the beginning of the month, she arrives in the sign of the Zodiac called the Ram), and the firmament in all its clearness, after several cloudy days, one says this formula: "Blessed be the author of creation." According to R. Yona this last prescription only applies during winter, when there has not been a serene sky for 3 consecutive days; it is to this that the following verse alludes (Job xxxvii. 21): *And now men see not the bright light, &c.* On seeing the new moon, say: "Blessed be He who renews the months." Up to what part of the month [9] may this be said? Until the moment, replies R. Jacob b. Aḥa, that it appears of half the size of the hand; according to R. Aḥa and R. Ḥanina it is until the moment that the hollow of the crescent becomes filled, or until the seventh day; the Cesarean Rabbis determine it by a division, the fourteenth of the month. R. Yosse b. R. Aboon says that the moon continues to complete itself, to become a perfect circle, until the fourteenth of the month. A man must therefore say the blessing in the 'Amidâ during the whole of this period. R. Yosse b. Nehorai (Lucius) said as a formula: "Blessed be He who sanctifies Israel and the Neomenias;" R. Ḥiya bar-Ashe also used these words. According to Samuel the following formula must be added: "Confirm upon us Thy blessing," as on festivals. Rab says that one must mention the object of the solemnity. R. Oshia supports and justifies these additions by this verse (Genesis i. 14): *And let them be for signs, and for seasons, and for days, and for years* (the last term but one has reference to the Neomeneas which, by apposition, one compares to the other solemnities, and which require the same additional formulæ). In passing a cemetery, say these words: "Be praised, O Lord, Thou who raiseth the dead to life." R. Ḥiya, in the name of R. Yoḥanan,

[7] The text has: Jonathan.

[8] See *Wayyiqra Rabba*, chap. xxiii.

[9] B., tr. *Synhedrin*, fol. 41 *a*.

prescribes the following formula: "Praised be He who is faithful to His covenant and raiseth the dead." The same author also said this formula: "He who knoweth thy number will discover the dust from your eyes and awaken you; praise be to Thee, O Lord, Thou who raisest the dead." R. Eliezer said this in the name of R. Ḥanina: "Blessed be He who has formed you with justice, who has kept you equitably, has taken you away, and will raise you up one day; He who knoweth your number will discover the dust of the eyes; be praised, O Lord, Thou who raiseth the dead." This, however, is only said for the dead of Israel; but for the dead of other nations they say (Jeremiah l. 12): *Your mother shall be sore confounded; she that bare you shall be ashamed.*

When one sees the rainbow one says: "Blessed be He who remembers His covenant" (not to send another deluge). According to R. Ḥiya, in the name of R. Yoḥanan, one must say: "Blessed be He who is faithful to His covenant and remembers it." R. Ḥiskia says, in the name of R. Jeremiah, that during the whole of R. Simon b. Yoḥaï's[1] life not one rainbow was seen (on account of his virtues, which alone would have saved the world from another deluge). The same author says that the supernatural power of this pious Rabbi was such that, if he desired a valley to be filled with pieces of gold, his wish was fulfilled.[2] This author also says that he heard some people saying to this Rabbi that very few people would be admitted to future life; if there be three, said he, I and my son will be among them;[3] and if there be only two, it will be I and my son. Finally, according to the same author, this Rabbi said: Let Abraham intercede with God to obtain pardon for all generations from his time to mine, and I will obtain the same from my time unto the extinction of all generations; if Abraham refuses, let Aḥia the Soolanite be with me, and we two will obtain pardon for the whole earth from the time of the patriarch until the end of time.

"One says the blessing for rain and good news, &c." Why does one compare here the rain with good news? R. Berakhia answers, in the name of R. Levi: because it is written (Prov. xxv. 25): *As cold water to a thirsty soul, so is good news from a far country.* How much rain should fall[4] that the blessing should be said? R. Ḥiya answers, in R. Yoḥanan's name, that, to commence with, enough should fall to fertilize the ground (which will be determined farther on), and to finish it the surface of the ground must be as it were washed (soaked). R. Yanaï bar-R. Ismael, in the name of R. Simon b. Lakish, indicates the same

[1] See *Shemoth-rabba*, section xxii.; Midrash on Psalm xcii.

[2] See *Bereshith Rabba*, chap. xxxv.

[3] This is one of those exaggerated expressions put by posterity into the mouth of Doctors who were incapable of such vanity. See Babli, tr. *Succa*, fol. 45 *a*, where this passage is modified.

[4] J., tr. *Taanith*, i. 3.

quantity to commence with; and to finish with, it suffices that the bung of the cask be soaked. But can the bungs (of the casks) be soaked? Are they not under shelter in the cellars? Verily, it is only supposed that they should appear to be soaked (without being so in reality). According to R. Yosse, in the name of R. Zeira, this measure was given so as in such a case to end the fast commanded to be observed in cases of want of water. R. Ḥiskia, R. Naḥoom, and R. Ada b. Abima being together, R. Naḥoom said to R. Ada b. Abima: Does it not seem to you that this measure was given for the blessing? Certainly, replied he. On the contrary, said R. Ḥiskia and R. Ada, does it not seem indicated in order to show that the fasting is to be stopped? He replied: Yes. Why then, said he to him, dost thou also reply affirmatively to R. Naḥoom's question? I approved of it, replied he, in his master's version, whose opinion it is; but, for me, I accept the explanation. Yet, said R. Mena to R. Ḥiskia, who is his master? R. Zeira. Now, according to the latter, it indicates the end of the fast.

R. Juda b. Ezechiel narrates that his father said the following words to obtain the rain: "May Thy name be exalted, sanctified, blessed, and praised, O our King, for every drop Thou causest to come down in our favour, and mayest Thou separate one from the other so that their quantity be not diminished," as it is written: *It shall be less* (Levit. xxvii. 18). R. Judan adds that He sends it in measure, as it is written: *He hath compassed the waters with bounds* (Job xxvi. 10). R. Yosse b. R. Jacob went to visit R. Judan Magdala. At the moment he arrived a heavy rain descended, and they heard hundreds and thousands of voices saying: "We must return thanks to Thy name, O our King, for every drop Thou sendest down to favour mortals who are not worthy of it." How knowest thou that? asked somebody. It is thus, was the reply, that R. Simon blessed the fall of rain.

It is said above that for an effective rain enough must fall to fertilize the earth. What does this measure represent? A full vessel containing the value of three palms; this is R. Meir's opinion. R. Judah says that, to commence, when the earth is dry the rain must penetrate the depth of a palm (i.e. much must fall); the second time, when the ground is already wet, a depth of two palms must fall, and the third time three. R. Simon b. Eleazar says: Not a drop falls from above but what it is replaced by two from the earth; the following verse indicates this (Ps. xlii. 8): *Deep calleth unto deep at the noise of Thy water-spouts.* R. Levi also says: The waters from on high are considered male, and those from the earth female. This seems to be indicated by the verse (Isaiah xlv. 8): *Let the earth open,* as the female opens herself to the male; *and let them bring forth salvation* by cohabitation; *and let righteousness spring up together* by the coming of the rain. *I the Lord have created it* for the good of the earth. R Aḥa taught, in the name of R. Simon b. Gamaliel, that the name *Rebiá*, is

given to the rain, because it fertilizes the earth (from the root *Raba'*, to enrich). R. Ḥanina b. Ika says [5] that the roots of the wheat penetrate three cubits into the earth, and those of the tender fig-trees grow even into the rocks. R. Ismael b. R. Eleazar teaches: the earth only absorbs what its hardness (dryness) requires (and therefore little in depth). How then are the roots of the caroubier and sycamore nourished (which are very deep in the earth and receive little water)? R. Ḥanina replies that once a month vapours arise from the deep and moisten these roots, in conformity with this verse (Isaiah xxvii. 3): *I the Lord do keep it; I will water it every moment.* According to R. Zeira, it has been taught elsewhere that: If there is an abundance of produce, cheap food, and that one river suffices to enrich an entire province, the following formula is said: "Blessed be the good and the kind." If one announces to any one the death of his father, he says: "Blessed be the righteous judge." If one inherit from the defunct, one says: "Blessed be the good and the beneficient.

3. (4). He who has built a new house, or bought new furniture, says, "Blessed be He who has kept us alive," &c.

R. Ḥiya b. Aba says that this blessing is said not only for new clothes, but also for old ones which are new relatively to the person who wears them. R. Jacob b. Zabdi says, in R. Ḥiya b. Aba's name, that this blessing is said when one buys them; but if one gets them as a present, one says these words: "Blessed be the good and the kind;" [6] this is also the opinion of R. Aba, father of R. Abamare. On dressing a man says this formula: "Blessed be He who clothes the naked." If a man constructs a *Succa* (a tent of leaves) for his own use,[7] he says this: "Blessed be He who has sanctified us by His commandments, and has commanded us to make the succa;" if it be for others, he adds these words at the end: "to construct the *succa* in honour of his Holy name." On going into it to sit down, he says: "Blessed be He who has commanded us to live in it." After having recited this formula on the first night of the festival, it is not repeated. Analogically, the following rules are established in preparing the *lulab*;[8] for himself a man says: "Blessed be He who has sanctified us by His commandments, and has commanded to us the precept of the *lulab*;" when a man appropriates it for others, he adds the words: "to prepare the lulab in His honour." When a man uses it the first day, he recalls the precept to take this bundle, adding this formula: "who has made us live and reach this solemnity;" and every time he takes the *lulab* he repeats the blessing which recalls this

[5] J., tr. *'Aboda Zara*, iii. 5.
[6] For that is still better; it is the formula of a greater satisfaction.
[7] See tr. *Succa*, i. 2 (3), and iii. 4.
[8] Leviticus, xxii. 40.

precept. The same ceremonial is observed, and the same series of blessings is recited when one puts into practice the commandment of the placing of the *mezuza* (inscription on the door-posts of the houses), on putting on the *tephilin* (phylacteries), the *tsitsith* (fringes of the garments), and on the taking off of the oblations to the priests and the tithes to the Levites.

He who cuts the throats of animals according to the prescribed rite must recall this precept in a blessing, also he who covers the blood and he who performs circumcision. The father of the child says this formula: "Blessed be He who has sanctified us by His commandments and ordered us to make him enter into the covenant of Abraham, our patriarch." The assistants say: "In the same manner as Thou hast made him enter into the covenant, Thou wilt make him enter into the bosom of the Law and pass under the nuptial dais." He who subsequently recites the blessing of the ceremony says: "Blessed be He who has sanctified His well-beloved from his mother's womb, who has made a law for his family and has put on his posterity, as a sign, the seal of the holy alliance. Therefore, in return for this action, the living God, who is our heritage and our support, has ordered us to save the flesh and blood of our well-beloved from the abyss of ruin. Be praised, O Lord, Thou who makest the covenant."

At what moment is the accomplishment of these precepts blessed? According to R. Yoḥanan, when one is about to accomplish them; according to R. Hoona, after the action. The latter conforms to Samuel's opinion, from whom we know, through R. Yosse b. R. Aboon, that every religious action must be blessed at the moment of its accomplishment,[1] excepting for the hearing of the *shophar*, for the bath of purification, and according to some opinions, for cohabitation. According to R. Yona, there is still another blessing: That one which, as some say, is recited before taking off the phylacteries from the arms, and before placing on those of the head. As for the slaughtering of animals, according to R. Yoḥanan, it is said when about to be effected; according to R. Yosse bar-Nehoraï, it is not recited until afterwards, for fear of the slaughtering not having been successful as regards the rite (for, in this case, the blessing would be unnecessary). If a man have this fear, should he not wait that the animal be examined to see if there is no defect? As a general rule the intestines are admittedly in good condition. And indeed, if after the slaughtering a wolf come and run away with the intestines before they have been examined, they are supposed to have been without defect, and the animal which has been slaughtered may be used for food. Neither is it feared that they were perforated, for, as R. Aba teaches, in the name of the Babylonian Rabbis, by R. Juda ben-Pazi, the intestines are always considered to be sound, until proof to the contrary has been given.

3. (5). One must bless for evil the source of good; and for good

[1] B., tr. *Pesaḥim*, fol. 7 *b*.

the source of evil. He who supplicates for what is past, such prayer is vain. How? His wife is pregnant, and he says, "God grant that my wife may bring forth a male child;" such prayer is vain. Or if one on the road hear the voice of lamentation in the city, and say, "God grant that it may not be my son, my house," &c., such prayer is vain.

3 (6). Whoever enters a fortified town must say 2 prayers, one at his entrance, and one at his departure. B. Azai says 4; 2 at his entrance, and 2 at his departure; he returns thanks for the past, and supplicates for the future.

At R. Janaï's school it was taught that the assertion of the Mishna relative to the pregnant woman only applies to the case in which she is near to be delivered; but before that time the prayer may sometimes produce the desired effect, according to this verse (Jeremiah xviii. 6): *Behold as the clay is in the potter's hand, so are ye, &c.* Verily, says Rabbi, in the name of R. Janaï,[1] Rachel, instead of bringing forth Dina, was previously to bear a boy; and it was thanks to her prayer that this child changed sex before its birth, as it is written (Genesis xxx. 22): *And afterwards she bare a daughter, and called her name Dinah.*[2] R. Juda b. Pazi adds, in R. Janaï's name, that our mother Rachel was one of the first prophetesses in foreseeing that she would have another child by her husband (ibid. 24): *And she called his name Joseph; and said, The Lord shall add to me another son;* she did not ask for several, but for a second one (which was Benjamin).

If a man be travelling and he hears people talking of misfortunes, he may only say: "I have the hope or the conviction that they do not concern my family." Hillel the ancient applied hereunto this verse (Ps. cxii. 7): *He shall not be afraid of evil tidings.*

"In passing through a village a man says two prayers: one at his entrance, and one at his departure." What does he say at his entrance? "Let it please Thee, O Lord, my God, and the God of our fathers, to let me enter in peace into this locality." At his departure he says: "I render Thee thanks, Lord my God, for having let me come out." According to B. Azai, 4 are said, thus: before entering he asks the favour to enter in peace; when he is entered, he thanks the Lord. The same for going out, he asks God the mercy to go out in peace, and thanks Him afterwards, adding the wish to arrive without delay at his home, or at a given place.

[1] See *Bereshith Rabba*, chap. lxxii.

[2] This is an example, at once the most curious and the most venturesome, of the diversion of the meaning of the Scriptures, from its biblical sense, effected by the Talmud for its exegesis; since it is not of Rachel, but of Leah, that this verse treats.

This series of blessings, however, is only to be used when travelling among pagans (often hostile), but not in a country inhabited by Israel. If it be a place where justice accomplishes capital punishment (where, in case of confusion, his life might be in danger) these blessings must be recited. Also in the same manner a man says a prayer on entering, and one on leaving a water-closet (where the angels who accompany men quit them momentarily). On going in a man says, in order to send them away: "Greeting to you, honoured attendants of the Most High, and blessed be the glory of the Lord." It is customary in these cases to tell those who accompany you to go on in front. On coming out say this formula of blessing: "Blessed be He who created man with wisdom," &c. In taking a legal bath, one also says two blessings; on going in: "May it please Thee, O Lord my God, and God of my ancestors, to drive away from me all danger, danger by fire, scalding, or destruction of the bath; that no misfortune happen to me, and if it were to happen, let my death be an expiation for my sins and save me from future condemnation in Heaven." On coming out say: "I render Thee thanks, O Lord God, and God of my ancestors, for that Thou hast saved me from fire." R. Abahoo says that this is only applicable to baths heated from below (where there is danger of fire), but not to an ordinary bath where there is only danger of scalding. R. Ḥelkia and R. Simon say, in the name of R. Josuah ben-Levi, that it is unnecessary to stand up for the blessing before bathing (it is said in going to it).

5. (7). Man is bound to bless God for evil, as he is bound to bless Him for good.[3] For it is said, "*And thou shalt love the Lord thy God, with all thy heart, and with all thy soul, and with all thy might*" (Deut. vi. 5). "With all thy heart" means, with both thy inclinations, the evil as well as the good. "With all thy soul" means, even should He deprive thee of life; and "with all thy might" means, with all the wealth. Another opinion is, that "with all thy might" means, whatever measure He metes out unto thee, do you thank Him with thy entire might.[4]

R. Berakhia establishes, in R. Levi's name, the reason of the following verse (Ps. xcii. 9): *But Thou, Lord, art most high for evermore;* that is to say, the right is always on Thy side. Generally, when a king is seated in judgment on diverse

[3] If a fortunate event occur, one says: "Blessed be God, the good and kind;" for a misfortune, one says this formula: "Blessed be He who is wise in His integrity." See B., *Meghilla*, fol. 25 *a* (Schuhl, *Sentences*, p. 209).

[4] This is a play upon the words *meöd* (much) and *midda* (measure).

cases, if he proclaims a clement decision,[5] everybody praises him; and if he decid on death, everybody murmurs at him; and why so? Because he has let himself be led away to make an outdo of justice; but as regards the Lord, it is not so: *Thou, O Lord, art eternally sublime.* R. Hoona, in the name of R. Aḥa, recalls the following verse (ib. ci. 1): *I will sing of mercy and judgment;*[6] *unto Thee, O Lord, will I sing.* David meant: If Thou judgest me favourably, I will sing unto Thee; if Thou judgest me severely, yet will I sing unto Thee; whatever Thy decisions, I wish to celebrate Thee. Thus, says R. Tanḥooma ben-Juda, is the following verse explained (ib. lvi. 10): *In God I will praise His word,* or, according to other versions, *I will praise the Lord,* &c. This divergence of expressions[7] explains itself, and its object is to show that he will praise Him as much for favourable judgments as for severe ones. The Rabbis also cite, in support of this thesis, the verse: *I will take the cup of salvation and call upon the name of the Lord; I found trouble and sorrow, then called I upon the name of the Lord* (ib. cxvi. 3, 4, and 13); that is to say: in either case I will call upon Him. According to R. Judan ben-Pedath, Job said the same thing (i. 21): *The Lord hath given, the Lord hath taken away; blessed be the name of the Lord.* When He gave it me, as when He took it from me, it was a favour; and, moreover, when He gave it me, He consulted no one; but when He took it away, He consulted the tribunal above. R. Eliezer says that, wherever it is written, *And the Lord,* it indicates that God was aided by the celestial tribunal; and it can be proved every time. Thus it is written (1 Kings xxii. 23): *The Lord hath spoken evil concerning thee.* Act therefore towards Him, either in fear or in respect,[8] for if thou hast hatred against Him, remember that thou must love Him, and a friend must not bear hatred; or else act with respect, for if thou rebel, thou wilt remember that thou must fear Him, and he who has fear doth not rebel.

There are 7 types of Pharisees:[9] 1st, he who accepts the law as a burden; 2nd, he who borrows, or acts from interested motives;[1] 3rd, he who counterbalances;[2] 4th, he who is sparing (ostentatiously); 5th, he who asks that one should show him a good action to be accomplished; 6th, he who acts by fear;

[5] For the words DIMOS, *demissus,* and *spicula* (torture), see *Bereshith Rabba* on Genesis xxxiii. 18, and *Pesikta* on Exodus xiii. 17; *Yelandenoa,* first verse of Deuteronomy; *Shoḥar tob,* chap. xxv.

[6] See Medr., *Shoḥar tob,* chap. xcviii.

[7] The term *Elohim* means: severe equity, and *Adonaï* means: mercy.

[8] J., tr. *Sota,* v. 5 (fol. 20 *c*); B., ibid. fol. 22 *b.*

[9] Upon Pharisees, see Derenbourg, *Essai,* &c. pp. 3, 119, 455, and M. J. Cohen's work, *Les Pharisiens* (vol. ii.).

[1] Perhaps the "flagellant," says M. Derenbourg, ibid. p. 71.

[2] It is explained by a commentary: he who strikes his head, to avoid seeing a pernicious person.

and 7th, he who is inspired by love. The following is a more detailed explanation: the 1st is like unto a man who would take the Divine commandments upon his shoulders, to carry them away;[3] the 2nd seems to say, Lend me (a moment, or wait), that I may accomplish a precept of religion; the 3rd says to himself, I am going to fulfil one religious prescription, and then violate another, and sets off one against the other; the 4th seems to say, From the little I have, I save enough to fulfil a religious precept; the 5th one, who is conscious of his duties, endeavours to efface his sins by his good conduct; the 6th one, like Job, acts through fear; the 7th, through love, like Abraham, and this last degree is the best of all. He resembles our patriarch Abraham, whose faith vanquished and converted, as it were, his inclinations to evil.[4] Thus it is written (Nehemiah ix. 8): *And foundest his heart faithful before Thee;* that is to say, the two inclinations. Indeed, says R. Aḥa, the patriarch had made a sort of compact with his instincts of evil, not to sin any more; for it is written (ibid.): *and madest a covenant with him* (and it is supposed, contrary to the customary meaning, that the pronoun *him* refers not to God, but to the inclination to evil). As David could not maintain the fight against it, he killed it, as it is written (Psalm cix. 22): *and my heart is wounded within me.*

R. Akiba was on the point of undergoing the last torture before the impious Turnus Rufus, when the moment to recite the Shema, arrived. He commenced to recite it and became very joyful. "Old man, old man, cried out to him the pro-consul, art thou a sorcerer, that the tortures make thee not suffer, or is it to brave me that thou smilest in the midst of thy tortures? Be easy, replied Akiba, I am neither a sorcerer nor a mocker; but all my life, when reading this verse of the Pentateuch, *Thou shalt love the Lord thy God with all thy heart, with all thy soul, and with all thy might,* I was sorrowful and said to myself: When shall I realize the three ways of adoring God, indicated in this profession of faith? I have proved that I love God with all my heart and with all my might; but I have not yet been able to prove to Him my love by giving Him my soul. I give Him, to-day, this proof at the very moment that it is customary to recite the words, which impose the duty upon us. Behold the cause of my joy." In saying these words, he gave up the ghost.

Nehemi Emsoni served R. Akiba 22 years,[5] and learnt from him the interpretations of even the most minute particle of the Bible (גם רק את אך). He explained to him, for example, the verse (Deut. vi. 13): *Thou shalt fear the Lord thy God,* where the particle את indicates that one must not the less respect the Law.

[3] That is to say: to disembarrass himself.

[4] He works with his evil instincts as it were a compact to sin no more (M. Ad. Franck's paraphrases in *Journal des Savants*, 1872, p. 563).

[5] B., tr. *Pesaḥim*, fol. 22 *b*.

5. (8). No man is to be irreverent, opposite the eastern gate of the Temple, for it is opposite the Holy of Holies. No man is to go on the mountain of the house with his staff, shoes, or purse,[6] nor with dust on his feet, nor is he to make it a short cut (*compendiaria via*); nor is he to spit at all.

We have learnt that when a man experiences the lesser want, he turns towards the north, and for the greater one, towards the south.[7] R. Yosse b. Aboon says that this rule only applies to a certain part of Jerusalem (out of respect for the sanctuary), beyond the *sophim* (point of observation of the Temple). R. Akiba says that it applies everywhere, and particularly to places not enclosed with walls. We have learnt also that, for the greater want, one must not turn the face to the east and the back to the west, but one must stand aside. According to R. Judah, this rule is only to be followed when in sight of the Temple; according to R. Yosse, only beyond the *sophim;*[8] according to R. Akiba, it is to be applied everywhere, and especially in a place which is not enclosed within walls. R. Akiba says: I followed R. Josuah to see how he acted in this matter, and I saw that he was seated having one side to the west (i.e. between north and south); he did not uncover himself until he was seated, and he did not sit down until he had dug a hole;[9] and finally he wiped himself, not with the right hand, but with the left. Simon b. Azaï also stated that, having once followed after R. Akiba, he saw him act in a like manner.

It has been taught, in a *baraïtha*, that a man must not go up to the hill of the Temple, neither with shoes, nor with dust on his feet, nor with money wrapped in a cloth, nor with a girdle on.[1] Why? In virtue of this verse (Ecclesiastes v. 1): *Keep thy foot when thou goest to the house of God.* R. Yosse b. R. Judah says that it is in virtue of the verse (Esther iv. 2): *For none might enter into the king's gate clothed with sackcloth;* now, if this be so for a mortal, with more reason must a man behave well before the Lord. Nor may a man make use of it as a short cut, and less still may he spit there; for it is a want of respect to pass there without a religious end in view, and it is self-evident that a man may not show any sign of disrespect.

[6] *Funda.* According to Obadia of Bertinoro it was a belt to keep money in (St. Matthew x. 9); according to others, it is a sort of vesture or surtout, which serves to protect the more expensive garments worn beneath it. Guisius remarks that we must distinguish the word used in the Mishna from its homonym, which is derived from the greek ἐπενδύτης, vestment. Cf. tr. *Shabbath*, x. 3.

[7] See *Sifri*, section *Ki*-Thetsé, §§ 257, 258.

[8] Observatory of Jerusalem. See De Saulcy, *Voyage en Terre Sainte*, vol. ii. from p. 150 forward.

[9] See Deut. xxiii. 14.

[1] Tossephta on our treatise, section 7.

5. (9). All the seals of the blessings in the Sanctuary used to say, "from eternity." But since the Epicureans[2] perversely taught, there is but one world, it was directed that men should say, "from eternity to eternity." It was also directed that every man should greet his friend in THE NAME (of God), as it is said, *And behold Boaz came from Bethlehem, and said unto the reapers, The Lord* (be) *with you; and they answered him, The Lord bless thee* (Ruth ii. 4). And it is also said, *The Lord is with thee, thou mighty man of valour* (Judges vi. 12). And it is said: *despise not thy mother when she is old* (Prov. xxiii. 22). And it is also said, (It is) *time for* (thee), *Lord, to work, for they have made void Thy Laws* (Ps. cxix. 126). R. Nathan says, They have made void Thy Law, because (it is) time for (Thee), Lord, to work.

They have taught that, instead of answering *Amen* in the Temple, men say: Blessed for ever be the name of His glorious reign. How is it known that one does not answer *Amen* in the Temple? Because it is written (Nehemiah ix. 5): *Stand up and bless the Lord your God,* &c. And how do we know that this was said after every blessing? Because it is written (ibid.): *He is exalted above all blessing and praise.* R. Josuah of Darôm says: There are three things which are decreed by human tribunals, and confirmed by the tribunal above; they are: the ruin of Jericho, the obligation to celebrate the festival of Esther, and the necessity of saluting one's neighbour by the name. For the ruin of Jericho it is said (Joshua vii. 20): *Israel hath sinned,* &c. Was it not Joshua who put Jericho under an interdiction? His decision has therefore been approved of by the tribunal on high. As regards the obligation to celebrate the festival of Esther, we read that the Jews *ordained and took upon them and upon their seed, and upon all such as joined themselves unto them, so as it should not fail that they should keep these two days* (Esther ix. 27). Rab says that the acceptance was expressed in the singular number,[3] that is to say, by the celestial tribunal alone. As proof of the salutation in the name of God, we read this: *Boaz came from Bethlehem and said unto the reapers, The Lord be with you;* and the proof of the confirmation of this by the tribunal on high is this, viz. that it is written elsewhere (of Gideon): *the Angel of the Lord appeared unto him, and said unto him, The Lord is with thee, thou*

[2] These Epicureans (*minim*, heretics) are as likely Sadducees as Pharisees, according to Geiger and Schorr, cited by M. Derenbourg, *Essai,* &c., p. 131. Cf. *Revue des Etudes juives,* vol. vi p. 73.

[3] Rab takes into account the method of writing the word KBL in the text, or *Ketib,* which has the plural sense according to the reading. Cf. *Rabba* on Ruth ii. 4.

mighty man of valour (Judges vi. 12). R. Aboon says, in the name of R. Josuah b. Levi, that it is the same with regard to the tithes, since it is written (Malachi iii. 10): *Bring ye all the tithes, &c., and there shall not be room enough to receive it;* now, says R. Yosse bar-Simon bar-Aba, in the name of R. Yoḥanan, an object, of which it cannot be said there is too much (DAI), is an effect of the celestial blessing.[4] R. Berakhia, R. Ḥelbo, and R. Aba b. Ilaï say, in the name of Rab: Your blessings shall be so numerous that you will get tired of returning thanks for them.

It is written (Prov. xxiii. 22): *Despise not thy mother when she is old.* This, according to R. Yosse bar-Aboon, signifies that if the explanation of the Mosaic precepts seems old to thee, thou must not despise them on that account in virtue of the above verse. R. Zeira explains it thus: If thy nation be weakened, rise up to sustain it. Thus Elkana urged Israel to enter into the Temple during the three great feasts, as it is written (1 Samuel i. 3): *And this man went up out of his city yearly, &c.*

It is also written (Ps. cxix. 126): *When it is time to work for the Lord, destroy even your Law.*[6] R. Nathan transposed this verse to explain it: Destroy your Law, says he, when it is time to make a manifestation to prove the existence of God (in the same manner as Elias sacrificed to the Lord to this end on a height far from Jerusalem, which was generally forbidden). R. Ḥilkia says, in R. Simon's name, that, according to this verse, the meaning of *destroy the Law* is to study it at intervals of time too distant one from the other. In this same verse, according to what was taught, R. Simon b. Johaï found the following interpretation: If thou seest, said he, the manifest sign that men have abandoned the study of the Law, have the courage to approach it, and thou wilt attain as much recompense as all the men together, because it is written: *Destroy the Law when it is time to act for the Lord.* Hillel the ancient said: When the wise men assemble together (to study amongst themselves), scatter abroad sacred knowledge; but when the wise men propagate science, be attentive. Hillel also said: If thou seest that Israel loves the Thora, and that all rejoice in it, pour out thy teachings; in the contrary case, keep to thyself. R. Eleazar says: Even as a child must be suckled every hour in the day, so also must every man in Israel occupy himself at every moment with the Law. R. Yona says, in the name of R. Yosse b. Nezera: All superfluous words are bad, but those of the Law are good;[7] ordinarily silence alone is good,[8] but regarding the Law it is not so.

[4] See J., tr. *Taanith*, chap. iii. § 9; *Wayyiqra Rabba*, chap. xxxv.

[5] By a play upon words between IMKHA, *thy mother*, and OOMATHKHA, *thy nation.*

[6] Here, as is often the case, the exegesist has diverted the usual sense of the verse to meet the exigencies of his thesis.

[7] It is not possible to speak too much while studying the Law. See *Medrash Yalqut* on the Psalms, § 878 (Schuhl, *Sentences*, p. 251).

[8] Certain editions have, instead of the word silence, כרביא or ברכיא, "all contentment

R. Simon b. Lakish says: I found in the *Meghillath ḥassidim* (devotions for pious people)[9] this maxim: *If thou abandonest Me for one day, says God to man, I will leave you for two days.*[1] This is like two individuals who having journeyed, the one from Tiberias, and the other from Sephoris, meet together in the first place in an inn; they then continue their road. Before they have well accomplished a mile each on their respective roads, they are separated by a distance of two miles; and again if a woman wait for him whom she loves, she will wait as long as he thinks of her; as soon as she hears that he does not think any more of her she hastens to espouse another.

We have learnt, in the name of R. Meir: Every Israelite recites one hundred blessings a day; thus, he says blessings before and after the reading of the Shema', before and after meals; he recites thrice the eighteen blessings of the 'Amidâ; and he accomplishes other precepts which he blesses (the total reaches a hundred). Also, says R. Meir, there is no Israelite that is not as it were enveloped in religious symbols; he carries the phylacteries on his forehead and arms, the *mezuza* on the posts of his door, the circumcision on his body, the four fringes on his garment. Thus said David (Ps. cxix. 164): *Seven times a day do I praise Thee, because of Thy righteous judgments;* and he also says (Ps. xxxiv. 8): *The Angel of the Lord encampeth round about them that fear Him and delivereth them.* In entering into a bath the psalmist remarked, in his state of nudity, that he carried on his body no religious symbol, and he said to himself: Alas, I am stripped of every Divine precept. But on noticing the circumcision he began to praise the Lord (Ps. xl. 1): *To the chief Musician, a psalm of David.* R. Eleazar says, in R. Ḥanina's name: People who study contribute to the peace of the universe, as it is written (Isaiah liv. 13): *And all thy children shall be taught of the Lord; and great shall be the peace of thy children.*

is good, but the contentment in study is bad" (a man must never think himself clever enough). The sense adopted here is in accordance with the parallelism, and it is confirmed by the text of the Lehmann edition.

[9] See Derenbourg, ibid. p. 2, note 1, for the analysis of this collection, which is now only met with in the Talmudic books, in the shape of mementoes there mentioned.

[1] Medrash Samuel, chap. i.; Sifri, section *Eqeb*, chap. xlviii.

END OF THE FIRST PART.

OMISSIONS.

Page 5, line 21, add, (Exodus xix. 21).
„ 40, line 18, add, (Eccles. iii. 2).
„ 56, line 20, add, morning flutes.
„ 82, line 4, add, And R. Zinoon was ordered to proclaim the close of the meeting.
„ 97, line 19, . . . in the name of R. Yoḥanan and his companions the following verse, "*O Lord of Hosts, blessed is the man that trusteth in Thee*" (Psalm lxxxiv. 13). R. Ezekia said in the name of R. Abahoo.
„ 98, line 3, *Blessed are they that dwell in Thy house* (Psalm lxxxiv. 4), and afterwards once. . . .

ERRATA.

Page 2, lines 28 and 31, read, Nehemiah iv. 15, 16.
„ 40, line 12, read, Amos iv. 12.
„ 56, line 1, read, Deut. xvi. 3.
„ 64, line 5, read, Deut. vi. 9.
„ 73, line 18, read, Psalm lv. 18.
„ 74, the last two lines, read, Jerem. xxvii. 18.

ALPHABETICAL INDEX OF THE SUBJECTS.

A.

AB-BETH-DIN, vice-president of the Supreme Tribunal, 83.
Abel. See Mourner.
Abraham, his name rectified, 28; from him comes to us the morning-prayer, 74-5; his intercession near God, 102.
Adam and the creation of the earth, 145, 151,157.
Additional prayers, or Mussaph, 76-9, 93-4; of *Amida's* end, 83.
Admission in the enclosure of the school very severe under R. Gamaliel, 82.
Adoration of God at the risk of the life, 149.
Agrarian repose year, or *Shmeta*, 18.
Akoom, idolator, 147, *n.*
Albino. See Seeing.
Amen, liturgical confirmation, 94-5, 109, 133, 145, 148, 171.
'Amida, eighteen benediction prayers, 2, 11, 16, 22, 23, 41-6, 85-8, 107; morning, 73, 94; exemptions, 55-62; at fixed hours, 73; afternoon, 74; evening, 81; a summary, 79, 85-9, 90; of Sabbat, 89, 138; with ten persons, 94; and reverence, 95-6.
Amoraim, orators who transmit the oral teaching, 81, 84.
Angels, their feet are 515 miles long, 152; An angel took the form of Moses, 153.
Asp, what gave birth to it, 144.
Assembly (Grand), its number, 43, 134. See *Minian*.

B.

BABYLONIANS despised, 32, 119.
Balustrade erected on the roof for the safety of the inhabitants, 64.
Bath-kol, a mysterious voice in favour of Hillel, 20.
Bath (legal) of purification, 66-9, 165; exemption, 72; warm, 90.
Beauty, on seeing it, one blesses God, 156 7.
Bedsteads, many sorts, 57.
Benedictions and maledictions in the Pentateuch, 80.
Beth-din. See School.
Bible, merit to read it, 18.
Bird's-nest, sent away the mother, 106.
Blessings, formulas, 155-9; beginning and ending, 20, 25; of *'Amida*, 23-4, 43-5; of *Shema'*, 31; of phylacteries, 38; after meal, 47, 63, 65, 117, 127-9, 143; by a Cohen, 59, 109, 110; of products, 111, 125, 137, 144; by many men together, 132-6; how long is one obliged to bless, 147; their seals, 171; how many every Israelite recites a day, 173.
Body (human) divided in 248 limbs, 91.
Bread, to cut a loaf was an honour, 141.
Bridegroom exempted from reading the *Shema'*, 48, 53-4.
Bug is useful as a leach, 159.
Building a house, say a form of blessing, 164.

C.

CAB, measure for water, 66.
Cahana, power attributed to his prediction, 52.
Cemetery, to respect it, 39; in passing through say a formula, 161; a Cohen must not go there, 61.
Child, when submitted to religious duties, 129, 130.
Circumcision, while performing it, one blesses God, 165; is a religious symbol, 173.

TABLE OF GEOGRAPHICAL AND PROPER NAMES.

BIBLICAL CONCORDANCE

(IN ACCORDANCE WITH THE HEBREW TEXT).

Levit. xxvii. 18, p. 163.
Numbers vi. 23, p. 110.
xv. 38, 39, pp. 15, 35; 37, pp. 26, 34; 39, p. 64.
xvi. 21, 24, p. 133.
xvii. 10, p. 133.
xix. p. 126, *n.*
xxiii. 22, 24, p. 21.
xxviii. 4, pp. 75-6.
xxxi. 19, p. 13.
Deuter. i. 6, 8, p. 39.
iii. 25, p. 127.
iv. 5, 9, p. 99; 6, p. 42; 7, pp. 152-3, 155; 32, p. 150.
vi. 4, p. 63; 5, pp. 167-8; 7, pp. 18, 96; 9, p. 64; 13, p. 169.
vii. 3, p. 156; 14, p. 148.
viii. 8, p. 119, *n.*; 10, pp. 2, 64, 127.
xi. 12, p. 158; 13, pp. 34, 73; 19, pp. 37, 63; 21, p. 8.
xiii. 2, p. 19.
xiv. 25, p. 47.
xvi. 3, pp. 26, 56.
xvii. 11, p. 19.
xxii. 6, 7, p. 106; 9, p. 112.
xxiii. 5, p. 99; 6, p. 100; 14, p. 170, *n.*
xxviii. p. 80; 2, p. 100.
xxxii. 3, p. 128; 35, p. 147.
xxxiii. 23, p. 136.
Joshua ii. 6, p. 124; 15, p. 91.
vi. 12, p. 171; 23, p. 91.
vii. 20, p. 171.
xxii. 22, p. 151.
Judges vi. 12, p. 172.
vii. 12, p. 9.
xviii. 30, pp. 160-1.
1 Sam. i. 3, p. 172; 12, p. 78; 13, pp. 73, 152; 22, p. 77.
ii. 3, p. 89; 10, p. 86.
ix. 13, p. 128.
xxvi. 6, p. 149.
2 Sam. vii. 12, p. 33.
xii. 24, p. 28.
xiii. 5, p. 113, *n.*
xv. 32, p. 90.
xix. 3, p. 49.
xxvi. 6, p. 149.
1 Kings v. 3, p. 92.
viii. p. 86; 28, p. 90; 30, p. 92; 44, pp. 90-2; 48, p. 92; 54, p. 23.
xiii. 2, p. 28; 11, p. 161.
1 Kings xvii. 1, 21, p. 101.
xviii. 1, p. 101.
xix. 11, p. 160.
xxii. 23, p. 168.
2 Kings ii. 11, pp. 96-7.
iii. 15, p. 10.
iv. 10, p. 91.
xx. 2, p. 90.
Isaiah i. 15, p. 78.
vi. 2, p. 137.
x. 34, p. 45.
xii. 6, p. 26.
xiv. 23, p. 149.
xxvi. 19, p. 102; 20, p. 131.
xxvii. 3, p. 164.
xxviii. 22, p. 53.
xxix. 23, p. 43.
xl. 2, p. 96; 22, p. 79; 17, p. 156.
xliii. 18, 19, p. 28.
xliv. 9, p. 147; 27, p. 77.
xlv. 7, p. 42, *n.*, 146; 8, p. 163.
xlvi. 7, p. 152.
xlix. 21, p. 157.
l. 4, p. 147.
li. 21, p. 96.
lii. 10, p. 151.
liv. 13, p. 173.
lv. 6, p. 98; 7, p. 43.
lvi. 7, pp. 43, 92.
lvii. 16, p. 159; 19, p. 111.
lxv. 24, p. 88.
lxvi. 90, p. 98.
Jer. iv. 19, p. 91.
vii. 17, p. 74.; 18, p. 3, *n.*
viii. 4, p. 167.
x. 10, p. 34.
xviii. 6, p. 166.
xxi. end, p. 96.
xxiii. 7, p. 27.
xxv. 30, p. 158.
xxvii. 18, p. 74.
xxxi. 13, p. 99.
l. 12, p. 162.
li. 29, p. 159; 39, p. 156; 49, p. 78.
Ezek. i. 7, p. 6, 152; 26, pp. 15.
viii. 16, p. 92.
xviii. 32, p. 39.
xxxvi. 8, p. 44.
xli. 1, p. 92.
xliii. 8, p. 91.
Hosea iii. 5, p. 44.
v. 15, p. 92.

Printed in the USA
CPSIA information can be obtained
at www.ICGtesting.com
LVHW022211101123
763606LV00005B/473

9 781019 371275